HARVARD EAST ASIAN MONOGRAPHS

82

CRIME AND PUNISHMENT IN MEDIEVAL CHINESE DRAMA
THREE JUDGE PAO PLAYS

CRIME AND PUNISHMENT IN MEDIEVAL CHINESE DRAMA
THREE JUDGE PAO PLAYS

by

George A. Hayden

Published by
Council on East Asian Studies
Harvard University

Distributed by
Harvard University Press
Cambridge, Massachusetts
and
London, England
1978

Copyright © 1978 by
The President and Fellows of
Harvard College

This book is produced by the John K. Fairbank Center for East Asian Research at Harvard University, which administers research projects designed to further scholarly understanding of China, Japan, Korea, Vietnam, Inner Asia, and adjacent areas. These studies have been assisted by grants from the Ford Foundation.

Library of Congress Cataloging in Publication Data

Hayden, George A   1939–
    Crime and punishment in medieval Chinese drama.

    (Harvard East Asian monographs; 82)
    Bibliography: p.
    Includes index.
    1. Chinese drama—Yüan dynasty, 1260–1368—
History and criticism.   2. Chinese drama—Ming dynasty
1368–1644—History and criticism.   3. Pao, Cheng,
999–1062—Drama.   4. Trials—China—Drama.
I. Title. II. Series.
PL2384.H3   895.1'2'409353   77-23880
ISBN 0-674-17608-1

For My Parents

FOREWORD

Crime and punishment was an important theme in traditional Chinese literature, perhaps more important than in any other of the world's literatures before the heyday of the Western detective story and crime story. Its popularity extended through all levels of Chinese society; it is found in classical, vernacular, and oral literature, and in virtually all narrative and dramatic genres.

The literature of crime and punishment naturally reflects Chinese conceptions of justice, particularly the Chinese conception of law as embodying ethical norms and of crime as violating the social order and, by implication, the cosmic order as well. In the broadest terms, we can say that a species of moral fable underlies a great deal of Chinese fiction and drama, and that the crime and punishment literature merely represents the fable in its purest and starkest form. But the fable, of course, is an abstraction and not the work itself. What we value in this literature is not the abstraction, but the particular sense of rude and passionate life that the works evoke, whether squalid or noble, comic or pathetic or horrible, as the unspeakable crime is committed and justice tantalizingly but inexorably responds.

The agent of justice is that remarkable figure, the Chinese official, who combined in his person the roles of prosecutor and judge, and, on occasion, of detective as well. The plot turns on his ingenuity.

But also on more than his ingenuity. In much of this literature there is an extra dimension, the bringing to justice of criminals who, in practical terms, are above the law by reason of their political power and influence. It required integrity and courage on the judge's part, as well as ingenuity, to bring them down. The hero is more than a brilliant detective and judge; he is also the very model of a courageous official.

The Northern operatic drama of the Yuan and early Ming dynasties (roughly the fourteenth century A.D.) contains some of the earliest and, by common consent, the best of the Chinese crime and punishment literature. The theme itself implies a literary structure, and the compact form of the Northern drama was admirably suited to it. Professor George Hayden, who teaches Chinese literature at the University of Southern California, completed a Ph.D. dissertation in this field at Stanford in 1971 and has published scholarly studies of it. His book gives us a selection of the finest Northern plays of this type, in a translation which pays due attention to the stylistic variety of the originals. It will interest students of Chinese thought and society as well as students of literature.

Patrick Hanan

PREFACE

This book is the product of an interest, professional or non-professional as the case may be, in Chinese colloquial language and literature, the detective story, and the drama and will, I hope, add to the knowledge and appreciation of all three. The study of Chinese drama in English has reached the stage where we can begin to concentrate more of our attention on specific topics and groups of plays within a fairly closely defined historical period, in this instance courtroom plays of the Yuan and early Ming dynasties (roughly from the thirteenth to, at the latest, the early fifteenth centuries). My aim, extending well beyond the scope of this book, is to identify categories within the drama of this period according to form and theme, and this study, by isolating one such category, should make the larger task easier.

Chinese drama relating to crime has much to tell us about pre-modern popular conceptions of justice and its instrument, the investigating hero. No other body of Chinese literature, classical or colloquial, provides this information in quite the same way, that is to say, quite as "dramatically." Later fiction centers on judges and crime but scarcely with the same ironic humor and single-minded passion for the victory of right over wrong. In this sense these plays are unique.

As examples I have chosen three Judge Pao plays that have never before been translated. In general format and theme they are typical courtroom plays, but in characterization, plot device, and lyrical tone each stands by itself. In each case I have tried to approximate the tone of the original by using conversational English, without slang but with abundant contractions and, in one or two places where the character of the speaker seemed to demand it, faulty grammar. The translations use a double system of notes: footnotes for a basic understanding of the text and endnotes to furnish selected philological and textual data.

Most of the research for this book was done for my doctoral dissertation at Stanford University on roughly the same topic, although the re-application of that research has often produced different results. It is therefore only fitting that a large part of my thanks goes to those who helped me with the dissertation. Professor Patrick Hanan of Harvard University, as the chairman of my dissertation committee, patiently guided and inspired me through all of the stages of my work, both before and after I received the degree. I still recall with affection our conversations on this and other subjects of Chinese literature at Stanford. Professors Shau-wing Chan and David Nivison of Stanford also gave me inestimable help as members of my committee. The demands of all three for translations of high quality have resulted, finally, in completely revised versions. While writing the dissertation, I had the good fortune to study under Professor Tanaka Kenji of the Kyoto University Research Institute of Humanistic Studies under the auspices of the U.S. Department of State and the Fulbright-Hays Committee in Japan. Besides opening the resources of the Institute to me, he gave up much of his valuable time in carefully reviewing my translations and vocabulary, thereby enabling me to avoid many errors and giving me a new awareness of the vocabulary and grammar of late medieval Chinese. To the late Professor John L. Bishop and to the other members of the Editorial Committee of the *Harvard Journal of Asiatic Studies* goes my appreciation for suggesting that I explore the ethical implications of courtroom drama. Special acknowledgment is due my good friend and colleague Professor Laurence G. Thompson of the University of Southern California, without whose encouragement this book would probably remain a plan for the future. Finally, I should like to thank my editor, Olive Holmes, for all of her help and her patience.

An earlier version of Chapter One appeared in the *Harvard Journal of Asiatic Studies* and that of Chapter Two in *Studia Asiatica,* while a less extensively annotated translation of *Ghost of the Pot* can be found in *Renditions.* Bibliographic details are in the Bibliography. I should like to thank the editors or publishers of these publications, Donald H. Shively, Robert Irick, and Stephen C. Soong respectively, for permission to use the revised versions here.

Los Angeles, California   G.H.
May 27, 1977

CONTENTS

FOREWORD   vii

PREFACE   ix

1. Courtroom Plays of the Yuan and Ming Periods   1

2. The Legend of Judge Pao from the Beginnings through Yuan-Ming Drama   16

3. *Ch'en-chou t'iao mi* (Selling Rice at Ch'en-chou)   29

4. *P'en-erh kuei* (The Ghost of the Pot)   79

5. *Hou-t'ing hua* (The Flower of the Back Courtyard)   125

Appendix A: Courtroom Plays (*Tsa-chü*)   179

Appendix B: Courtroom Plays in Yuan and Early Ming Accounts   181

Appendix C: Late-Ming Anthologies in Which Courtroom Plays Appear   182

NOTES   185

BIBLIOGRAPHY   217

GLOSSARY   229

INDEX   237

Chapter 1

COURTROOM PLAYS OF THE
YUAN AND MING PERIODS

During the more than one hundred years of Mongol occupa-
tion in North China (1234–1368), a form of sung and spoken
drama appeared from origins obscure today to open a new chapter
in the history of Chinese literature.[1] Although the Yuan (the
dynastic name of Mongol rule in China) was not the first period to
witness theatrical activity, Yuan drama is unique in one respect:
its texts are the first to survive with any certainty as to the approximate dates of original composition.[2] The plays come under the
general title in Chinese of Yuan *tsa-chü,* "variety drama"; a more
convenient term might be "northern drama."[3] Their common
structure, for all we know, took shape in the Yuan period but
persisted, with some occasional alterations, well into the Ming
period.[4] This structure enjoys several advantages: it is long enough
to unfold a plot of some complexity, yet sufficiently compact to
concentrate dramatic focus on a single train of events and avoid
digression into subplots and other ramifications. By its arrangement of the singing roles, it is able at the same time to unify
dramatic vision within a limited number of major characters.
Yuan–Ming northern plays could easily have been performed in
their entirety within a single afternoon or evening, although our
ignorance of the speed of performance makes this statement only
a reasonable guess. At least this relatively short span of performance time is inconceivable in the case of the much longer plays
that supplanted the northern drama in popularity by the sixteenth
century.

Northern drama as a genre includes songs, for the most part
of popular and northern provenance, as well as dialogue and some
chanted poetry. A typical play consists of four song sequences, or
sets, each sequence containing several songs (perhaps ten to twelve)
of the same musical mode and holding to a single rhyme based on

1

northern pronunciation. Usually one actor or actress, playing a major character, sings throughout the play, although the character he or she portrays may change from sequence to sequence according to the demands of plot.

Two hundred and twenty-six plays ascribed to Yuan dramatists[5] share this format. Their characters range from emperors to prostitutes, from valiant warriors to simple tradesmen. In theme we find tragedy, comedy, suspense, and swashbuckling adventure, and sometimes mixtures of all these within one play. The style may be elegant and literary, filled with subtle allusions to China's classical literature; or it may be plain, outspoken, and even filled with slang. Within this spectrum can be identified a group of twenty-seven plays similar enough in form and theme to be classified under one category, or sub-genre. Included in this number are the three plays translated here, as well as eight of the nine remaining Judge Pao plays.

Anyone weary of hearing that the Chinese invented almost everything long before the West will be dismayed to learn that the Chinese were writing detective stories at least three hundred years before Edgar Allen Poe and courtroom drama about two hundred years before that time. "Courtroom drama" is the name chosen here for these twenty-seven plays. They could as easily be called "crimecase drama." Indeed, modern Chinese literary historians, among them Hu Shih and Cheng Chen-to, have borrowed a term used in the sixteenth century in reference to the detective story: *kung-an,* "crimecase," in describing the category as they see it.[6] "Courtroom drama," a term that incorporates the one element shared by all the plays, the courtroom scene, seems particularly suitable and will be used exclusively in this study.

This is the world of crime and punishment, as viewed by the popular imagination, a world of murder and corruption and also of justice tinged with mercy. Other northern plays may present characterizations that are delicately balanced and flavored with slight nuances in song and dialogue. The courtroom plays are different: they are frank and vigorous appeals to the basic emotions of fear, pity, outrage, and the delight of revenge. Avoiding inner

psychological conflict or moral irony, they act out literally a life
and death struggle between good and evil, a basic dichotomy that
in a variety of modes forms the very essence of later popular literature. Melodrama, then, and a stereotyping of characters are the
possible dangers in this type of theater and for that matter in detective literature as a whole, Eastern and Western. Characterization
often has some difficulty in this medium competing with the
requirements of plot. Although the limitations of the category
should not go unnoticed, they should be placed in a certain per-
spective, that is to say, as against the larger theme of the plays as a
group. What the authors collectively are trying to say and what
they are assuming about the emotional responses of their audience
make up this common theme. Its determination will be the ulti-
mate task of this chapter and, by extension and example, of the
following chapter and the translations as well.

Any literary category or sub-genre is not a rigid set of rules
but a general heading for a group of literary works similar in form
and theme, and some variation and blending with other categories
are to be expected.[7] With this proviso in mind, an initial definition
of the courtroom plays is possible. All have three essential ingredients: (1) a crime, a specific infraction of the legal statutes of the
approximate time in which the plays were written, (2) the crime's
solution and punishment in a courtroom situation, and (3) a judge
or courtroom clerk who solves the crime and, in the case of a judge,
punishes the guilty and rewards the meritorious. In addition, courtroom drama presents the crime and its solution and punishment on
stage, and the agent for its solution, the judge or clerk detective, is
a significant character in the plot. The crime occurs early in the play
and in full view of the audience. It is the central element in the
plot, and its successful detection concludes the play. Focus on a
crime and its detection and punishment produces a theme centered
on justice, as opposed to mystery, and directs itself to an audience's
interest in courtroom procedure as a means to the redress of legal
wrongs.[8]

In contrast to a favorite Western device, "whodunit" plots do
not figure in Chinese drama. Chinese playwrights have tried to

people their conflicts with consistently identifiable characters and
to spell out the cause of each action as it happens. The emphasis is
not on the problem of who performed the crime or why but on
whether and how the crime will be solved. The playwright sparks
the audience's desire for solution purely on ethical and emotional
and not on intellectual grounds.[9]

Also, established usages of jurisprudence as they exist in
reality are not important in their own right; they serve instead
only to project through verisimilitude an ambience that ultimately
sets the tone of each play. An audience highly receptive to this
ambience must have been well established by the Yuan and early
Ming. Court cases have fascinated the Chinese reading audience
since at least the Sung, when two case manuals appeared.[10] But
lacking in these earlier accounts is the emotional impact of the
drama. One ingredient that surely provoked an emotional response
among the theater audiences of the time derives from popular
conceptions of jurisprudence: the awe and even dread aroused in
the minds of ordinary citizens by the tribunal. The law court was
meant to intimidate through threat of physical punishment characters like Chang the Headstrong in *P'en-erh kuei* (The ghost of the
pot), especially since it automatically took a dim view of anyone
so morally careless as to involve himself, however innocently, in
any crime. As Judge Pao says to Wang Ch'ing in *Hou-t'ing hua* (The
flower of the back courtyard), "If you haven't done anything
wrong, then what are you doing here in my K'ai-feng Tribunal?"

As the central and determining element of the plot, the crime
usually occurs early enough, most often in the second act, to
furnish suspense until the ensuing official discovery and then the
sentencing in the fourth and final act.[11] All but five of the twenty-
seven plays deal with murder. In the majority of cases the murder
is committed with a knife. The playwrights seem to have found
that only a depiction of cold-blooded murder could produce the
feelings of outrage at the crime's occurrence and relief at its solution that they desired in their audiences. Thus, they universally
presented the murderer as irredeemably evil, either at the very outset or as a result of character development.[12]

Some modern scholars[13] have suggested that many Yuan dramatists were delivering veiled attacks against their Mongol rulers when they portrayed the criminal as a member of a highly privileged class and invulnerable to punishment by ordinary process of law. Nothing but circumstantial evidence has yet been offered to support this speculation. One should consider, first of all, the danger at that time in playing a criminal as a Mongol or other foreigner on stage. Aside from ethnic considerations, the depiction of an extremely powerful antagonist can certainly be justified and appreciated for its dramatic appeal alone. Also, privileged classes have never been the unique property of any one dynasty; reference to them may well have been a convention inherited from earlier practice. An example is the appearance of scions of influential and therefore legally immune families as criminals in a Sung record of famous court cases, *Che-yü kuei-chien* (Guide to the solution of crime cases) by Cheng K'o. Also, an anecdote related in the next chapter concerning Judge Pao and stoppages along a canal in the capital shows that in legend and possibly in fact a judge as popular hero did confront rich and powerful families in the Sung. Finally, even if the Yuan rulers were the targets of such criticism, courtroom plays of this type would have to be considered the exception, since they would number only six of the twenty-seven.[14]

The thesis, then, is not quite refuted. Some or all of the plays, of course, may have been written against the historical background of Mongol oppression. The Yuan period was a dark age for China in many respects. The Chinese, a conquered majority, were subject to discrimination in all respects, criminal justice included. But these plays are not just historical commentary, and if they deserve to be read at all today, it is because they reaffirm civilized man's abhorrence of cruelty and injustice, at any time and in any culture.

The fact is that evildoers in the courtroom plays are not restricted to any one class or even sex (although a male usually commits the physical act of murder). The only attribute these villains share is a black heart. This is offset by the white of the judge. The man in the middle, the victim, usually a peasant, servant, or small tradesman, evokes the audience's sympathy. Sympathy and something more, respect, are due the detective. His moments of confusion and error may delay the bestowal of this respect, but in the end he sees everything clearly. Occasionally he is gifted with extraordinary powers of perception that enable him to see ghosts or to have revelatory dreams. He frequently possesses the symbols of total power (i.e., a sword of execution and a golden badge or bronze blade) and with these embodies law and order.[15] His role will come into sharper relief upon a close look at the scene in which he assumes his proper significance.

The one ingredient that best typifies the sub-genre is the court-room scene.[16] It is in the full use of the structural and thematic possibilities of this scene that the category distinguishes itself primarily from the rest of northern drama.

In its varied forms the courtroom scene can serve as the locus for three stages in plot development: conflict, revelation, and reso-lution. In plays with more than one such scene, these stages may be apportioned to different segments of time; in others, the same scene may perform all three functions, always necessarily in the above order.

The courtroom is sometimes the setting for the fundamental conflict of a courtroom play, that between the criminal and his victim. Since the dramatists place the crime early in the play, the tribunal is not the first occurrence of this conflict but is rather its extension into another area, in which protagonist (the victim or his champion) and antagonist confront each other in the context of formal trial. This is the scene of official inquiry, which can take two forms. In one, a stupid, venal, or tyrannical judge, almost always relying on a scheming courtroom clerk, misjudges an inno-cent defendant, someone who is closely allied with the victim of the crime and who is mistakenly suspected of this same crime. In the other form, the true agent of justice, judge or clerk, first investi-gates the case and sets about tracking down the real criminal. In either form (both may appear in this order within one play), this scene is a means by which the dramatist can heighten tension and more fully substantiate characterization.

Immediately following the mistrial, when it occurs, is the true courtroom scene, in which an honest representative of imperial justice determines by investigation the actual circumstances of the case (revelation) and lays the groundwork for eventual reward and punishment (resolution). This obligatory scene may occur anywhere subsequent to the crime, but all plays save one[17] include it in the last act, where it is also the setting in which a judge pronounces sentence. There need be no restrictions in locale for this scene, particularly when it appears in the final act. Since the judge or clerk as hero carries the law with him at all times and appears in no other capacity but that of criminal investigator, wherever he happens to be at a given time might well serve as a courtroom. Most of the plays are set in K'ai-feng-fu, the seat of all legal authority in the Northern Sung period. According to these playwrights, the prefectural tribunal there was the highest in the land for the common citizen. Yet all too often the dramatist fails to point out exactly where a scene takes place. If a scene presents a courtroom milieu, no matter how makeshift, in which a detective investigates a crime or a magistrate passes sentence, it qualifies as a courtroom scene. A courtroom scene can therefore be set outside the tribunal proper, in which case the judge eventually establishes a provisional courtroom.

According to the usual pattern, the magistrate gathers the testimony of plaintiff and defendant, along with that of witnesses and other investigators, and, in either the same or a subsequent courtroom setting, makes proper adjudication. The process of detection itself varies in length. In its briefest form it concludes the final act, and the role of the detective is correspondingly limited to judging passively the evidence brought before him. In other plays, the detective's more active search for the truth allows for considerable expansion of the scene. In *Selling Rice at Ch'en-chou* the courtroom "scene" can be interpreted to extend over three acts, to include Judge Pao's journey to Ch'en-chou and his on-the-scene investigation.

Some playwrights saw even in the courtroom scene proper an opportunity to give additional play to tension and characterization prior to the dénouement. They did this by placing within the first

half of the investigation scene a variation of the mistrial, with all
of its emotional impact but without its usual outcome. Here the
honest magistrate, supposedly the epitome of legal wisdom, unwit-
tingly takes the place of the incompetent judge of other scenes. By
letting appearances temporarily confuse him into misjudging guilt
and innocence, he becomes, initially at least, yet another antagonist and only plunges the innocent defendant further into despair.
Notably effective in this role is Judge Pao, who is famous otherwise in popular legend for his intelligence. In four plays, Pao has
particular difficulty in sorting out true and false at the outset of
his investigation. In three of these (one is *The Flower of the Back
Courtyard*) he directs the wrath of his tribunal against the wrong
person.[18] If this victim then cries out in dismay at Pao's lack of
understanding, it is because Pao's reputation for sagacity, always
presumed in these plays, appears to be groundless. As an unjustly
accused heroine sings to Pao in one trial scene,[19]

> Your Honor, in your heart you clasp a bright mirror,
>> in your palm the punishments of law.
> In judging the cases of the realm, never have you
>> erred.
> . . .
>
> On no basis at all you would make me into the root
>> of misfortune.

In his temporary antagonism toward an innocent suspect, the
judge serves a purpose. He highlights the dramatic character of this
suspect and is for this reason relegated to a secondary role. Concerning the role of his detective, the playwright has a choice, and this
choice is dictated solely by the demands of plot. One option allows
the detective to dominate a courtroom scene and even an entire play.
Judge Pao as a legendary figure is especially qualified for this
prominence; in four plays he has the singing role during at least one
act (cf. *Selling Rice at Ch'en-chou* and *The Flower of the Back
Courtyard*).[20] But he is only one example among others[21]; taken as
a whole, these show that the detective as a character type, rather
than as a particular personality from folklore, can be the center of
the playwright's attention in a given act.

The privilege of the singing role in northern drama carries with it a certain obligation, however. The character who sings must deserve the audience's moral sympathy. To be more precise, he must feel some kind of devotion to a moral ideal, a devotion bordering on passion, that transcends weakness and confusion and whose intensity merits and sustains an entire lyrical sequence. No matter how lowly in worldly position or how potentially comic he may be, when he sings he automatically attains a nobility of stature. The dramatist, then, can direct the audience's sympathy toward the detective, even while he is floundering in the complexities of a crimecase, just so long as his idealism still predominates. For example, Judge Pao, although confused in *The Flower of the Back Courtyard,* sings in the last two acts. In this instance, the focus is on Pao's quest for true justice and on his sense of frustration when only a legally expedient but morally unsatisfactory solution presents itself: to judge an innocent student guilty of murder and have done with the case. Pao suspects that all is not as it appears and, furthermore, knows that he is bewildered.

Pao does not always have this dual awareness. In the other three plays in which he sings, he is driven initially by a desire for a rapid solution. He succumbs to the temptation of seizing the first likely suspect or, in one of the plays, of adhering to the letter of the law regardless of extenuating circumstances.[22] The assignment of roles in the courtroom scenes of these three plays duplicates that of any mistrial scene. The suspect sings and the judge does not, no matter how well known he may be outside the drama, or how crucial he may be to the resolution. The playwright, then, may borrow a character like Judge Pao from popular legend but at the same time is free to manipulate this character as he sees fit, even in a direction contrary to normal expectation. In fact, the more famous the judge, the more startling is the effect when he suddenly turns against someone the audience knows from the first to be blameless.

The occasional fallibility of the judge serves another purpose: to keep his characterization within mortal limits. Otherwise, given the extraordinary fame of a popular hero like Judge Pao and his inevitable triumph, the playwrights might have been tempted to elevate the judge to a superhuman level. Actually, they come close to drawing a line between their judges on the basis of supernatural power, but demarcation here owes less to the nature of the judge himself than to the setting of the courtroom scene that he attends. Two plays place the final courtroom scene in the realm of the spirits,[23] but in the other twenty-five plays, investigation and trial are set in the mortal world and are conducted by mortal detectives.

Within these twenty-five plays, the interpretation of the judge is far from uniform. In some instances he is liable to mistaken judgment; in others he is gifted with a special kind of clairvoyance that enables him to see ghosts of murder victims in a temporal setting. In some plays, it is not clear that this ability is the judge's alone[24]; in three of the Pao plays, on the other hand, *Ghost of the Pot* among them, Pao states that no one but he can see the manifestation of a spirit.[25] The implication here is that Pao, as a terrestrial agent of divine justice, has the power to see what others can only hear. Within any one courtroom play, the judge's fallibility and his clairvoyance are mutually exclusive. Examples are these three Pao plays, in which Pao never comes to a wrong decision. Although this mutual exclusion may be only the result of coincidence, it is more likely that it represents two divergent tendencies at work: one, to portray the judge as approaching the superhuman, in which case he is extraordinarily perceptive; the other, to make him more human, wise and honest, to be sure, but as susceptible to error as any other mortal.

Another supernatural element in some of the plays is the dream of the judge. In three plays, before the judge is aware of the true circumstances of a murder case, he has a dream that either exposes the facts all at once or alludes to them in tantalizing obscurity.[26] The latter variety includes a metaphor from nature for the actions of the principals[27] and a word game on the name of the criminal.[28] These last two dreams, especially, presuppose a superhuman force acting indirectly for human justice. Unlike a visitation by a spirit, however, they do not make a demand as stringent as intellectual perfection on the judge. Naturally he must have the intelligence to connect the dream to actual events, but before he does so, he is free to misinterpret testimony.

Although acknowledged in these plays to be extraordinary phenomena, prophetic dreams and the appearance of ghosts at the same time assume a perfectly natural place in the drama as literature. What courtroom drama takes to be truly unnatural is not these marvels but rather the human act that sets them into motion: calculated murder. This throws the natural order "out of joint" and stirs up energies, sometimes working through miracles, that move inexorably toward restitution. In the enormity of his crime, the murderer pits himself not only against the laws on earth but, unknowingly, against these same laws in Heaven as well, and he is doomed from the start. As if taking their cue from the dictum of Ch'eng I, a Sung Neo-Confucian philosopher, that the extremely stupid, who destroy themselves, cannot be changed,[29] these laws offer no hope of salvation to the killer but demand instead that his debt of blood be repaid in kind—with his own life.

Northern drama is well known for its innovative and even daring reversals of orthodox attitudes, especially on the subject of romantic love. But in the matter of justice, these courtroom plays are devoted heirs to Chinese tradition, in both its elite and popular forms. Chinese culture has tended to view human society as a delicately balanced organism, complex in its relationships but working always toward stability. An axiom of this view is that, as every cause has its effect, so every action results in its appropriate reaction, leading in time to a new equilibrium. This means that anything given will be replaced, and anything taken away must eventually be returned.[30] The courtroom plays regard a crime as a taking away and even more as a debt awaiting payment by the criminal. When Confucius advocated justice rather than kindness as the reward for unkindness, he struck a note that would find its echo in courtroom drama in the proverb "As a debtor pays his debt, so a murderer pays with his life." The drama introduces an elaboration on this theme, however. Now, in the frustrations expressed by detectives like Judge Pao, appears a sense of urgency in the redressing of grievances. For every moment that a debt stays unpaid, a murderer runs free, and a wronged spirit remains unavenged, humanity suffers in its disequilibrium. Obviously the inevitability of divine action is not enough, that is, if the human tribunal is to have any relevance in the governing of mankind. Assurance that the universal order will sooner or later bring the criminal to task is all very well, but Chinese culture has never been any more content with that assurance than has any other form of civilization. The detectives of northern drama are never willing to sit back and allow events to take their course. Some of them actually seem afraid of losing the opportunity to perform as an agent of providence, as if they might be found culpable of having let heavenly justice falter.

The note of inevitability is softened, and the dramatic appeal of the plays accordingly enhanced because the instrument of natural vengeance, the detective, is almost always a human being, with all of the unpredictability that this term implies. For all his failings, however, he is armed with the one weapon, a basic intelligence, that is demanded of his role in the victorious resolution. This is more than the capacity to think clearly or, as judges often do, to devise clever solutions to various dilemmas. It would appear to reflect an equation of intelligence (an equation strongly Neo-Confucian in tone) with man's innate ability to distinguish right from wrong.[31] In its most extreme form, this insight allows the detective to determine from a mere glance at a subject's physiognomy and bearing his innocence or guilt. In all plays it gives the detective the means by which to weigh evidence and solve the crime, a means that may exceed the bounds of ordinary logic and rely instead on intuition.

If we are correct in tracing this intuition to Neo-Confucianism as at least one of its sources, it presumably belongs to all men in a perfect state. That which distinguishes the detective as the crime-solving agent from other characters in the same play would then be the relative purity of this universal intelligence in him. The mere possession of authority without insight is, as we have seen, meaningless. Any judge can let ethical distinctions be obscured by complexity, as in *Flower of the Back Courtyard,* or, with far more serious implications, by desire. Desire, the root of all human evil according to the Neo-Confucians, can take more than one form in courtroom drama. As selfishness, it produces the corrupt and comic judge of some mistrial scenes, while inhumane desire for a rapid solution, regardless of mitigating elements, results in the excessively severe judge of other such scenes, including some with Judge Pao. The scenes with Pao differ only in eventual outcome, and this outcome is predicated on his ability alone to clear away the cobwebs of confusion and legalistic zeal and restore his mind to its pristine clarity. The confusion and error of a judge can be said, then, to be a kind of lapse that, before being rectified, does help to alleviate the penchant of courtroom plays for melodrama. Ultimately, of course, the virtue of the judge in its original purity confronts the evil of the criminal, and the absence of any redeemable moral qualities in the latter makes his character, at any rate, highly melodramatic. Even so, the Neo-Confucian theory that all men are by nature good could also be applied to the criminal, so long as one assumed that his wickedness is not fundamental or self-existent but due only to a lapse from grace more extreme than that of the judge or, in other words, that it differs in degree but not in kind. At least the criminal never has a Prince of Darkness on his side, although the detective has Heaven on his.

By associating these attitudes of the courtroom playwrights with Neo-Confucianism, I am not saying that they necessarily derive from this philosophy through any conscious, direct, or even consistent process. I do suggest that some images and broad concepts of the dominant school of thought of that time may have found their way into vernacular literature, even in the trappings of popular legend, for example, the detective's mirror, often identified with that of the Taoist Yellow Emperor. One of the favorite images of the Neo-Confucians for man's original mind is a mirror, which need only be polished to remove the impure obstacles to perfect knowledge. And a stock metaphor in courtroom drama for the detective's wisdom is a crystal-clear mirror, which victims of crime and injustice hope will shine through superficialities and reflect all things in their true proportions.[32]

If all men have an inherent ability to separate right from wrong, and if the mortal detective is set above others only in the

degree to which he preserves this ability, it would be misleading to
see him in any absolutely superhuman role. The courtroom plays
illustrate that the principle of justice, while existing on an extra-
terrestrial plane, pervades human society in all its forms and in fact
cannot be distinguished as to level. Courtroom drama places the
human tribunal of K'ai-feng, the subterranean court of justice of
King Yama, and the celestial Hall of Purgatory on Mt. T'ai side by
side, not in comparison only, but in positive identification as three
spheres of a single reality informed equally with the principle of
justice. Four plays[33] have variations on a stock entrance poem of
the judge:

>   The court drum booms,
>   While clerks line up on either side.
>   (This is) Yama's Hall of Life and Death,
>   The Hall of Purgatory of the Eastern Mountain (Mt. T'ai).

In all-pervasive justice is accomplished the unification of (1) the
Chinese Triad: Heaven, Earth, and Man, and (2) the three religions:
Confucianism (the detective), Buddhism (King Yama), and Taoism
(Mt. T'ai). References in courtroom drama to the universality of
justice are numerous, especially in songs, poems, and classical
quotations. Even the most comic of all the detectives, Chang Pen,
is in earnest when he says these lines of verse:

>   Heaven's mind I deduce up above
>   And the spirit of earth down below.
>   As in the light follow trouble and joy,
>   So the dark holds ghostly reward.
>   . . .
>   The people below may be easy to cheat
>   But never so Heaven on high.[34]

Crime, especially murder, disturbs the natural balance at all levels
by going against the principle of justice. Disruption in turn may or
may not produce supernatural events but, in any case, demands
immediate correction. And the agent for this correction, the detective, is a man of two aspects. As a deputy of Heaven he is in concert
with the divine principle of good, while as a champion of the

oppressed he places the otherwise forbidding tribunal on a secure basis of human sympathy and benevolence.

The courtroom plays of northern drama ceased to be written by known playwrights by the early-Ming period, although the plays by anonymous authors may date from this time and after. This is not to say that the plays had no effect on later drama, but among the few long plays of the Ming that include criminal and court-room themes, a change in tone from the northern plays is obvious. We find in them a tendency to revive the murdered protagonist by means of magic at the end of the play.[35] No longer is the emphasis on crime and justice, since the device of reviving the murder victim at the end of the play obliterates the crime and any sense of wrong it may have engendered in the audience. The northern plays end on a note of triumph, of course, but the murder victim, however satis-fied he may be in spirit by legal vengeance on his murderer, remains dead. His loss of life gives meaning to the resulting acts of reward and punishment and leaves the onlooker with a lasting regret that the crime should ever have occurred. In this sense, a note of tragedy persists, even in the ultimately comic tone of the happy ending and in spite of the many instances of humor interspersed among scenes of moral outrage and pathos.

Chapter 2

THE LEGEND OF JUDGE PAO
FROM THE BEGINNINGS THROUGH YUAN–MING DRAMA

The historical figure Pao Cheng (999–1062; courtesy name
Hsi-jen) is probably no stranger to students of Northern Sung (960–
1127) history. Pao's name appears frequently in connection with
various fiscal, military, and bureaucratic issues during the reign of
Jen Tsung, and the account of his official career gives a fascinating
picture of a man in constant battle for the ideals of honesty and
dedication in public service.[1] Most Chinese, however, probably
know of Pao Cheng, not as the minister and political critic of documented history, but as the courtroom judge of popular drama and
fiction, that relentless foe of evil and injustice in the *Lung-t'u
kung-an* (Crime cases of the Lung-t'u judge) stories of the late
Ming and in the plays of Peking and other local theaters of the late
Ch'ing.[2] In tracing the figure of Judge Pao in Chinese popular
imagination throughout the formative period of his legend (from
the Northern Sung through the Yuan and early Ming periods), we
can find the connection between history and legend.

This period of development may be divided into two chrono-
logical stages: (1) Pao's own lifetime and a century or so thereafter,
that is, the Northern and Southern (1127–1279) Sung dynasties, and
(2) the Yuan and early Ming eras. The late-Ming period, although
producing popular literature on Pao in some quantity, seems to
have been ignorant of previous contributions to the legend. It
indeed might be said to form a separate, although related, tradition.
The literature of each stage, including the late Ming, made its own
unique contribution to the growing legend, but the late-Ming short
stories and long plays change the direction of the Pao legend. To
examine Judge Pao in dramatic literature before that point, then,
is one aim of this study; another is to indicate, by way of conclusion,
exactly what kind of shift took place.

The Sung Period

Material written about Pao during and shortly after his lifetime provides a background that, throughout later developments,
never changes in at least three aspects: his official career, his personality, and his wisdom as a judge. According to available evidence,
Pao has never been considered apart from his official capacities,
either in orthodox histories or in popular literature. Details of his
career, such as titles of posts, are subject to almost whimsical alter-
ation in drama and fiction, but at least Pao is always identified
with a particular governmental function.

That function, as seen in the long series of positions and ranks
in Pao's documented career, can be described in one phrase: devoted
service to the Sung empire. Whether magistrate, political censor, or
fiscal minister, Pao Cheng pitted himself against official corruption
and incompetence as well as crime and injustice, and actually seems
to have enjoyed his many confrontations with the enemies of good
government, no matter how powerful. (This quality, incidentally,
comes through strongly in the drama.) He never achieved the very
highest levels in the bureaucracy, nor was he spared an occasional
demotion or embarrassment.[3] Upon his death, however, a grateful
emperor gave him the honorary rank of Minister of Rites (*Li-pu
shang-shu*) and the posthumous title of Filial and Reverent Duke
(*Hsiao-su-kung*).

Official titles and matters of governmental policy, however,
separate from the heroic attitude that lay behind them, count for
little in the Judge Pao legend. What caught the imaginations of even
the Sung chroniclers, to say nothing of later writers of popular
literature, was Pao's personality. Sung sources delight in presenting
Pao as morally severe, supremely conscientious, and without the
slightest grain of humor. This personality, softened as it is by a
deep but unsentimental concern for human suffering, produces a
gently humorous and reassuring effect which, paradoxically enough,
can sometimes be found in ferocity—when tinged with compassion.
Any other aspect of Pao, such as personal warmth as a friend,
father, or husband, will be sought in vain. The dominant portion of

his entire makeup was made to represent the whole, and although we may be dissatisfied with such caricaturization today, it does seem to have helped to guarantee Judge Pao's place in later plays, stories, and novels.

An excellent example of this point is the section in the *Sung shih* (History of the Sung dynasty) biography of Pao on the subject of his personality:

> Stern and impatient by nature, he hated the high-handedness of clerks and strove toward sincerity and generosity. He loathed evil, yet he was ever ready to apply good faith and sympathy. He would not toady to the opinions of others, nor would he try to please them with false words and manners. Because he never responded to personal requests for favors, his friends and relatives all broke off relations with him. Even when he was in high position, his clothing, utensils, food, and drink were like those he had used as a commoner. He once said, "Should any of my descendants be guilty of corruption in office, they may not return to their home, nor may they be buried in the family plot. Whosoever does not follow my ideals is no son or grandson of mine.[4]

Helping to give these traits some degree of individuality and poignancy are various remarks and stories concerning his administration as prefect of the Northern Sung capital, K'ai-feng-fu, from 1056 to 1058. Here he became famous locally as a strict and scrupulously fair administrator, so much so that eunuchs, powerful families, and courtroom clerks supposedly shrank back at the very sound of his name. He was known as the Clear-sighted Investigator (*Ming-ch'a*) and as Pao *Tai-chih* (this from his former title of Academician-in-waiting [*tai-chih*] of the T'ien-chang Pavilion). A saying on the theme of his honesty became popular: "Bribery will get nowhere,/ For Old Pao, the King of Hell, is here" (*Kuan-chieh pu tao,/ Yu Yen-lo Pao-lao*). A current joke was that a smile from his lips was as common as clear water in the Yellow River.[5]

Four incidents of legendary flavor illustrate Pao's rule of K'ai-feng-fu. The first is set on the day he arrived to assume his duties

as prefect. During the opening ceremony, when the clerks asked him if there were any taboo words that they should avoid saying, such as the personal names of his ancestors, Pao glared and replied that the only thing to be avoided was corruption by clerks.[6]

According to another anecdote, a dishonest clerk secretly made a proposal to a criminal who was about to be beaten: for a certain sum of money the clerk would share the punishment. The gullible man, eager to reduce the number of strokes of the rod, accepted but became angry when he was sentenced the original number of blows by Pao. Before the criminal could raise an out-cry, he was shouted down by the clerk, who told him to take his punishment and get out. Pao became so enraged at the brazen clerk that he had him beaten instead of the criminal, who was pardoned.[7]

The third incident involved the stoppage of a local river and a consequent flood; the disaster had been caused by gardens and pavilions built by officials and rich families on land fills. When Pao had these obstructions removed, many owners protested, using falsified land titles as proof. After determining which documents were bogus, Pao promptly punished or reported the offenders.[8]

After intimidating the clerks and powerful families, Pao had only one more potentially troublesome group to deal with: local ruffians. During a fire, when all hands were needed to fight the flames, some street types chose the moment when the blaze was at its worst to have a joke with Pao. They approached him and asked where they should get the water to douse the flames, in the Sweet Water Alley or in the Bitter Water Alley. Pao, obviously failing to appreciate the humor in their question, had them executed on the spot.[9]

Pao's administration of the capital probably was not as repres-sive as these stories suggest. A good instance of the "sympathy" mentioned in the *Sung shih* account would be his innovation in courtroom procedure. In order to ensure justice for everyone, regardless of wealth or position, he dispensed with the require-ment that litigants report a case first to the outer clerks; he instead allowed them to come directly into the courtroom through the

main gate.[10] The effect of this reform, or at least of the intent behind it, on Pao's later role in popular literature may have been considerable.

Pao's moral qualities as magistrate are the requisites for an attribute that would play a crucial part in the development of the tradition: his wisdom as a judge at law. If we are to believe one anecdote, he showed early in his life a talent for finding the truth among the complexities of legal testimony. While Pao was serving in one of his first official appointments, that of county magistrate, a man reported to him that his ox's tongue had been cut out. Pao secretly told him to go home, slaughter the animal, and sell the meat. After this was done, another man came to court and accused the first man of secretly slaughtering a beast of burden. But when Pao turned about and accused the accuser of cutting out the tongue of another man's ox and making a false charge for personal revenge, this second man turned pale and made an immediate confession.[11]

Pao in his own lifetime, then, became known throughout the capital as a champion of justice; and from there, presumably, his reputation soon spread to outlying areas. Although we have no solid evidence from the time, his prominence in contemporary miscellanies and in later popular literature suggests that during the remainder of the Northern Sung and throughout the Southern Sung and Kin periods he was a favorite topic of storytellers, chanteurs, and actors in the marketplaces and entertainment districts. Pao himself might have been surprised, to say the least, to know that his rather crusty personality would eventually assume legendary, even mythic, proportions and, long after his K'ai-feng Tribunal had lost its glory, would continue to satisfy his countrymen's traditional hunger for justice.

The Yuan and Early Ming

Roughly by the time the Mongols won control of North China during the first half of the thirteenth century, a striking change had taken place in Judge Pao. He was now not only the human magistrate of recorded history but an immortal judge of dead souls as well. The Kin and early-Yuan poet Yuan Hao-wen (1190–1257)

relates that in 1240 Pao once appeared through a medium as overseer of the "Court of Prompt Retribution of the Eastern Mountain (Mt. T'ai)" (*Tung-yueh Su-pao-ssu*),which position he had earned by his exemplary honesty.[12] An inscription of 1285, commemorating the chapels of the Seventy-five Courts of Justice (Ch'i-shih-wu Ssu) on the hill Hao-li in the environs of Mt. T'ai, reinforces this item. The surname given for the director of the thirteenth court, the Court of Prompt Retribution, is Pao.[13]

From at least the Latter Han, Mt. T'ai in its awesome grandeur was associated in Chinese folklore with control over life and death and various other aspects of fate.[14] By the Tsin period, the more anthropomorphic Lord of Mt. T'ai had come to preside over the trials of dead souls in order to determine the span and level of their next existence.[15] This item of Taoist mythology seems to be a copy of the Buddhist King of Hell, King Yama (and, of course, of the Buddhist concept of *karma*); in fact, the gods came to be very closely associated in Yuan–Ming drama.

The medieval Chinese believed that the death of a hero did not necessarily put an end to his service to mankind. In a manner of speaking, the termination of such a man's life on earth signified a supreme bureaucratic advancement into the plane of spirits and the afterlife, where he could now benefit both the living and the dead. The earliest reference that this writer has found to this Chinese humanization of the pantheon is in the *Sui shu* (Book of the Sui dynasty) of the early T'ang, in which a Sui general named Han Ch'in-hu is reputed to have become King Yama after death.[16] Similar accounts of other notable officials' attaining the rank of Yama or some such post appear with some frequency in Sung sources.[17] In the aggregate, these give the impression of a duplication in Heaven or Hell of Chinese bureaucratic procedure in the world of men: a deserving man after death fills for a time a divine post, perhaps an expanded version of his earthly one, and, after an allotted term of office, turns his duties over to a just-deceased successor. Although this is the usual case, it does not seem to apply to Pao in his new role. Indications are that, at least during the Yuan, he was permanent judge of the Court of Prompt Retribution.

Given Pao's supernatural fame in the Yuan, we might expect to find some mention of it in the rich body of dramatic literature surviving from and ascribed to this period. Pao Cheng is a significant character in twelve plays of the northern genre of the Yuan and early Ming. Yet only one of these plays, *The Ghost of the Pot,* and the southern *Hsiao Sun T'u* (Young butcher Sun) make the slightest allusion to any otherworldly capacity of Pao's, and this is his ability to judge wronged spirits after dark (and during his lifetime only). In the former play, the spirit of a murder victim says to Pao in verse,

> By day you have decided among the world of light,
> And at night you have judged phantoms in the realms
>> of darkness.

In another Yuan northern play, *Young Butcher Chang,* a play in which Pao is not an actual character, the servant of a god points to Pao's image at the temple on Mt. T'ai and explains in dialogue and song,[18]

> Madam, over there is a god, who was Judge Pao in life
> but now, after death, is divine. This, then, is the Court
> of Prompt Retribution.
>> (Melody: *Erh-sha*)[19]
> This is a man who once kept the peace of the
>> realm, who has cured injustice where Heaven
>> and Earth have been lax.
> His robe is of purple silk, his tablet of whit-
>> est ivory, and about his waist is a golden
>> belt.
> His glaring eyes are black as rain clouds, and
>> the silken hair of his temples is white
>> as snow.
> Solemn is his majesty, great his wisdom.
> In the courts of Hell ghosts would do his bid-
>> ding,
> And at K'ai-feng no people's money would he touch.

It is highly probable that Pao as judge of spirits on Mt. T'ai

was common knowledge to Yuan and early-Ming dramatists. If so, their relative silence on this aspect of their dramatic hero may have been a matter of choice, and this choice was for the human being who lived and died during the Northern Sung dynasty, not for the demi-god of a sacred mountain.

The twelve northern plays of this approximate period that include Pao as a character of some significance are Plays 2, 8, 10, 14, 15, 18, 19, 20, 21, 22, and 27 of Appendix A, and the anonymous play *Lu Chai-lang,* which does not belong to the courtroom sub-genre. All of the plays are set during Pao's tour of duty as prefect of K'ai-feng-fu and involve him in the dramatic action purely as a judge of criminal cases. All include a crime; in all but two plays this crime is murder, either real or suspected.[20] Pao solves this crime by a variety of judicial, extra-legal, or even supernatural methods and, in the courtroom plays, brings the play to a tidy conclusion upon his assignment of rewards and punishments.

As soon as Pao enters, he makes clear in a few lines of monologue, dialogue, verse, or song that, at least in spirit, he is very much the Pao Cheng of history. Like any other character in medieval Chinese drama, Pao wastes no time in establishing the moral tone of his characterization, as in *Hui-lan chi* (The chalk circle):[21]

> I am honest, capable, pure, and upright, staunch and
> firm in my integrity. Eager to serve my country and
> scornful of devotion to riches, I associate only with
> loyal and filial men and have nothing whatever to do
> with slanderers and flatterers.

In *The Ghost of the Pot* a stock entrance quatrain places Pao's moral superiority in a definitely Confucian context,

> When laws are just, Heaven's heart's in accord;
> With ethical purity comes an unblemished world.
> My brush exalts sons loyal and true,
> And my sword beheads the guilty.

Some of Pao's special loathings are true to his historic image:

powerful criminals, for example, because they all too often are immune from punishment for their crimes. As Pao sings in *Selling Rice at Ch'en-chou,*

> I have made it clear to my sovereign
> That those who lust for power are my mortal foes.
> . . .
>
> They are bandits who plunder the homes of the people,
> But a fierce watchdog am I.
> Money and possessions are all they desire,
> But never shall they keep this hound from tracking them
>   down.

Against venal courtroom clerks, Pao seems to speak in these lines from *Shen-nu-erh* for all the innocent victims who have ever found themselves in a medieval tribunal,[22]

> You clerks, in your infinite love affair with money,
> Taking in secret your gifts of gold and silver,
> Will you ever look on a plaintiff with impartial eyes?
> I shall get rid of you all, root and branch.

Pao's hatreds merely push into sharper relief his one overriding concern, in the drama as well as in earlier legend: the welfare of the helpless citizen, beset by the forces of privilege and corruption. His way of helping his fellow man in the drama is to remove injustice by means of investigation and trial. He deals with two kinds of injustice, both of which become points of dramatic conflict: the first, which always occurs, is the crime committed on an undeserving victim; the second, which is optional, is the miscarriage of justice mentioned in the preceding chapter. Of the Pao plays, *The Chalk Circle* and *Shen-nu-erh* have a mistrial scene, but in *Hu-tieh meng* (The butterfly dream), *Liu hsieh chi* (The sign of the slipper), and *The Chalk Circle* again, Pao's initial investigation resembles the mistrial scene in its antagonism toward the innocent, if not exactly in the judge's motive, which in Pao's case is pure even if betrayed by an overly zealous approach.

The temptation to stylize characters is very great in medieval Chinese drama, particularly in a type of play with a morally repugnant crime, a criminal, a victim, and a detective, as are the Pao plays. The playwrights of *Lu Chai-lang* and *Ho-t'ung wen-tzu* (The contract) seem to have given in to the temptation to stylize their Judge Pao, perhaps because their attentions were directed elsewhere. Each has given Pao an idealized and mechanical role as administrator of justice, hence someone with sufficient authority to tie up the loose ends of plot in the context of trial and adjudication. But a Judge Pao capable of momentary confusion, as in *The Flower of the Back Courtyard*,[23] or downright error, as in *The Butterfly Dream, The Sign of the Slipper,* and *The Chalk Circle* is a more well-rounded and human character. By reducing his stature to this degree, these dramatists at the same time show an interest in Judge Pao as an individual.

This interest might even be interpreted as affection. Some playwrights have a little fun with "Old Pao" before allowing him, as always, to emerge victorious at the resolution. In his solemnity and almost overpowering dedication, Pao makes an excellent "straight man" to the clownish antics of courtroom attendants. In *Sheng-chin ko* (The tower of fine gold), he is accidentally pummeled on the leg by his retainer,[24] and throughout the play his humorless personality provides a contrasting backdrop to the buffoonery of this retainer and a courtroom attendant. In *Selling Rice at Ch'en-chou,* Pao journeys in disguise to the scene of murder and corruption and finds himself leading the donkey of an old prostitute, being strung up on a tree by the villains, and very nearly receiving a beating. The image of pokerfaced Pao dangling from a tree (at least in the imagination of the audience, if not actually on stage), while eavesdropping on his retainer's attempt to extort a bribe from the criminals, shows the liberties that one playwright took with this august deputy of imperial power. In fact, in this play Pao actually makes a joke.[25]

Because Pao does represent the authority of the emperor and, by implication, of Heaven as well, his nominal power is almost limitless. In five plays,[26] Pao holds the symbols of supreme power: a sword of authority and a golden badge (or a bronze blade), as do some other judges in courtroom drama. With these instruments he can order an immediate execution of a criminal without having first to get permission through official channels. Pao's normal judicial procedure would then be relatively simple: to gather evidence and testimony, weigh them according to his own eye for ethical distinctions, and impose an appropriate sentence. Apparently dissatisfied with this potentially mechanical approach, some authors have devised situations in which the sword and the badge are not enough. True to the Pao tradition, they test their hero against a criminal's influence and privilege. Certain villains in these plays regard themselves as fully entitled by position or wealth to act with impunity, knowing that high connections or full-scale bribery will save them. These formidable obstacles demand extraordinary measures, which take the form of some kind of dissembling by Pao. This subterfuge may be the trip under cover in *Selling Rice at Ch'en-chou;* a surreptitious transference of a crime to an already condemned criminal, as in *The Butterfly Dream*[27]; an outright lie, as in *The Tower of Fine Gold*[28]; or even the falsification of an official document, as in *Lu Chai-lang.*[29] So long as the cause was just, apparently, audiences encouraged this type of extra-legal, even illegal behavior on the part of the judge.

A judge's craftiness, however, should not be confused with his wisdom, which transcends his mistakes and trickery and gives him his unique status. As is indicated in the preceding chapter, Judge Pao, like his counterparts in the courtroom drama as a whole, is the human counterpart to the two other components of the Chinese Triad, Heaven and Earth; in his wisdom he is attuned to the same moral laws in all three levels. In these plays he could never become a god on Mt. T'ai or King Yama in Hell (as in the *Crime Cases of the Lung-t'u Judge*). Although wise, Judge Pao as a human is not blessed with godlike infallibility. Rather, he is saddled with a sense of duty to mankind that, in spite of his momentary shortcomings, constantly spurs him on to his eventual triumphs over evil.

The Yuan and early Ming northern drama marks a high point for the Judge Pao legend, at least in its moral implications. Pao would appear in later drama and particularly in the collection of short stories built around him, the *Crime Cases of the Lung-t'u*

Judge.[30] New developments would occur: Pao as King Yama or his deputy during Pao's lifetime, Pao in opposition to imperial in-laws, or Pao in magical combat against fantastic demons, to give three examples. But in the often more sensational Pao literature from the late Ming on, the atmosphere of urgency of the northern plays is missing, an atmosphere given substance by a strong and even earthy colloquial style. The crimes in later drama and fiction lack the sense of needless and tragic loss that is so striking in the earlier drama and so lack also the driving need for recompense. In this sense, the moral tone, indeed the very motive, of the Judge Pao legend had been set out long before and would never be surpassed.

CH'EN-CHOU T'IAO MI

(Selling Rice at Ch'en-chou)

INTRODUCTION

Among the twelve Judge Pao plays under consideration, *Ch'en-chou t'iao mi* (Selling rice at Ch'en-chou) devotes the most attention to Pao as hero and central character. Pao's is the singing role for three acts, or song sequences, out of the four. In only two other courtroom plays does the detective enjoy a comparable position: in *Yen-an-fu,* the judge has the singing role in all four acts, while *K'an t'ou-chin* (Investigating a head cloth) duplicates this play exactly in assigning to its detective, a clerk, the singing role in Acts 2, 3, and 4.

The authors of all three plays, by allotting to their detectives the majority or even totality of the singing roles, show their high regard for the dramatic possibilities in crime detection as a theme. Nowhere in northern drama are these possibilities used to greater effect than in *Selling Rice at Ch'en-chou.* First, the crime itself is repugnant enough: the cold-blooded murder of an innocent and righteous man through a combination of greed and a sheer delight in power. Then the secondary theme of "one man against the multitude" appears, as Pao with the authority of the throne (and Heaven) behind him struggles against the benign indifference of his fellow officials and the malign interference and antagonism of privileged criminals. The playwright keeps his hero on a human level, lightens the tone of his play, and intensifies suspense by involving Pao in some comic and potentially demeaning episodes, while insuring that Pao never loses his dignity or seriousness of purpose.

The humor of this play corresponds quite closely to Western notions of "comic relief" by maintaining some distance from scenes of moral outrage and pathos (compare *P'en-erh kuei* [The ghost of the pot], the second play translated, for a different approach). The villains, for example, are comic in some scenes, as are their counterparts in many courtroom plays (but with a venom and a flippancy that only accentuate their inhumanity). The grim

31

humor associated with them disappears momentarily, however, during the murder scene, which is consistently serious.

The comic scenes with Pao hold integral positions in the thread of suspense running from the murder to its punishment by appearing in the contexts of movement and quest. Chang Ch'ien's soliloquy and his exchange with Pao in Act 3 take place while both characters are traveling to Ch'en-chou to solve the case. The scene with Pao and the prostitute is also set during this journey, as is that in which Pao is strung up on a tree by the villains. The author thus includes these episodes in the train of events leading to the solution of the crime and the conclusion of the play, thereby maintaining the pace of the narrative.

Before the journey begins, the pace takes a little time to develop. At the start of the play, a convention seemingly more theatrical than dramatic introduces the officials Han Ch'i, Lü I-chien, and Lord Liu one after the other, with rather lengthy soliloquies and frequent recapitulations of plot. This formula, which might be called "arrival in series," occurs often in northern dramatic texts and probably was more effective on stage than on the written page, particularly in military plays with their elaborate costuming. Even in this play, the serial introduction of the characters in Act 2 builds in intensity as the appearance of Lord Liu precedes that of Judge Pao himself, the last to mount the stage. It is here, also, that suspense begins, as Pao at first refuses to undertake the assignment and engages in his sparring dialogue with Liu.

Any antecedents of *Selling Rice at Ch'en-chou* are unknown. No source of the Yuan or the early or middle Ming mentions a northern play of this title, although a play of the *hsi-wen* genre with the same title existed in the Yuan or the early Ming.* The only surviving edition of the northern play is that of *Yuan-ch'ü hsuan.***

*A play featuring Pao's journey to Ch'en-chou to sell rice is mentioned in a song in the *hsi-wen Huan-men tzu-ti ts'o li-shen,* surviving in the *Yung-le ta-tien;* see *Sung Yuan hsi-wen chi-i,* "Ch'ien-yen" (Introduction), p. 5. The text is not extant.

**Yuan-ch'ü hsuan, I, 32–52; or *Ch'üan Yuan tsa-chü,* III, iv, 1319–1408. The play's vocabulary is annotated in *Yuan-jen tsa-chü hsuan,* pp. 509–548.

SELLING RICE AT CH'EN-CHOU

Wedge[1]*

        (*Enter* Fan Chung-yen *with attendants.*)

  FAN:

      (*in verse*)

      All books have met my eye, the Classics in depth;

      Gloriously have I shone in service to the realm.[2]

      To the Palace I offered my Plan of Exalted Peace;[3]

      Of the names of foremost candidates, the first was mine
          alone.**

I, of the surname Fan and with the given name Chung-yen and the courtesy name Hsi-wen, am from Fen-chou.[4] I have devoted myself to scholarship from childhood and know the Classics and Histories down to the last detail. Since winning the Doctorate of Letters in a single try, I have served the throne for many decades. His Majesty's favor has granted me the office of Minister of Finance with the rank of High Scholar of the T'ien-chang Pavilion. I now have a letter from the officials of Ch'en-chou,[5] telling of the three-year drought there, the shortage of grain,[6] and the misery of the people, who in desperation have been nearly reduced to cannibalism. All this have I reported to the throne; I have the emperor's command to confer with the ministers at the Secretariat.** This morning a man honest officials to open the state granaries and sell rice at Ch'en-chou. By imperial order the price has been set at an ounce of silver per bushel of hulled rice.[8] By now the man that I sent to invite the ministers should have performed his task. Attendant, keep watch outside the gate and tell me[9] who is arriving.

    ATTENDANT: Yes, sir.

---

*The translation of a term that perhaps was borrowed from southern drama or from fiction. As used in dramatic texts of the late Ming, it indicates an optional song, appearing before, between, or (rarely) after the song sequences, but usually at the beginning of a play.

**A reference to the imperial examinations for state service, specifically the Doctorate of Letters (*chin-shih*) examinations given in the capital, which was almost *de rigueur* for aspirants to high office in the Sung.

(*Enter* Han Ch'i.)

HAN: My surname is Han, my given name Ch'i, and my courtesy name Chih-kuei; I am a man of Hsiang-chou.[10] During the reign of Chia-yu,* when I was just twenty-one, I received the Doctorate of Letters. At that precise moment, an imperial astronomer reported to the throne that a rainbow-colored cloud had appeared at the capital; for this reason the Court has entrusted me with important duties, and I am now Prime Minister with the title of Duke of Wei. This morning as I was relaxing at home after morning audience, a man from his Honor Fan Chung-yen came with an invitation, and I am obliged to comply and learn what the business is at hand. Now that I am here—attendant, inform your master that Han, the Duke of Wei, is at the gate.

ATTENDANT: I beg to inform you that Han, the Duke of Wei, has arrived.

FAN: Ask him to enter. (*approaches*[11] Han) Please sit down, your Excellency.

HAN: What is the occasion, I wonder, for your invitation?

FAN: I should like to open the discussion once everyone has arrived, your Excellency. Attendant, go back to the gate and keep watch.

ATTENDANT: Yes, Sir.

(*Enter* Lü I-chien.)

LÜ: I, Lü I'chien, have seen continuous service since graduating in the first rank and, by the favor of his Majesty, enjoy the office of Chief Councillor of the Secretariat.** This morning a man from Fan Chung-yen, the T'ien-chang Scholar, came with an invitation, and I felt that I should go learn what it might concern. Now that I am here—attendant, go tell your master that Lü I-chien has arrived.

ATTENDANT: I beg to inform you that Councillor Lü has arrived.

---

*The Chia-yu reign of Emperor Jen Tsung of the Northern Sung lasted from 1056–1063.

**The Chief Councillor of the Secretariat was in fact the prime minister of the Northern Sung government.

FAN: Ask him to enter. (*approaches* Lü)

LÜ: Ah, I see that your Honor is here already. Well, Scholar Fan, what matter do we have to discuss today?

FAN: Please take a seat, sir. Once everyone is here, we can start.

(*Enter* Lord[12] Liu.)

LIU:

(*in verse*)

A prince among all scoundrels,[13]

A prodigal supreme

Just to hear the name will give an ache to any head

Lord Liu am I, a man of might and influence to spare.

Lord Liu, that's who I am. I come from a long line of power and wealth; I can kill a man as easily as lifting a piece of tile off a roof and will get off just as free as you please. While I was relaxing at home, a man came with an invitation from the Scholar Fan Chung-yen, and I thought I had better go find out what's the matter. While I've been talking, I've come to the spot. Attendant, inform your master that I've arrived.

ATTENDANT: I beg to inform you that Lord Liu is at the gate.

FAN: Ask him to enter. (*approaches* Liu)

LIU: So you are all here, gentlemen. Scholar Fan, what business have you called us here to discuss?

FAN: Please take a seat, Lord Liu. I have asked all of you here for one particular item: a letter has come from the officials of Ch'en-chou informing us of the drought, famine, and suffering there. Upon my report of this to the throne, the emperor has ordered me to send two honest officials to open the granaries and sell rice at the set price of an ounce of silver per bushel. Now what I have asked you here to discuss, gentlemen, is whom we can send to Ch'en-chou to take charge of the granaries and sell the rice.

HAN: Since this is a matter of emergency relief, only the most scrupulous of men will do.

LÜ: I concur wholeheartedly.

FAN: What is your opinion, your Lordship?

LIU: My dear sirs, allow me to suggest the two most scrupulous individuals I can think of: my two boys, one my son-in-law Yang Chin-wu, the other my own son, Liu Te-chung. If we send them, nothing can go amiss. How do you feel about it, gentlemen?

FAN: Lord Liu has recommended his two sons, Young Liu and his son-in-law, Yang Chin-wu, to go to Ch'en-chou to sell the rice. Since I've never seen your sons, your Lordship, I wonder if I might trouble you to call them here and let me have a look at them.

LIU: Attendant, call my sons here.[14]

ATTENDANT: Yes, sir. Let the two young masters come forward.

(*Enter* Young Liu *and* Yang Chin-wu.)

YOUNG LIU:

(*in verse*)
The vast blue heavens I know full well,
Three hundred and sixty-seven feet o'erhead.
I get on a ladder, and what do I see?
Just a blue and white stone, is all.*

I'm[15] Liu Te-chung, son of Lord Liu, and this is my brother-in-law, Yang Chin-wu. Under the protection of our father, we thieve and grab, pocket and pinch, meddle and loaf, riot and run amuck. Oh, everybody knows who I am, all right! As soon as I lay eyes on somebody's nice piece of goods—an antique, maybe, or gold, silver, jewelry, whatever—just as long as it's worth something, then I'm a regular chip off the old block; I take it for my own, scot free. If somebody won't hand it over, I start kicking and hitting and pulling hair; I flip him over and stamp on him a few times for good measure. Then I pick out the good things and make off with them. He can make his complaints to any magistrate he likes, I don't care; if I ever let anybody like that scare me, I'm the son of a scabby toad. Right now my father's calling for me, and I'd better go find out what he wants.

YANG: If Father's calling for us, he's probably counting on us to pull him out of some scrape he's gotten himself into. Well, here

---

*Young Liu gleefully admits here that he is of small moral stature.

we are. Attendant, announce that Squire Liu and his brother-in-law Yang Chin-wu are here.

ATTENDANT: I beg to inform you that the two young masters have arrived.

FAN: Have[16] them come in.

ATTENDANT: You may go in.

(Young Liu *and* Yang *approach the others.*)

YOUNG LIU: Why have you called us here, Father?

LIU: Now that you're here, you might pay your respects to everyone.

FAN: So these are your sons, your Lordship; from a look at them, I should hazard a guess that they're not quite suitable for the task.

LIU: Gentlemen, Scholar Fan, hear me out. Do you suppose that I don't know my own sons? I guarantee that they're honest enough to sell the rice.

HAN: Scholar Fan, those two will never do.

LIU: Your Honor, surely you're aware of the saying, "No one knows a son like his own father." They will be just fine.

LÜ: Let's leave the matter up to the T'ien-chang Scholar.

LIU: Scholar Fan, I'll even draw up a written guarantee that my boys will sell the rice, and I'll submit to punishment along with them if anything should go wrong.

FAN: Very well, since Lord Liu has guaranteed you, kneel toward the palace and listen to the imperial decree: "Because of the drought, famine, and suffering in Ch'en-chou, we are sending you there to open the granaries and sell rice at the set price of one ounce of silver per bushel. Take care that you hold to the law and keep the public welfare constantly in mind, that in governing the people you act with compassion."[17] Today is an auspicious time to begin your long journey. Face the palace and give thanks for his Majesty's favor.

(Young Liu *and* Yang *bow.*)

YOUNG LIU: Our thanks to all of you for your support. We go as pure as ice and jade and shall return when our task is done. We know you will applaud what we're about to do.

(*They go out the gate.*)

LIU: Come over here, boys. My rank is nothing to complain about, but the family finances could use a little help. Now when you get to Ch'en-chou, you might as well get some private advantage out of a public transaction: on the sly, change the official price set by Scholar Fan from one ounce of silver to two. Give them the full measure, all right, but mix a little dirt and chaff into the grain first. Make each bushel short by six quarts and add thirty per cent to the scales. Let them try crying to Scholar Fan; I'll be working from this end, so you can start your trip with peace of mind.

YOUNG LIU: No need to say a word, Father; we know what to do. You see, I'm even sharper than you are. Just one thing: if the people at Ch'en-chou don't go along with us, how can we put them in line?

LIU: Good point, son. I'll take it up with Scholar Fan. (*steps up to Fan*) There is only one problem, sir: the people of Ch'en-chou are hard to control, and if they give my sons trouble, how do you suggest they be put in line?

FAN: I have anticipated your question, your Lordship; I have already brought the matter up before the throne. If the people of Ch'en-chou should prove hard to control, there is always the gold[18] mace, a gift from the emperor; executions carried out with that are not subject to judicial review.* Attendant, bring it to me immediately. This, sir, is the gold mace. Give it to your son, but tell him to act with caution.

YOUNG LIU: With those words in mind, we'll be setting out today, then, for Ch'en-chou to open the granaries.

(*in verse*)
An ounce a bushel — that's the price they set;
Two ounces a bushel — that means some for us.
Our father has guaranteed it, nothing can go wrong;

---

*Normally capital punishment in the Sung and, nominally at least, in the Yuan could be carried out only after review at the provincial and metropolitan governmental levels.

Well, we're just a couple of grafters, after all.

(*Exit with* Yang.)

LIU: Well, sir, my sons are starting off now.

FAN: Yes, Lord Liu, indeed they are.

(*Hsien-lü* mode, Melody: *Shang hua shih*)

From year upon year of plagues of nature, famine dire,

Most of the people have had to run far away.

Hence it is that to sell rice at Ch'en-chou,

You would offer your sons;

Yet it gives me pause — are they indeed the ones to share

Our sovereign's sore cares?

Attendant, my horse; I am off to report to the emperor.

(*Exit with* Liu.)

HAN: I doubt very much, your Honor, that those two are going to do the people any good; rather, that they'll do them a good deal of harm is far more likely. If we should get any more bulletins from the region in the future, I have another plan of action in mind.

LÜ: The salvation of the people rests with you, your Honor.

HAN: Now that Scholar Fan has gone to court to report to the emperor, we might as well go back to our homes.

(*in verse*)

The relief of famine is no light task;

Through integrity shall the people be saved.

LÜ:

(*in verse*)

Future winds of rumor, should they reach our ears,

Shall you and I submit to the crown, each and every one.

(*Exeunt.*)

ACT ONE

(*Enter* Young Liu *and* Yang Chin-wu *with a servant bearing the gold mace.*)

YOUNG LIU:

(*in verse*)

Oh, what a splendid noble am I!
Not a thought for the commonweal, only for cash.
When all is found out and my head hits the ground,
A big piece of plaster should cover the gash.

Little Lord Liu, son of Lord Liu, that's me. My brother-in-law
Yang Chin-wu and I are here in Ch'en-chou to open the granaries
and sell rice. The price was supposed to be one ounce of silver per
bushel, but it's two now. We'll give out a full measure, but with
some dirt and chaff thrown into the bargain. Each bushel will be
short by six quarts, and the scales heavier by thirty per cent. If the
people raise a fuss, no need to fear; we have the gold mace, the gift
from the throne. Servant, call for the granary clerks.[19]

SERVANT: Let the local granary clerks come forward.

(*Enter two* Granary Clerks.)

FIRST CLERK:[20]

(*in verse*)

A clever granary clerk am I,
Lifting some rice for the wifey dear.
I don't exactly haul if off by the bale,
Just stint on the measure is all.

We two are the clerks of the granary here. The authorities think
we're as honest as they come and don't have an eye for even a grain
of rice, and so they keep hiring us year after year. They say the two
newly appointed granary officials are something to be reckoned
with. We'd better go find out what they want us for. (*approaches*
Young Liu) Your Honor, what may I do for you?

YOUNG LIU: So you're one of the clerks, are you? Well, I have
some instructions for you. The price set by the throne for a bushel
of rice is two ounces of silver, and there's no way we can deduct[21]
even a bit of that for ourselves. What we *can* do is change the measure and the scales on the sly, making the measure smaller by six
quarts and the scales heavier by thirty per cent. Most of the take
will go to me, of course. Sixty-forty should about do it.

FIRST CLERK: Of course, sir. Even then you'll be helping me
make a tidy bundle. I'll just open the granary now and see who
comes along.

(*Enter three* Rice Customers.)

CUSTOMER: We, the people of Ch'en-chou, are suffering terribly from the three-year drought and the failure of the grain harvest. Fortunately his Majesty has graciously sent two officials to sell rice from the granary. The authorities said the price determined by the throne was to be one ounce of silver for a bushel of rice. The trouble is, it's now two ounces; what's more, the rice has dirt and chaff mixed in it, the measure we get is six quarts short, and the payment in silver is thirty per cent extra. We know very well that this is no way to do business, but the granary is the only place where we can get any rice at all, and we're not about to endure starvation. The only way out is to gather everybody's silver together and buy some rice to keep us from death's door. And so here we are.

FIRST CLERK: Where do you people come from?

CUSTOMER: We're the people of Ch'en-chou, here to buy rice.

YOUNG LIU: Take a good look at their silver, you two. I don't care what else they try to pass off on you, just watch out for the stuff with lead on the inside; don't let them hoodwink you is all I ask.

SECOND CLERK: All right then, how much silver have you people gotten together?

CUSTOMER: All we have between us is twenty-four ounces.

FIRST CLERK: Put it on the scales.—Oh no, it's far too short. You have only fourteen ounces here.

CUSTOMER: Our silver is a five cash weight.*

YOUNG LIU: These people are getting hard to handle. Get out the gold mace and give them a whack.[22]

CUSTOMER: Don't beat us, sir; we'll add a little more and be done with it.

FIRST CLERK: Then do it and be quick about it. I want my forty per cent.

---

*The customer apparently is explaining that each piece of silver is half the standard weight, since by usual reckoning ten cash (or penny-weight), not five, made up an ounce. The line may be a joke based on the customer's ignorance or on his attempt to put something over on the clerk.

CUSTOMER: (*adds the silver*) Six ounces more.

SECOND CLERK: Still short by a little but never mind.

YOUNG LIU: Now that they've paid in full, give them their rice.

SECOND CLERK: Five bushels, ten, fifteen, twenty.

YOUNG LIU: Don't give them a full measure. Put the containers on a slant and scoop a little out of the middle.

FIRST CLERK: I know what you mean. I have things well in hand.

CUSTOMER: The rice is two bushels short that way, plus the fact that dirt and husks are mixed in. When we grind that up, we're not going to get much more than five bushels out of it. Ah well, let it be; it's our fate, after all, to be mistreated like this. As they say, "In curing the wounds before your eyes, you carve out the flesh from your very heart."*

(*Exeunt.*) (*Enter* Chang the Headstrong[23] *and* Young Chang.)

CHANG:

(*in verse*)

A hundred patches mend and piece the tatters of the poor,

While springtime robes of venal clerks are sweeping on the ground.

I wonder who it is that makes the crops go dead and spoil,

Who makes the storms lash out and wreck the labors of my hand.

I am a man of Ch'en-chou named Chang. My personality is a little difficult, and so people all call me Chang the Headstrong. I have a son named Chang Jen. Because of the shortage of grain here in Ch'en-chou, a couple of granary officials were sent by a few days ago. I hear tell that with the emperor's set price of an ounce of silver for a bushel of rice, they were supposed to relieve every-

---

*That is, in order to alleviate immediate suffering, one must make drastic and painful sacrifices.

body's misery. Now those two have changed it to two ounces and made the measure short and the scales extra heavy. I've just managed to scrape up some odd silver from around my farm into these few ounces to go buy some rice.

YOUNG CHANG: Just one word of caution, father: since you're always so headstrong, when we get to where we buy the rice, you'd better not say a word.

CHANG: What the Court intended as a favor to help the people, they're using to enrich themselves. Now tell me, am I supposed to let them go ahead with it?

> (*Hsien-lü* mode, Melody: *Tien chiang-ch'un*)
> Those officials know of the crime;
> Inside and out, they act in accord.
> But let me unite the poor as one,
> Name names, on paper for all to see,
> Then straight to the Secretariat shall I go to appeal.

YOUNG CHANG: Father, what could we possibly have to say in the face of officials like these?

CHANG:

> (Melody: *Hun chiang lung*)
> "When the top beam is crooked, the lower's awry."[24]
> Self-seeking at work fuels hatred intense.
> Should they try to cause us some trouble or pain,
> Don't think I won't raise all hell.
> Nothing is gentler than a river or stream,
> But on rocky ground then loud is its roar.[25]
> They are bent on breaking the decrees of the crown.
> They're rats set loose in the grain house,
> Flies that lap pus and foul blood. (*approaches the clerks*)

We're here.

FIRST CLERK: Hey, old man, if you're here to buy rice, let me weigh your silver.

CHANG: (*gives him the silver*) Here it is.

FIRST CLERK: (*weighs the silver*) Hey, old fellow, you've got only eight ounces here.

CHANG: Twelve ounces weighs out at eight? I don't

understand how it could be that short.

YOUNG CHANG: We brought twelve ounces with us; how could it come out to just eight? Be fair, brother.

SECOND CLERK: Don't give me that. It's eight right there on the scales. What do you think I did with the rest, swallow it?

CHANG: (*sighs*) It was twelve to start with; how can you make it out to be eight?

(Melody: *Yu hu-lu*)

O custodian of the granaries, don't turn me down
When I ask you to let me work the scales on my own.

FIRST CLERK: Don't you have a brain in your head? If your silver's on the short side, am I expected to make it come out more on the scales? I mean, there are standards, after all.

CHANG:

Who in the present day is not the cleverest of men?
But I twist and turn, irresolute,
Like mounting Remembrance Peak.*
I falter as I walk,
As if entering the Crystal Well.**

FIRST CLERK: On a scale like this one, it doesn't come to even eight ounces.

CHANG:

The silver comes out light,

(*The clerks measure the grain.*)

SECOND CLERK: I'm giving you a hollow measure, and I've scooped out a little extra.

YOUNG CHANG: Father, that one there has scooped out some of the rice!

CHANG:

Ah, and the amount of rice unfair,
With that short measure of theirs, the heavy scales.

---

*In folklore, the souls of the dead in the afterlife climbed this peak to gaze back upon the world of the living.
**Obviously another item from medieval folklore, but its origin and its meaning here are obscure.

Over a shortage of even two ounces of silver,
Why shouldn't I fight after all?

FIRST CLERK: The two granary officials are as honest as the day is long and take nothing from the people. Just as long as they get some ready cash, they have nothing but the best interests of the people at heart.

CHANG: What officials are you talking about?

FIRST CLERK: Don't you know? Those two over there are the granary officials.

CHANG:

(Melody: *T'ien-hsia le*)
Next to Pao Lung-t'u[26] of K'ai-feng-fu you cannot even
    hope to compare.

FIRST CLERK: Watch your tongue, old man. Don't provoke them. They have power and privilege to spare.

CHANG:

Boast all you like of your honest officials,
But when the law is set in motion,
A little sweetening will keep anyone from guilt.

SECOND CLERK: Too much rice here. I'll just scoop out a little more.

YOUNG CHANG: He's scooped out some more rice, father!

CHANG:

A peck here, a few quarts there,
By insulting others he only disgraces himself.

SECOND CLERK: Open up your pocket, and I'll measure some out for you.

CHANG: What kind of measurement is that? We didn't come here to buy rice just for ourselves, you know.

FIRST CLERK: So you didn't come just for yourselves. Fine. We're on official business and aren't selling it just for ourselves either.

CHANG:

(*Chin chan-erh*)
On official business, so you say;
For your own good is what *I* say.

This handful of rice that we treasure is the staff of several
  lives,
Not a mere mountain buck, not a deer of the plains, for
  all to wrangle about.
You're stealing scraps of bone from the jaws of a starv-
  ing wolf,
The dregs of broth from the bottom of a beggar's bowl.
A few pints, yes, I might give that up but no more;
Why then do you give up your good name, for nothing
  but profit alone?

FIRST CLERK: Old man, you're an idiot. Speaking against the granary officials, are you? I'll just go tell them that. (*starts to report*)

YOUNG LIU: What do you two clerks have to say?

FIRST CLERK: I must inform you that an old man here to buy rice came short of money and then started calling you names.

YOUNG LIU: Bring him here. (Chang *approaches* Young Liu.) You're playing with fire, you thief! You're short of money, and you dare call me names?

CHANG: The two of you are plundering bandits, the bane of the people, and of no good whatsoever to the realm!

FIRST CLERK: As you can see, your Honor, I wasn't lying. He's calling you names all right!

YOUNG LIU: The old peasant is going to be rude, is he? I'll just use the gold mace on him. (*beats* Chang)

YOUNG CHANG: (*raises* Chang's *head*) Father, can you hear me?[27] What did I tell you? I asked you not to say anything, and now you've been beaten with the gold mace. Oh, father, you are lost to me now!

YANG: The blow was too light. If I'd had my way, he'd have beaten his brains out in one bash and made mincemeat out of him.[28]

CHANG: (*gradually comes to*)
    (Melody: *Ts'un-li ya-ku*)
    The golden mace fell
    Like a clap of thunder overhead,
    And over my body blood pours.

What can I do? How can I fight them?

Where did it strike, on the back, on the skull, on the
    shoulder?

I feel only the pangs of a tooth lanced through, the pain
    of a carved-out chest, the ache of trampled bones.

The signs, oh the signs that my long life is through!

Why have you beaten me, when I came only to buy rice?

YOUNG LIU: What does your life matter, something worth no
more than a blade of grass? You can tell any courtroom you like
that I was the one who hit you. I couldn't care less.

YOUNG CHANG: What are we to do, father?

CHANG:

(Melody: *Yüan-ho ling*)

We are guiltless who buy the rice;

The guilty are you who sell it.

YOUNG LIU: I was the one who hit you, all right, but I'm not
worried, not worried at all. Go ahead and inform on me. See where
it gets you.

CHANG:

Prison and exile, whip and staff are the punishments for
    crime,

And don't they say that before each man's gate lies a
    fathomless moat?

Fill it in as you will,

In it you shall go, pushed all the harder for that.

YANG: We're as pure as water and white as flour,* praised by
everybody at Court, civil and military alike.

CHANG:

(Melody: *Shang ma chiao*)

Ah, pure, yes, pure on the surface you are,

As the turnip is green above soil,[29]

YOUNG LIU: I look more like a weed than anything else. Who
do you think you're calling a turnip?

*The concluding segment of this expression, left off in the original text, is
found elsewhere in northern drama. Water and flour mixed together produce
a turbid paste, the symbol of stupidity and immorality.

CHANG:

> Sitting there in your money-grubbing audience hall,
> Smearing your mirror of office in a dish of flour paste.

YANG: I'll have you know we're famous for our unimpeachable purity and honesty.

CHANG:

> Ah, still back on that purity of yours,
> Like ice in a pitcher of jade?*

YOUNG LIU: It's precisely because we're the epitome of purity that every single minister at Court recommended us for this job.

CHANG:

> (Melody: *Sheng hu-lu*)
> Chicanery is all you are after;[30]
> Who of you would really aid the Court?

YANG: Old peasant, trying to pressure us with talk of the Court, but you don't scare me a bit.

CHANG:

> One fine day you'll feast on the headsman's sword.
> Then, your money spent, friends gone, family split
>   asunder,
> Then will come remorse for a lifetime of greed.

YOUNG LIU: This miserable wretch is a sty in my eye, a thorn in my flesh. Getting rid of him would be about as consequential as squeezing a rotten persimmon.

CHANG: Hold your tongue!

> (Melody: *Hou-t'ing hua*)
> The poor to you are sties in the eye,
> And the good, goiters 'neath the jaw.

Have you people no moral standards whatever?

> Have your fill of your wine and your meat,
> But keep gold and silver far away from the scales.

My son, take this matter to a magistrate.

YOUNG CHANG: You know how much influence they have,

---

*A jade pitcher was the traditional symbol of ethical purity.

father. I don't think we stand a chance of making a complaint
against them.

CHANG:

    Hurry, son, lay plaint and fear not.

YOUNG CHANG: If I did, who would be my corroborating witness?

CHANG:

    The mace of gold shall prove your case.

YOUNG CHANG: We may have some corroboration, but where
should I take the complaint?

CHANG:

    Straight to the provincial court of appeal

    Go with your grievance and shout it out loud.

    Put forth the true plight we bear.

    Some lord or minister there

    Will surely sanction your plea.

YOUNG CHANG: If not, where else should I go?

CHANG:

    Though the ravenous beasts

    Would use guile and foul tricks

    To block your access to all courts in the land,

    The emperor's throne is your last resort, there to beat
        the Drum of Appeal.

(Melody: *Ch'ing-ko-erh*)

Neither winning nor losing is allowed in the strife,

Yet clear are rewards for deeds done.

Was the gold mace intended to slaughter the good?

Though I lie in the realms of dark death,

My memory shall always live on,

Till the gods, once informed,

Haul the thieves to Hell's Court,

Extract their confessions of guilt,

And strike their lives off against mine.

Only then shall sore hatred be calmed.

Else never shall dim these hawk's eyes of mine.

I haven't much longer to live, my son. Be sure to make this case known.

    YOUNG CHANG: I shall.

    CHANG: The plundering bandits, they extract their salaries from the emperor but do nothing to share his woes. Instead they persecute people like us. Oh Heaven above!

    (Melody: *Tsuan sha-wei*)

    Stupid are they who seek riches in office;

    Honest and bright are the ones who do not.

    Corrupt officials like you

    Take his Majesty's pay in vain.

You plundering bandits, have you ever stopped to think just why you were sent to open the granaries and sell rice?

    It was to save us from famine.

    Ask yourselves, then,

    To what purpose you laid open my skull with the mace.

    YOUNG CHANG: When should I set out to make the appeal?

    CHANG:

    Be on your way today

    Straight to the imperial seat.

    They say, "No more formidable foe than father and son."

    Choose a man of probity and keen mind

    And give the lie to these robbers of the people.

    YOUNG CHANG: Which tribunal should I go to, father?

    CHANG:

    To rid the Ch'en-chou people of harm

    Only the impartial Judge Pao, with face of iron,[31] only

       he will do.

    (*Exit.*)

    YOUNG CHANG: (*weeping*) My father is dead, and I'll never stop until I have revenge! I don't think the local officials here in Ch'en-chou can do anything about this, so I'll go all the way to the capital, pick out an important tribunal, and swear out my complaint there.

    (*in verse*)

    What they say is they're relieving disaster;

> What they did was to put my father to death.
> I was born of no miracle but of parents dear,
> Whose revenge I must have if my name's to be Chang.
> (*Exit.*)

YOUNG LIU: Clerk, the old man wanted his son to report us. I figure that he'll take it to the capital, where my father is. What's more, Scholar Fan is a good friend of my father's. One person be damned, why, we could kill ten and still get away with it.[32] Well, nothing to do here; let's go to Powderface[33] Wang's place at Dog Leg Bay and have something to drink. As they say,

> Granaries and storesheds
> Make you rich in a trice.
> Powderface Wang's
> Makes a patron feel nice.
> (*Exeunt.*)

ACT TWO

(*Enter* Fan Chung-yen *with attendants.*)

FAN: I am Fan Chung-yen. Ever since Lord Liu recommended those two sons of his to open the granaries and sell rice at Ch'en-chou, it has turned out to my surprise that as soon as they arrived there, they broke the law by taking graft and spent their time drinking and carousing. His Majesty has ordered me to send someone else to Ch'en-chou, someone honest this time, who will settle this case. To accomplish this, the throne will confer upon him a Sword of Authority and a Gold Badge,[34] and with these he can perform summary executions without going through channels beforehand.[35] Today in the Conference Hall I plan to meet with the various ministers, who should be here by now. Attendant, stand watch at the gate and tell me when they have arrived.

ATTENDANT: Yes, sir.

(*Enter* Han Ch'i.)

HAN: I am Duke Han of Wei. Fan Chung-yen, the T'ien-chang Scholar, is at the Conference Hall and has sent someone for me. I thought it best to come and find out what he has in mind. Ah, here's the gate.

ATTENDANT: Duke Han of Wei has arrived.

FAN: Ask him to come in. (Han *approaches* Fan.) Welcome, your Honor. Please have a seat.

(*Enter Lü I-chien.*)

LÜ: I am Lü I-chien. While I was relaxing at home, a man from the Scholar Fan Chung-yen came with a request to go to the Conference Hall, and here I am.

ATTENDANT: Prime Minister Lü is here.

FAN: Ask him to enter.

(Lü *approaches* Fan.)

LÜ: So you are here, your Honor. Scholar, may I ask why you have called me here today?

FAN: Gentlemen, the matter concerns the sale of rice at Ch'en-chou and Lord Liu's recommendation of his sons as granary officials, their avarice, lawlessness, drinking, and carousing. I have His Majesty's orders to call the ministers together and propose an honest official to proceed to Ch'en-chou and put the matter to rest. Now that everybody is present, we can put our heads together and come up with someone.

HAN: You must have chosen someone by now, and we of course will go along with your recommendation.

(*Enter* Young Chang.)

YOUNG CHANG: I'm Young Chang. My father and I went to buy some rice, but the two granary officials beat my father to death. When he was about to die, my father commanded me to appeal to Judge Pao. People say he's an old man with a white beard. I'm now waiting at this thoroughfare to see who might come along.

(*Enter* Lord Liu.)

LIU: I am Lord Liu. I haven't heard a word from my boys since they left for Ch'en-chou to sell rice. Now someone is here saying that Scholar Fan wants to see me. I'd better go find out what the matter is now.

YOUNG CHANG: That white-bearded old man must be Judge Pao. I'll go up and make my appeal to him. (*kneels*)

LIU: Well, young fellow, what's your problem? I'll do what I can for you.

YOUNG CHANG: I've come from Ch'en-chou. My father and I went to buy some rice with twelve ounces of silver, and my father was murdered with a blow of the gold mace by the granary officials. No one there dares to touch them, but since you must be Judge Pao, you can help me.

LIU: I'm Judge Pao, all right, young man. I'll help you. Just stay right there and don't tell anybody else about this.

YOUNG CHANG: (*rises*) Yes, sir.

LIU: (*aside*) Oh, I suppose those two bastards have gotten themselves into some kind of mess! Attendant, announce that Lord Liu is at the gate.

ATTENDANT: Lord Liu is here.

(Lord Liu *approaches the others.*)

FAN: A couple of fine, upstanding officials you've recommended, Lord Liu!

LIU: My two boys really *are* fine, upstanding officials, Scholar. I'd never try to put anything over on you.

FAN: What I hear, your Lordship, is that those two sons of yours have done nothing at Ch'en-chou but drink and carouse, ignore their duties, take graft and flout the law, and mistreat the people. Are you aware of all this?

LIU: Don't listen to what other people say, your Honor. Nobody I recommend would ever do things like that.

FAN: It seems that he still isn't convinced, gentlemen.

YOUNG CHANG: (*to* Attendant) Say, brother, the one who just went inside—he must be his Honor Judge Pao, right?

ATTENDANT: That was Lord Liu. If you want Judge Pao, he hasn't shown up yet.

YOUNG CHANG: Good lord! I wanted to report Lord Liu, and where do I end up but in the jaws of the tiger himself! I'm finished now!

(*Enter* Judge Pao *with* Chang Ch'ien.[36])

PAO: My surname is Pao, my given name Cheng, and my courtesy name Hsi-wen. I come from Lao-erh Hamlet, Ssu-wang

Village, Chin-tou Commandery.[37] With the rank of Academician-in-waiting of the Lung-t'u Pavilion, I hold the office of magistrate of the Southern Court[38] of K'ai-feng. I have just returned from a tour of inspection in Wu-nan[39] on his Majesty's orders and must now go to the Conference Hall to see the ministers.

CHANG: I was wondering, your Honor, when you plan to open and close court?

PAO:

> (*Cheng-kung* mode, Melody: *Tuan-cheng hao*)
> From the first hour of the cloudy morn
> Straight to evening with its fading sun
> Without cease my head will be immersed in the records,
> My hands caught up in my purple robes,
> And I know now what service entails.

> (Melody: *Kun hsiu-ch'iu*)
> If you take no bribes, you disappoint others;
> But to go after money is not my desire.
> This salary of mine is scarcely enough to allow me to
>   please friends and kin.

CHANG: Your Honor has never dodged the rich and powerful.
PAO:

> 'Gainst the mighty I have hatred as high as the hills,
>   as deep as the bed of the sea:
> I had one named Lu get the ax in the square,
> Had another named Ko sent to jail,[40]
> And what do I get for all of this but some curses bitter
>   and foul.

CHANG: Your Honor is old now, but you still have your ideals.
PAO:

> All that is over now.
> From this time on
> If things do not touch me I'll say not a word.
> I shall give a curt nod to the world of man
> And roam in freedom complete.[41]

Here we are at the door of the Conference Hall. Take my horse, Chang Ch'ien.

YOUNG CHANG: Someone I asked said this was Judge Pao.
(*kneels and shouts*) Help me, my lord; I am the victim of injustice!

PAO: Who are you, my boy? What problem do you have? Tell
me the truth and I'll help you.

YOUNG CHANG: I'm from Ch'en-chou and am the son of Chang
the Headstrong. Two officials have opened up the Ch'en-chou granary and are selling rice. The price set by the emperor was an ounce
of silver a bushel, but they changed it to two ounces. Our family
scraped together twelve ounces of silver to buy some rice, and they
weighed it out at only eight ounces. When my father went up to
them and protested, he was beaten to death in a single blow from a
gold mace. I wanted to make an accusation against them, but
people said they were members of a rich and powerful family and
nobody there could touch them. As my father was dying he said,
"My son, when my life is over, go straight to the capital, find his
Honor Judge Pao, and make your appeal to him." Now that I have
seen you, sir, it is as if through the parting clouds I see the sun
once more, as if a dull mirror has been polished anew.[42] You must
help me!

> (*in verse*)
> If I could but tell you how I feel — —
> But my voice is choked back by sobs.
> The golden mace took my father's life,
> And hard is the grievance I bear!

PAO: Stand aside.

> (Young Chang *pulls on* Pao.)

YOUNG CHANG: If you won't help me, my lord, who will?

PAO: Yes, yes, I understand. (Young Chang *pulls on* Pao *two
more times.*) Attendant, announce that Judge Pao is at the gate.

ATTENDANT: Judge Pao has arrived.

FAN: Good, good, Pao Lung-t'u is here. Hurry and ask him to
come in.

> (Pao *approaches the others.*)

HAN: Now that you've just returned from your inspection trip
to Wu-nan, Judge, you must be exhausted.

PAO: Yours is the difficult task, gentlemen.

LIU: Welcome back from your long journey, Magistrate.

PAO: Oh, I beg your pardon, your Lordship.

LIU: (*aside*) Now why did the old fellow give me that look?
He couldn't have seen the boy making the accusation, could he?
I'll just feign ignorance.

PAO: After I got back from my inspection of Wu-nan yesterday, I saw his Majesty, and today I've made it a point to pay my
respects to you gentlemen.

FAN: I wonder, Judge, how old you were when you took up
official service, and how old you are now. Please go into it in some
detail.

PAO: How old was I when I became an official and what is my
age now, you ask. Well, it's not a very interesting story, but I'll tell
you all about it, as you wish.

> (Melody: *T'ang hsiu-ts'ai*)
> Since taking my degree at thirty-five or six,
> I've served now to the age of seventy-eight or nine.
> Haven't you heard? "At middle age, all things come to
>   a halt."
> I have studied the lore of the T'ang and the Han, read
>   the *Spring and Autumn Annals;**
> In my career all these have been my guides.

FAN: You've been in office many years and have such broad
experience.

LÜ: You have served your country with the most loyalty;
you have attacked evil and raised the standard of honesty. So it is
that in the Court and beyond, the sound of your great name strikes
fear into the rich and powerful families. You are truly an example
of the honest statesman of ages past!

PAO: I am nothing.[43] I think back on the statesmen of virtue
in former dynasties, men who met an undeserved death; after all,
brashness like mine has never been the way to preserve one's life.

FAN: Tell us about them.

---

*The annals of the state of Lu from 722 to 481 B.C. The work was supposedly
edited by Confucius and forms part of the Confucian classics. The name came
to signify historical writings in general and may be so employed here.

PAO:

(Melody: *Kun hsiu-ch'iu*)
Ch'ü Yuan of Ch'u died in a river;
Kuan Lung-feng came under the sword.
Pi-kan's heart was cut out by Chou,
And Marquis Han was beheaded in Wei-yang Palace.[44]

LÜ: Judge, Chang Liang planned strategy while sitting in a
tent and won battles hundreds of miles away.[45] He assisted the
first emperor of the Han to found the empire, but when he saw one
of his comrades, Han Hsin, executed and another, P'eng Yueh,
made into pickle, he abdicated his noble title and vowed to follow
the immortal Ch'ih-sung-tzu in his wanderings. In my opinion, he
had a great deal of foresight.

PAO:

If Chang Liang had not hurried home,

HAN: And it was well for Fan Li of the Kingdom of Yueh
that he sailed the five lakes in his skiff.[46]

PAO:

And if Fan Li had not secretly fled,
Neither would have ended with his corpse in one piece.
I am a fish that has escaped the net;
How dare I swallow the hook once more?
Best to return to the mountains at once.
I only fear that I shall not fulfill my duties
And that I serve in vain.

Gentlemen, I am far too old to be an official. When I next see his
Majesty, I'll request relief of my duties and permission to retire.

FAN: You're making a mistake, Judge. After all, how many
at Court these days even approach your honesty? Moreover, you're
hardly senile. Your age is just right for official service. Why, then,
request to be relieved?

PAO: Scholar, I have something that I should like to speak
with you about.

LIU: You're right, Magistrate, you're not getting any younger.
You'd be much happier if you gave up office and requested relief
and retirement.

FAN: What was it that your Honor wanted to talk to me about? I'm ready to listen.

PAO:

> (Melody: *Ai ku to*)
> I have made it clear to my sovereign
> That those who lust for power are my mortal foes.

FAN: How would you deal with them?

PAO:

> They are bandits who plunder the homes of the people,
> But a fierce watchdog am I.
> Money and possessions are all they desire,
> But never shall they keep this hound from tracking them
>   down.
> If they could have me die this day and vanish the next,
> They would feel untrammeled and free in a hundred, a
>   thousand ways.

FAN: You may go home for now, Judge. I am afraid that I have other matters to discuss here.

PAO: (*takes his leave*) Forgive my rudeness, gentlemen; I'll take my leave. (*leaves through door*)

> (Young Chang *kneels at doorway and shouts.*)

YOUNG CHANG: Help me, my lord!

PAO: I'd almost forgotten. Go on home first, my boy; I'll join you later.

YOUNG CHANG: (*shows his gratitude*) Now that I've seen Judge Pao, he'll help me for sure. He told me to go back home first, so I'd better not stay here any longer but go to Ch'en-chou and wait for him there.

> (*in verse*)
> Now I've seen the Lung-t'u Judge
> And told of my father's cruel death.
> Now to return to Ch'en-chou and wait till he comes
> There to beat the criminals with the golden mace.
> (*Exit.*) (Pao *turns about and re-enters.*)

FAN: I thought you had left. Why are you back?

PAO: Just as I was about to leave for home, I heard that

corrupt officials and wicked clerks were victimizing the people of Ch'en-chou. I wonder, have you sent any capable officials to Ch'en-chou?

HAN: The Scholar sent two.

PAO: And who might those two be?

FAN: I don't suppose that you could have known about it, but since the time you left for the inspection trip to Wu-nan, the Court has been temporarily short of men, so we sent Lord Liu's son Liu Te-chung and his son-in-law Yang Chin-wu to Ch'en-chou to sell rice. It has been some time now since we've heard from them.

PAO: I hear that the officials and clerks of a certain county of Ch'en-chou are dishonest and the people are restless. Wouldn't it be wise to send another man to Ch'en-chou to investigate those officials and clerks and calm the people?

HAN: For your information, Judge, it is precisely for this reason that we officials are gathered here today.

FAN: I have received his Majesty's orders to send another official to Ch'en-chou, an honest one this time, first, to sell the rice and second, to judge this case. Since I doubt that anyone else could accomplish the task, I have to trouble you to make the trip. How do you feel about it?

PAO: I can't go.

LÜ: If you can't, whom can we send?

FAN: Judge Pao is adamant. Defer to him this once, Lord Liu, but you had better go if he doesn't.

LIU: Of course. Why not make the trip to Ch'en-chou, Judge?[47]

PAO: Since your Lordship is so insistent that I go, I'll do it for your sake. Chang Ch'ien, prepare my horse; we're off to Ch'en-chou!

LIU: (*startled, aside*) What!! If the old fellow really does go, what will become of my two boys?

PAO:

> (Melody: *T'o pu-shan*)
> Hot tempered and stubborn am I,[48]
> Just like pouring oil on fire.
> With despotic officials I love to lock horns,[49]

So my thanks to you, sir, for vouching for me at the
    Court.

LIU: I did no such thing!

PAO:

    (Melody: *Hsiao Liang-chou*)

    With heart beset by care for the realm,

Chang Ch'ien, my horse!

    CHANG: Yes, sir!

PAO:

    Off I go to Ch'en-chou,

    For my heart drives my thoughts onward.[50]

    So cleverly have they worked behind the scenes,

    A pity they haven't long to enjoy the results.

Gentlemen, your attention please. I'll make the journey, but if the
rich and the powerful prove hard to deal with, what would you
have me do?

    FAN: That is no cause for worry. His Majesty will give you a
Sword of Authority and a Golden Badge, as well as the right to
perform summary executions. Take this Sword of Authority and
this Golden Badge, please, before setting out for Ch'en-chou.

    PAO:

    (Melody: *Refrain*)

    Thanks be to his Majesty for his concern for the people.

    Sword, no need to hold back at Ch'en-chou;

    You'll have your taste of raw human flesh.

    Ah, there! That animal, devoid of conscience,

    First to fall should be his, a traitor's head!

    LIU: Magistrate, when you get to Ch'en-chou,—the two gra-
nary officials are members of my family. Look after them for my
sake.

    PAO: (*gazing at the sword*) Of course; I'll look after them with
this.

    (Liu's *request and* Pao's *action and reply are repeated
    twice.*)

    LIU: Are you totally without human feelings? I've asked a
favor of you two or three times now, but all you do is look at the

Sword of Authority and say you'll look after them with that.
Would you dare kill my two boys? As far as rank is concerned, I
have nothing to fear from you, and I'm certainly richer than you!

    PAO: How could I ever compare with you?

       (Melody: *Shua hai-erh*)

       You have amassed gold and silver into a pile higher than
          the Dipper

       And would hope to endure with Heaven and Earth.

       You'll see how your toils for family and country shall
          end.

       Your every word is devoid of shame.

       With just my brush I struggle for trifling pay;

       By what sword did you ever win your title and your
          rank?

    LIU: I am not afraid of you.

    PAO:

       Stop your bragging!

       Though you cause one-man havoc,

       On my shoulders alone shall lie the worries of Ch'en-chou.

    LIU: Magistrate, you don't know how difficult it is to be a
granary official.

    PAO: I am well aware of the troubles[51] of granary officials.

    LIU: If so, then tell me.

    PAO:

       (Melody: *Sha-wei*)

       Take away that grain on the river bank;

       Pile up those tallies in the storehouse.

       Be sure to fatten your own pockets;

       Don't let the skin and bones of the people get you down.
When I get there,

       I'll have them gather up their baskets and stop their weigh-
          ing.[52]

       (*Exit with* Chang Ch'ien.)

    LIU: Gentlemen, this affair is turning out badly. When the old
fellow gets there, he's going to show no mercy to my boys.

    HAN: There's nothing to fear, your Lordship. Just take your

problem to Scholar Fan. Prime Minister Lü and I shall be going
now.

> (*in verse*)
> My lord, don't be sick at heart;
> Take it up with the T'ien-chang Scholar.

LÜ:

> (*in verse*)
> Even when phoenixes alight on the parasol tree,*
> Someone will always be there with a comment to make.[53]
> (*Exeunt.*)

FAN: Set your heart at ease, Lord Liu. I'll speak before His
Majesty and have you take his orders there in person, along with a
document that pardons all but the dead.[54] I guarantee that nothing
will come of this.

LIU: In that case I thank you, Scholar.

FAN: Come with me to see his Majesty.

> (*in verse*)
> Don't be concerned about Judge Pao.
> First ask for the letter of pardon.

LIU:

> (*in verse*)
> I place all my trust in a half sheet of paper
> To save my whole family from woe.
> (*Exeunt.*)

ACT THREE

> (*Enter* Young Liu *and* Yang.)

YOUNG LIU:

> (*in verse*)
> Do nothing wrong by the light of the day,
> And a nighttime knock needn't strike you with fear.

---

*According to legend, phoenixes would alight only on the parasol tree, and
such an event was held to be a good omen. Lü is telling him not to be need-
lessly pessimistic.

I am Lord Liu's son. Ever since the two of us came to Ch'en-chou to open the granary and sell rice, we've followed my father's advice by changing the price, adding chaff and dirt, and pocketing a lot of money for ourselves, and when we get home how are we ever going to spend it all? For the past few days we've just been drinking and amusing ourselves. I've heard that his Majesty has sent Judge Pao here. Brother, you don't want to provoke that old boy. He's always cutting people's heads off without going through the proper channels, and we've been a little too obvious in what we've been up to. Right now let's go to the reception point to meet old Pao.

> (*in verse*)
> Ferocious is old Pao's disposition;[55]
> Not many have angered him and lived.
> If he can't put up with us,
> Then there's nothing to do but run!
> (*Exeunt.*) (*Enter* Chang Ch'ien *with a sword slung on his back and* Pao *on horseback.* Pao *is listening to* Chang.)

CHANG: Chang Ch'ien, that's me. I've just gotten back from a tour of inspection in Wu-nan Route with his Honor Judge Pao. Now he's being sent to Ch'en-chou to sell rice with the Sword of Authority and a Gold Badge. There he is back there, while I'm a good distance up front. You have no idea how honest his Honor is, how he won't touch anything that belongs to the public. All right, so he doesn't want money, but he[56] might at least eat something! As soon as he gets to a prefecture or whatever and opens court, the officials and village elders lay some food out and he doesn't even look at it. Three meals a day, and nothing but thin gruel![57] You're old and can't eat anything else, but I'm a young man. These two feet of mine have to keep up with the four hooves of the horse, and wherever that horse goes, no matter how far, there I go. But on a meal of thin gruel I can't make over a mile before I get hungry! Now that I'm up in front, at the first house I get to, I'm going to say, "I'm with his Honor Judge Pao, who is on his way to Ch'en-chou to sell rice. With the Sword of Authority I'm carrying on my back and the Golden Badge we can behead anybody we like without authorization. So hurry up and lay out some food for me—fat partridge and tea wine!"[58] When I get my fill of that meat and wine, I'll be able to grit my teeth and cover fifty or sixty miles at a stretch!—Oh, I'm just a damn fool! I've never eaten anything like that. What am I blabbering away[59] about? What if Judge Pao back there happened to hear all that?

PAO: What was that, Chang Ch'ien?

CHANG: (*timidly*) I didn't say anything.

PAO: Something like "fat partridge"?

CHANG: I didn't say anything like "fat partridge," sir. I was just walking along and came across somebody, and when I asked him how far it was to Ch'en-chou, he said I still had a far trudge. When did I ever say anything like "fat partridge"?

PAO: Something on the order of "tea wine"?

CHANG: I didn't say anything like "tea wine," sir. I saw a man while I was walking along and asked him how we get to Ch'en-chou, and he said down the road in a beeline. I never said anything like "tea wine."

PAO: I'm getting old and hard of hearing, Chang Ch'ien. Since I'm an old man, I can't have a proper meal; thin gruel is good enough for me. But there *is* something up ahead of me that you might eat and enjoy to your heart's content. That's what I'll give you to satisfy your hunger.

CHANG: Something to satisfy my hunger, sir? What would that be?

PAO: Have a guess.

CHANG: Well, sir, you said, "There is something up ahead of me that you might eat and enjoy to your heart's content." And that's what you'll give me to satisfy my hunger. Could it be bitter tea?

PAO: No.

CHANG: Dried turnip leaves?

PAO: No.

CHANG: Oh, I know! How about thin gruel?

PAO: No again.

CHANG: If it isn't any of those things, sir, what is it?

PAO: What are you carrying on your back there?

CHANG: The sword.

PAO: That's what I'll have you eat!

CHANG: (*timidly*) I think I'd settle for thin gruel, sir!

PAO: Chang Ch'ien, now that responsible officials and clerks, soldiers and civilians in all the empire have heard about this secret journey of mine, are they happy, would you say, or are they worried?

CHANG: It wouldn't be my place to bring it up, sir, but since you ask—now that the people have heard that his Honor Judge Pao has set out for Ch'en-chou to sell rice, there isn't a single one who doesn't say in deep reverence, "Somebody who will help us is on the way!" But why should they be so happy, is what I'd like to know.

PAO: You'd have no way of knowing, Chang Ch'ien, so I'll tell you.

> (*Nan-lü* mode, Melody: *I-chih hua*)
> Now people in forced labor are happy,
> And officials with undeserved salaries are not.
> But in all this urgency, no satisfaction do I feel,
> As long as, try as I might, I can get no permission to
>   retire.
> Now, in the evening years of life,
> I feel the fatigue of the saddle.
> Now, all through the land, they say, "Pao Lung-t'u is on
>   his secret journey,
> And some officials are shaking with fear!"
>
> (Melody: *Liang-chou ti-ch'i*)
> They get their salaries of fifty or sixty thousand strings
>   of cash[60]
> And commit murder for twenty or thirty years
> In the capital and every part of the realm.
> Since our gracious lord began his reign and I took up my
>   post,
> Often have I reviewed the cases at law,
> Searching out facts in all their detail:

No more than just farmers who fought over land
Or brothers dividing the family wealth.
We now—we were the the officials of the Sung, officials
    high and low.
They now—they were dunned by you usurers for profit
    and interest.
And you—you never dreamed that the poor would cry out
    in bitterness and wrath.
Now that we are not far from Ch'en-chou,
Even should someone mistreat me,
Just blink[61] your eyes and pay no mind.
Ride the horse, wear the badge, and continue on your way;
No need to roll up your sleeves, stick out your fists,
    and put on a show of force.[62]

We're getting close to Ch'en-chou, Chang Ch'ien. You ride the horse and wear the badge; go on into town ahead of me, but don't hurt anybody.

CHANG: Yes, sir. I'll be riding off now.

PAO: Come on back, Chang Ch'ien. I have some more orders for you. I'm going to stay behind, and if someone should bully or hit me, you're not to interfere. Remember what I've told you now.

CHANG: Yes, sir. (*rides off*)

PAO: Chang Ch'ien, come back here.

CHANG: Sir, if you have something to say, say it all at once,[63] why don't you?

PAO: Remember my instructions.

CHANG: I'll go into town ahead of you then, sir.

(*Exit.*) (*Enter* Wang Fen-lien.)

WANG: I, Wang Fen-lien, live here at Dog Leg Bay at the Southern Gate. The only business I know anything about is selling my smiles for a living. The authorities have sent two officials here to open the granaries and sell the rice: one is Yang Chin-wu and the other young Lord Liu. They spend all their money at my place, and all I have to do is ask for anything and they give it to me ten times over—they really throw their money around.[64] They're so rich and influential, loafers stay away from my door. My house cuddles up to them and gets all their gold and silver cash. Several days ago they pawned a gold mace with me; if they don't have the money to redeem it, I'll make some hairpins and rings out of it and get a tidy profit. Some of my sisters have asked me over for a few cups of wine and sent somebody with a donkey to get me,[65] but when I mounted it, all of a sudden it brayed, gave a kick, and bucked me right off. I hurt my willowy waist and it's so painful! Since nobody was around to help me up, I had to scramble up somehow. The donkey's run away, and I have no way of catching up with it. I wonder if I can get somebody to stop it for me.

PAO: That woman there doesn't look very respectable to me. I think I'll catch that animal[66] for her and put some questions to her, just to see where it might lead.

WANG: (*approaches* Pao) Stop that donkey for me, old-timer!

(Pao *catches the donkey.*) (Wang *expresses her thanks.*)

WANG: Thanks a lot, sir.

PAO: Where do you hail from, sister?

WANG: He's certainly a rube if he doesn't know who I am. I live at Dog Leg Bay.

PAO: And what do your people do for a living?

WANG: Try and guess, old fellow.

PAO: All right, I'll have a guess.

WANG: Go ahead then, guess.

PAO: Are you oil grinders, perhaps?

WANG: No.

PAO: Pawnbrokers?

WANG: No.

PAO: Cloth merchants?

WANG: No again.

PAO: Well, if it isn't any of those, what *is* your business then?

WANG: At my place we sell quail!* Where do you live, old man?

---

*Lit., "skin quail." The use of "skin" here is puzzling, but otherwise "quail" means exactly what it does in English slang: prostitute.

PAO: I had just one wife—she is long dead—and have no children. I just beg for something to eat wherever I go.

WANG: Come along with me, old-timer; I can use you. Just stay with me, and all my good wine and meat are yours.

PAO: Fine, fine, I'll go along with you. How might I be of service to you?

WANG: Come home with me, my fine old man, and I'll dress you up. I'll make you a stiff shirt and a new hat, a brown belt, and a pair of leather boots. You'll sit at the gate on a stool and be my doorman. You'll be doing very nicely indeed!

PAO: Tell me, sister, what sort of men come around your place?

WANG: The other customers, merchants and travelers, aren't so important, but I have two men, both granary officials, who have influence and money both. Their father's at the capital, a very high official, and they're here selling rice at the high price of two ounces of silver a bushel. Each half bushel is short by three quarts, and their scale is thirty per cent heavier. But I've never gotten any of their profits from all that.

PAO: Even if you haven't gotten any of their money, have you by any chance received anything else from them instead?

WANG: They haven't given me any money, it's true, old fellow, but they *have* given me a gold mace. If you just took a look at that thing, it would scare the life out of you!

PAO: I've lived all this time, and I've never seen anything like a gold mace. Would you mind letting me have a look at it, so that I can stamp out trouble and crime?

WANG: One look at that, old man, and you'll stamp out trouble and crime all right, or whatever you're talking about. Come home with me, and I'll show it to you.

PAO: I'll go along with you then.

WANG: Have you had anything to eat, old man?

PAO: No, I haven't.

WANG: Come along with me, old fellow. Those two have laid out a banquet for me up ahead, and when we get there, you can have all the wine and meat you want. Help me onto the donkey now.

(Pao *helps* Wang *onto the donkey*.)

PAO: (*aside*) Who in all the empire doesn't know that Judge Pao is magistrate of K'ai-feng-fu? And now here I am in Ch'en-chou catching a donkey for this woman. What a farce!

> (Melody: *Mu-yang-kuan*)
> One day I leave the leopard tail ranks;*[67]
> The next I draw near Dog Leg Bay.
> What difference between me and a common groom?**
> I only fear an Intendant will happen by, a Censor might
>   come along.
> Why, he would ask, is our Lung-t'u judge
> Entranced with this demon of fleshly delight?
> Am I in disgrace to end my career?

WANG: Come with me, old man, and I'll show you the gold mace.

PAO: Very well, I'll go with you. Just show it to me, and I'll eliminate trouble and crime.

> (Melody: *Ko-wei*)
> To listen to her makes my heart shake with ire,
> And for a long while the anger blocks the words in my
>   mouth.
> Using imperial grain of the storehouses they work their
>   ill,
> But even if they have none,
> For the people *I* have pity enough.
> Like fat men wrestling,[68]
> I'll have them gasping for air.
> (*Exit with* Wang.) (*Enter* Young Liu *and* Yang *with*
> Granary Clerks.)

YOUNG LIU:

> (*in verse*)
> Both my eyes are twitching;***
> Bad luck is sure to come.

---

*High rank in Imperial service. I have kept the original metaphor in order to provide a parallel with "Dog Leg Bay" in the following line.
**Lit., "behind the horse and before the donkey," a common phrase ridiculing mindless servants.
***In popular belief, a sign that disaster was imminent.

If an honest official should happen along,
The rafters are bound to fall.

We're here to welcome old Pao. I don't know why it is, but my eyes are twitching, and I've just had some wine[69] to calm my nerves while we settle down to wait for him.

(*Enter* Pao *and* Wang.)

PAO: Isn't this the reception hall, sister? I'll wait for you here.

WANG: Yes, here we are at the reception hall. Help me off the donkey, old man. Wait for me here while I go in and bring out some wine and meat for you. Just hold the donkey for me. (*sees* Young Liu *and* Yang)

YOUNG LIU: (*smiling*) There you are, sister!

YANG: Sweetheart, you've had a long trip!

WANG: Damn you anyway! Why didn't you come and get me? On the road I fell off the donkey and almost killed myself. And the donkey ran off. It was a good thing I met an old man, who caught the donkey for me. Hey! I almost forgot about him; he hasn't eaten yet. I'll give him some wine and meat first.

YANG: Clerk, take some wine and meat to that old man with the donkey.

(First Clerk *takes wine and meat to* Pao.)

FIRST CLERK: Old fellow, you, with the donkey, come here and I'll give you some wine and meat.

PAO: Tell your granary officials that I'll have none of it and am giving it all to the donkey instead.

FIRST CLERK: (*angrily*) Huh! The old hick doesn't have any manners at all! (*approaches* Young Liu) Officer, I just took some wine and meat to the old man pulling the donkey, and instead of eating it himself, he gave it all to the donkey!

YOUNG LIU: Hang the old man up on that locust tree, clerk, and we'll give him a hiding at our leisure after we meet old Pao.

FIRST CLERK: Yes, sir. (*hangs* Pao *up*)

PAO:

(Melody: *K'u huang-t'ien*)
Lord Liu recommended his son,
But why did Scholar Fan issue the imperial order?

Now the thieving granary officials enjoy honor and
    wealth
And care nothing about the sorrows of the people,
Always whoring it up in the brothels.[70]
The blackguards don't follow the imperial standard but
    add to their profits instead,
Steal granary rice and expropriate official funds,
Which they give to the whore, the whore Wang Fen-lien.
But I have stolen upon them unawares,
And they'll not get off lightly with me!

(Melody: *Wu-yeh t'i*)
First they shall taste my virgin sword.
No place in Heaven shall they find.
Lord Liu, what kind of favor would you like me to do?
I've reached the end of the case
And find that it's no rumor at all.
I fear not your influence with the T'ien-chang Scholar
Or that to seek imperial grace you would mount the Chin-
    luan Hall.*
For I, Pao Lung-t'u, with face of iron,
Shall list your names in the Forbidden City and send you
    to perdition in the Yellow Springs.

CHANG: "If you receive somebody's trust, you have to do the
job right." His Honor ordered me to go into town ahead of him
and look for Yang Chin-wu and young Lord Liu. I went straight to
the granary after them, but I can't find either one of them. I
wonder where his Honor is now? I'll just take a look in this reception hall. (*sees* Young Liu *and* Yang) I was just searching for those
two, and here they are having a drink. I'll go over and put a little
scare into them, have a few cups of their wine, and get me a bribe
in the process. (*approaches them*) What a fine sight, you here drinking! His Honor Judge Pao is going to get you two. You see, I know
everything!

*The location of the Han-lin Academy during the T'ang period.

YOUNG LIU: If you can see fit to help us out, brother, I'll treat you to a drink.

CHANG: What a couple of idiots! You must know that asking the servant for a favor is better than asking the head man.[71]

YOUNG LIU: You're right there, brother.

CHANG: I've been making some inquiries into your affairs. Just set your hearts at ease; I'll help you out. Judge Pao just sits around; *I'm* the real Judge Pao. Just leave it to me.

PAO: So you're the "real Judge Pao," are you?

(Melody: *Mu-yang-kuan*)

The rascal had little to say before my horse.

Today at the station he boasts and brags.

Truly, everyone must have a little authority!

Ah! You charlatan[72] of retainers, would you gain
          immortality by posing as an immortal?

CHANG: (*pours a libation*) If I don't save you two, may my life be like this wine! (*sees* Pao *and becomes frightened*) That scared the life out of me!

PAO:

His fright turns his face the color of yellow paper; his
          gestures turn berserk.

When all is said and done, a rat after all has no nerve,

And how can a monkey sit and meditate?

CHANG: You two fools, you came to Ch'en-chou to sell rice. The official price originally was the imperial standard of one ounce. So how come you changed it to two? And when Chang the Headstrong made a few objections, why did you have him beaten to death? You were about to buy wine and treat me to a drink. And you took the law into your own hands by hanging up the old man with the donkey. Now Judge Pao on his secret mission has entered the city through the East Gate. Aren't you going to greet him?

YOUNG LIU: What'll we do now? Well, since Judge Pao has entered the city, let's go greet him.

(*Exit with* Yang *and* Clerks.) (Chang *unties* Pao.)

WANG: Now that they've gone, I'm going home. Bring me my donkey, old man.

CHANG: (*curses* Wang) You thieving slut! Even if it were the death of you, you'd still want his Honor to pull your donkey for you!

PAO: Hey there, don't say anything more! I'll help you up on the donkey, sister. (*helps* Wang *onto donkey*)

WANG: Thank you, old man. If you're too busy, then forget about it; but if you have some time, do come over to my place and have a look at that gold mace, won't you?

(*Exit.*)

PAO: Those rotten thieves have a lot of nerve!

(Melody: *Huang-chung sha-wei*)

They give no thought to the cares of ruler and subject

But love only money for sex and for drink.

Today ruined homes and people near death are common
    sights.

I'll have you villainous, thieving hawks

One by one brought forth

And your lives offered to the Sword of Authority.

Don't resent me for having no mercy;

Just blame the strumpet of the house of Wang.

She shouldn't have asked me to catch her donkey and
    walk such a long, long way.

(*Exit with* Chang.)

ACT FOUR

(*Enter* Prefect *and* Secretary.)

PREFECT:

(*in verse*)

I'm not a bad prefect at all.

I strut and stride when I judge a case;

And only two things do I like to eat:

Turtle and crab boiled in wine.[73]

My surname is Liao and my given name Hua.[74] I serve in the post of prefect of Ch'en-chou. Today his Honor Judge Pao is opening court and presiding. Secretary, arrange every document nice and proper for signature.

SECRETARY: You give me these documents and tell me to arrange them nice and proper, but since I can't read, how can I understand what they say?

PREFECT: You deserve a good beating, you boob! If you can't even read, how do you think you can serve as secretary?

SECRETARY: Actually, I'm a substitute on temporary hire.

PREFECT: Pah! Brush off the court desk and be quick about it. His Honor is about to arrive.

CHANG: (*calling the court to order*) Silence, all in court!

(*Enter* Pao)

PAO: I am Pao Cheng. Since the corrupt officials and evil clerks of Ch'en-chou have hurt the people, I have received his Majesty's command to investigate those officials and clerks and calm the populace. This is no easy task.

(*Shuang-tiao* mode, Melody: *Hsin shui ling*)
With my head bowed low in the Chin-luan Hall I
        received my sovereign's charge
To proceed on my way to the place Ch'en-chou and save
        the people from harm.
My awesome name quakes with the earth;
My wrath comes on the tide of the frost.*
My hands grasp the Sword of Authority and the Golden
        Badge.
Oh, Lord Liu, place no blame upon me!
Chang Ch'ien, bring in Liu Te-chung and his associates.

CHANG: Yes, sir. (*seizes* Young Liu, Yang, *and the* Two Clerks, *who kneel before* Pao) Face the court!

PAO: Do you admit guilt?

YOUNG LIU: I do not.

PAO: Rascal, the price by imperial decree is how much silver for a bushel of rice?

---

*Pao's anger is like the cold air that "kills" vegetation. In traditional cosmology, autumn was the season for the administration of punishment.

YOUNG LIU: My father told me the price by imperial decree was two ounces a bushel.

PAO: The price by imperial decree was to be *one* ounce a bushel. You changed it on your own to two, cut the bushel by six quarts, and added thirty per cent to the scales. How can you deny guilt?

> (Melody: *Chu-ma t'ing*)
> Money and riches are all you desire,
> Unmindful of the people's poverty, oppressing them
>   without cease.
> Now that you find yourself in chains,
> For half a life of evil with your own life you'll pay.
> I watch him step forth, as if ascending the Hall of
>   Purgatory,*
> Then shy back, as if entering the Eastern Sea.
> Before your corpse is hacked asunder in the streets,
> I'll send your very soul aflight beyond the azure sky.[75]

Chang Ch'ien, go to the Southern Gate and get Wang Fen-lien and the gold mace.

CHANG: Yes, sir. (*brings* Wang *forth, who kneels*) Wang Fen-lien, face the court.

PAO: Wang Fen-lien, do you know who I am?

WANG: No, I don't.

PAO:

> (Melody: *Yen-erh lo*)
> Are you really such a dolt, Powder-face Wang,
> Not to know of the cleverness of Judge Pao?
> Off the granary officials you thought to get rich.
> Before a magistrate now, why have you lost all your
>   charms?

Who gave you the gold mace, Wang Fen-lien?

WANG: Yang Chin-wu.

PAO: Chang Ch'ien, pick out a large staff, take Wang Fen-lien's

---

*Lit., "Hall of Frightened Souls." In popular belief, this hall was a part of the Buddhist hell.

pants down, and give her thirty strokes. (Chang *beats* Wang.) After
you've done that, throw her out. (Chang *takes* Wang *off.*) Chang
Ch'ien, bring Yang Chin-wu up before me. (Chang *brings* Yang *forward.*) This gold mace has the emperor's script and the imperial
seal; why did you give it to Wang Fen-lien?

    YANG: Have mercy, your Honor! I didn't exactly *give* it to
her; I just pawned it for a few tarts.*

    PAO: Now, Chang Ch'ien, take Yang Chin-wu out, hang his
head in the market place, and report back.

    CHANG: Yes, sir.

    PAO:

> (Melody: *Te-sheng ling*)
> Ah, through the eyes of coins you squirmed and schemed,
> Now on the edge of the blade your corpse finds its place.
> You have flown in the face of the time-honored codes,[76]
>   and pardon is not for you.
> Though a strategist great[77] laid his plans for you, never
>   could he save you now,
> Your death you shall not delay,
> My sword is as quick as the wind.
> Your death is fully deserved,
> Who told you to pawn the gold mace for some wine?
> (Chang *seizes* Yang *and kills him.*)

Chang Ch'ien, bring Young Chang here.

    CHANG: Young Chang is before the court. (*takes hold of*
Young Chang, *who kneels*)

    PAO: Who was it that beat your father to death?

    YOUNG CHANG: Young Lord Liu, with the gold mace.

    PAO: Chang Ch'ien, bring Liu Te-chung here and let Young
Chang beat him to death with the gold mace.

    CHANG: Yes, sir.

    PAO:

> (Melody: *Ku mei-chiu*)
> For the wrongs by the young lord

---

*The double meaning appears to be intentional in the original text.

Bide your time, my Young Chang.

The blood feud between you is his fault alone, and how
    can he hope to escape?

It is only right[78] that his debt to your father accrue now
    in full to you.

(Melody: *T'ai-p'ing ling*)

The life of each man is Heaven's concern.

Could it ever allow him to slaughter the people like a
    tiger or a wolf?

The golden mace is here still;

Take it up and smash his skull,

And when flesh is torn and blood is spilled,

When such a punishment is carried out,

Only then will Ch'en-chou be at peace.

(Young Chang *beats* Young Liu.)

Chang Ch'ien, has he been beaten to death?

    CHANG: He has.

    PAO: Take Young Chang away.

    CHANG: Yes, sir.

    (Chang *takes* Young Chang *off.*) (*Enter* Lord Liu *in panic
    with a letter of pardon.*)

    LIU:

    (*in verse*)

    Full of worry on the long, long road,

    For a crisis have I left my gate.

I am Lord Liu. I've spoken before His Majesty and pleaded for a
letter of pardon that pardons only the living but not the dead. I
have traveled all night to Ch'en-chou to save my two sons. Stop the
execution! I have a letter of pardon here pardoning only the living
but not the dead!

    PAO: Who are the ones who are dead, Chang Ch'ien?

    CHANG: Yang Chin-wu and the young lord.

    PAO: And who is still alive?

    CHANG: Young Chang.

    LIU: What!? I've just pardoned somebody else instead!

PAO: Chang Ch'ien, release Young Chang.

(Melody: *Tien-ch'ien huan*)

Suddenly a shout that a pardon has come,

And I can't help but laugh in the wind.

To think of them, father and sons—relying on influence
and might,

And seeing their fortune now gone.

He hoped through the pardon to find a way clear,

Not dreaming that ere it was here

They might have been dead all along.

This time the tables were turned, he redeemed someone
else in their stead.

It is not that his plot was ill laid,

But the pattern of Heaven is clear.

Chang Ch'ien, take Lord Liu away. Hear my verdict.

(*in verse*)

Because Ch'en-chou suffered with drought and poor
crops,

The poor were cast forth in distress.

Lord Liu, a man of no worth,

And Yang Chin-wu, a sly rogue,[79]

Received the throne's orders to sell rice in Ch'en-chou,

But they changed the set price to squeeze out their own
gain.

The golden mace murdered a man good and true.

At the sound of his pain Heaven wept and Earth
mourned.

Was Scholar Fan to put up with these crimes?

He asked that our sovereign not pardon the dead.

Today with pure justice I judge,

And Young Chang has taken revenge in his hands.

Now do we see how the law of the realm

Can endure without favor through time.

P'EN-ERH KUEI

(The Ghost of the Pot)

INTRODUCTION

Selling Rice at Ch'en-chou illustrates one element of court-room drama and particularly of the Judge Pao plays: the detective's righteous struggle against powerful criminals. *P'en-erh kuei* (The ghost of the pot) illustrates another: the intervention of the ghost of a murder victim to help solve a case. Another reason for its selection here is that this play is an excellent example of the role of humor in courtroom drama.

In one respect *The Ghost of the Pot* is typical of much of northern drama. Like so many others of its genre, it is an inventive combination of conflicting tones and qualities as embodied in the best and the worst of human character and situation. Contrast, for example, the delicacy and sensitivity of the protagonist during his dream with the crudeness of the two villains in later scenes. This contrast avoids outright imbalance or lack of focus by virtue of the author's unifying moral vision: an abhorrence of cruelty in the midst of its comic portrayal. If we laugh at *The Ghost of the Pot,* we do so from shock and dismay and not from delight.

Other courtroom plays blend comedy and pathos within a single seriousness of purpose; *Selling Rice at Ch'en-chou* is one example. The usual technique is to alternate the two effects in dif-ferent scenes or segments. *The Ghost of the Pot* stands alone in its simultaneous evocation of horror and laughter in one scene, and if this clash of reactions is disconcerting, perhaps it was meant to be so. Anyone searching for Chinese versions of "black comedy" should turn to this play. It is at once the most gruesome and the most comic of all the courtroom plays, and it is certainly no acci-dent that it is one of the few northern plays to have survived rela-tively intact into later drama and fiction.

Other disconcerting notes involve the play's structure. What, for example, is the real significance of Kuo-yung's dream? Its primary function is to give the audience a sense of foreboding by presaging the murder, but why should Kuo-yung's drinking a draught of wine and picking a blossom bring about the villain's

81

(Chao's) anger and assault? These actions by Kuo-yung in the dream seem to have no counterpart in the rest of the play. They may be symbolic of later transgressions committed by Kuo-yung against Chao, specifically with P'ieh Chih-hsiu, the former prostitute and now Chao's wife. The dream may then be a surviving fragment of an earlier version of the play, in which Kuo-yung, in a sense, more nearly deserved his harsh treatment by Chao. If so, the nature of Chao's crime and its punishment by Judge Pao would have taken on quite a different ethical coloration. Perhaps Kuo-yung's actions in the dream merely stand for his defiance of fate, implicit in his decision to come within three hundred miles of home before the end of the predicted time limit.

A more serious question of structural unity concerns the second act, in which the Spirit of the Kiln harasses Chao and P'ieh. Since the agent of celestial justice is Judge Pao and not the Spirit, the necessity for the events in this act is not apparent, in spite of their delightfully raucous humor. To watch the villains squirm is entertaining, but they could be squirming as easily under Pao's relentless interrogation. Pao in any case is not so easily satisfied as this god, who settles for sacrifices to the victim's soul as atonement for murder. Viewed from the context of the entire play, the act seems awkward, because it has no immediate effect on the remainder of the plot. Possibly it was meant to conclude the spiritual side of the Chaos' debt before proceeding to the temporal. In this case, the Spirit would seem to be robbing Pao of his role as a divine agent, and indeed Pao does not enjoy the prominence in this play that he does in most others. But it is important to note that the scene with Pao concludes the play, as in all of the Pao plays, and in this scene the author succeeds in promoting Pao and his courtroom above the status of a god by making him even more credible as a moral force.

Of the two editions of this play available today (see Appendix C), that in *Yuan-ch'ü hsuan,* the more readable and complete, is the text for this translation.

THE GHOST OF THE POT

*Wedge**

    (*Enter* Yang Ts'ung-shan.)

TS'UNG-SHAN:

    (*in verse*)

    Summer goes, and winter comes, and after spring, the fall.

    The evening sun sinks to the west, and eastward flows the
        stream.

    Never trust the fine face of youth;

    Your hair turns white full soon.

I am a man of the capital,**[1] Yang Ts'ung-shan by name. My son,
Yang Kuo-yung,[2] went off to the market place this morning in
search of a friend of his, but he should be back by now. Well, I'll
just have to wait up for him.

    (*Enter* Yang Kuo-yung.)

    KUO-YUNG: I, Yang Kuo-yung, went to the market place this
morning to form a business partnership with a friend, but on the
way I came across a fortuneteller called Chia the Demigod. Everybody says that his predictions always come true, and so I felt I just
had to part with some of my cash and have my fortune told. As
soon as he came up with the prediction, he cried out, "Strange,
how strange! The fortune says that within a hundred days, blood
will glisten![3] And it looks as if there is no way out, either." I asked
him, "Demigod, would you try one more time, just to see if there
might be some way of escape or other?" After his fingers flew over
the divining board once again, he said, "If you can get three hundred miles away from home, you just might have a chance." As I
was about to leave, he called me back and told me, "Be sure not to
come back until the last day of the hundred is up. Remember what
I've told you, remember it now!" All this has frightened me very
much, and the only thing I can do is borrow five ounces of silver

*See note at foot of page 33.
**K'ai Feng, the capital of the Northern Sung dynasty.

from my cousin Chao K'o, buy some goods, and set out to avoid
trouble. Today happens to be an auspicious time, and once I've
said goodbye to my father, I'll have to be on my way. (*goes in and
approaches* Ts'ung-shan)

TS'UNG-SHAN: You're back, son.

KUO-YUNG: Yes, father, here I am.

TS'UNG-SHAN: Where have you been?

KUO-YUNG: Father, at the market place I met a man called
Chia the Demigod, a fortuneteller, who predicted that a bloody
calamity would befall me within a hundred days if I didn't go three
hundred miles away. That scared me, and I borrowed five ounces
of silver from my cousin Chao K'o, purchased some goods, and
shall go away to transact some business.[4] I'll be saying farewell,
then, father, and after the hundred days are past and I've escaped
trouble, I'll come home.

TS'UNG-SHAN: It's true what they say, son, "You can't believe
in fortunetelling, for if you do, all you get is a bellyful of grief."
My eyes, my arms, all of me exists for you alone. If you leave, who
will take care of me? Don't go, my son.

KUO-YUNG: Since people call that fortuneteller Chia the Demigod, it seems to me it would be wiser to take his word for it. I've
already made up my mind to go, and I'm afraid that if I stayed, I'd
only get sick or something. You must stop worrying, father. Wait
until the hundred days pass without incident, and I'll be home
again. (*takes his leave*)

> (*Hsien-lü* mode, Melody: *Shang hua shih*)
> Short of rice, lacking fuel, what are we to do?
> Hence I leave from this my home to engage in trade.
> With a handful of household funds
> I'll duck calamity
> And be a merchant too.

TS'UNG-SHAN: Come home as soon as you can, son.

KUO-YUNG:

> If I can get by unscathed,
> I'll come home to you soon enough.
> (*Exit.*)

TS'UNG-SHAN: My son is setting off now. I'll just gather up
some food and wine and send him on his way.

> (*in verse*)
> His heart drives his thoughts on before him,
> And to hold them back would make us foes.
> Let him go, then, on his way.
> With profit our woes will cease.

(*Exit.*)

ACT ONE

(*Enter* Inn boy.)

INN BOY:

> (*in verse*)
> Others brew wine with rice alone;
> For our wine, water's just as good.
> Toss it down and out puffs your gut.

You may never get drunk, but you'll never feel starved.[5]
I'm an inn boy. I run a little wine shop[6] here at Three Mile Stop
beyond the Northern Pass in Shang-ts'ai County,* where everybody
traveling north and south, wheelbarrow pushers, pole bearers,
merchants, and what have you, come to have a drink and stay the
night. It's a beautiful day today, and I've gotten up early to tidy
up the shop and order some fresh meat and vegetables to go with
the wine. I'll just hang out the straw broom**[7] to show we're
open for business and see who happens along.

(*Exit.*)

KUO-YUNG: I am Yang Kuo-yung. Since the time I left home,
said goodbye to my father, and set out to do business, it's been
three months now. I had to leave all of a sudden, without getting
used to the rigors of travel, and this bumpy[8] road has cut my feet
up badly.

---

*In present-day Honan province.
**The sign of a tavern.

(*Hsien-lü* mode, Melody: *Tien chiang-ch'un*)
On the twisting road
The heart of a traveler is troubled.
In all my haste
I've walked till my strength is gone.
It's getting late.
  And the evening sun do I spy, on its every dim descent.
Better keep moving, Yang Kuo-yung.
  (Melody: *Hun chiang lung*)
Fear is the lot of the wandering tradesman
As crows caw at dusk in the withered wood.
Look at the light of the sun, how fast it sinks.
  The sun is gone now,
  Nothing but a wisp of red.
  Over wilderness creeks I go, across a bridge, mile after
   mile,
Aren't those houses up ahead?
  In the distance, bamboo paling and thatched huts, two or
   three.
  Man relies on the roads of old, true enough,
  Like the wild goose that touches down upon its sandy
   plain.
  Past lonely hamlets and tiny paths,
  'Round distant bays afloat with rafts,
  I head for where the dogs are barking, a place of rest
   serene.
  Never has leisure been mine to have,
  As I stagger my way through life.[9]
Here's a wine shop; I might as well stay here for the night. (*calls at the gate*) Inn boy! Open the gate!
  (*Enter* Inn boy.)
  INN BOY: Who's calling there at the gate? I'll just open it up here. (*approaches* Kuo-yung) Where might you be from?
  KUO-YUNG: I'm from the capital. Would you have a nice clean room for me?
  INN BOY: Oh yes, sure enough. This one is pretty clean. What would you like to eat?

KUO-YUNG: Nothing to eat, but I would like you to light me
a lamp. All I want is a night's rest; I have to get an early start
tomorrow.

INN BOY: All right, I'll light a lamp for you, and have a good
rest. I'll be sleeping in back.

(*Exit.*) (Kuo-yung *goes to bed. He has a dream and gets
up.*)

KUO-YUNG: For some reason I can't seem to fall back to sleep.
I think I'll get up and wander around a bit. Here's a little doorway.
I might as well push it open and see where it leads. (*gives a look*)
Oh, a flower garden. What beautiful flowers!

(Melody: *Yu hu-lu*)

The light of spring fills my eyes, a lovely sight indeed,
As I stroll in the light of the moon.
Could this be willow floss blown by the wind, or the
dancing petals of the pear?

(*gives a start*) How strange!

Crab apple branches rustle against my cap;
Thorns of the rose cling to my robe.
Beyond a pavilion of cypress and pine
I see the blossoms of apricot and peach,
Terrace and plot of peony,[10] arbor of climbing rose,
While wending through flowery profusion.

Ah, in the midst of the flower bushes is a low table with fruit
dishes, cups, and plates. Wine and food are arranged so neatly that
I suppose the wine seller must have set them out.

(Melody: *T'ien-hsia le*)

Am I a wanderer through the wine shops of West Lake?
Who could it be
That put this in place?

I don't see any harm in having a cup for myself.

What harm if the one with the passion for flowers should
suddenly happen by?

(*picks up the wine pitcher*) Let me have a look. Why, it's full of
wine! I'll just pour myself a cup.

Into the goblet goes the fragrant brew,

As the proverb goes, "If you drink, drink a deep draught;

if you wear a flower, make it a full bloom."
> And into my hair goes the blossomed stem.
> We shall be drunk as one, you and I.

What excellent wine! What's the harm in having several cups? (*sits*)
> (Melody: *Na-cha ling*)
> Lay them out among the flowers,
> The seats and beds so soft.
> Place them on the table,
> The cups of jade so warm.
> Pour it down,
> Wine[11] of sweetest scent.
> This time of year, young spring's first bud,
> Counts more than a pile of gold.
> Ambrosia[12] have I drunk, many cups.

While I'm here enjoying this wine, I can't help wondering if my father back home has any wine as good as this.
> (Melody: *Ch'ueh t'a chih*)
> Before I go, I'll break off a branch in bloom
> And start off for home the next day.
> My concern's been for naught but the health of my trade,
> The balance of income and cost.
> (*Enter* Villain[13] *in stealth, who grabs* Kuo-yung.)

VILLAIN: Hey there! These flowers belong to somebody else!
KUO-YUNG:
> (*startled*)
> A shout that the flowers belong to someone else;
> Oh, Heaven above,
> A black-faced demon, a harrier from Hell!
> (Villain *holds up knife.*)

> (Melody: *Chi sheng-ts'ao*)
> In fright have I lost the sweet bliss of wine.
> In panic I've dropped the blooms from my hand.
> I see a giant, of malice chill,
> Gripping a shining blade of steel.
> The fear in my heart sets me atremble.

"Why?" you may ask, but why should I not bow my
    head?
After all, it's his low eaves that I find myself beneath.*

(Melody: *Lu-yao hsu*)
Ai-ya! I've taken a look
And seen his ghastly face:
Rolling eyes of a monster, crossed,
Nostrils aflare,
Clenching fangs,
Enough to kill by fright alone!
(Villain *seizes* Kuo-yung *by the hair.*)
Ai-ya! One hand has my hair,
The other pulls out the knife.
So the fortune comes true at last, and blood will shine
    this day;
So my life will be cast away, to the corner of the sea,
    the farthest edge of sky.
Have mercy, my brother, spare my life!
    VILLAIN: Don't blame me, but this same hour and day and
month next year will be the anniversary of your death!
    KUO-YUNG:

(*weeps*)
(*Refrain*)
We have no quarrel, you and I.
Why do you want me to die?
To come and view the flowers, I grant you, is something
    I shouldn't have done.
(Official[14] *rushes onstage and grabs hold of* Villain.)
    OFFICIAL: Don't kill him, don't, I say!
    KUO-YUNG:

He makes a sudden grab of the shoulder
And gives the shout, "Don't kill!"
Oh, who might his Honor be?

---

*Bowing one's head under low eaves, i.e., yielding to force.

OFFICIAL: Don't be frightened, sir!

KUO-YUNG:

> At the shout, "Don't be frightened, sir!"
> The bandit's[15] hands draw back.
> Oh, your Honor is the very Bodhisattva incarnate.
> Could you be the Lung-t'u Judge
> Of the court at K'ai-feng-fu?

(*Exeunt* Official *and* Villain.) (Kuo-yung *awakes.*)

Murder!

> (*Enter* Inn boy *in panic.*)

INN BOY: Where?

KUO-YUNG: Take a good look, brother; is my head still on my shoulders?

INN BOY: Look, sir, if you didn't have your head, do you suppose you could still talk?

KUO-YUNG: Whew, what a nightmare!

INN BOY: Tell me about it.

KUO-YUNG:

> (Melody: *Chin chan-erh*)
> Why all the clamor, you ask,
> Why startle you as well?
> Because of a weird dream, a moment ago,
> Of a hulk[16] of a man with a knife.

INN BOY: What was he going to do with the knife?

KUO-YUNG:

> He was about to kill me with one slash.

INN BOY: Well, did he?

KUO-YUNG: Luckily an officer of the court grabbed hold of him and shouted, "Don't kill him!"

> Expecting nothing in return, he saved my life,

This life of mine,

> Whose spark was rekindled from dead, cold ash,
> Whose bud grew again from withered branch.

INN BOY: They say springtime's the time for dreaming, just as autumn's the time for farting. You can't go by anything in a dream. What's to be frightened of?

KUO-YUNG: It's just that an unlucky dream like that one gives me a sense of foreboding. Well, it's light out now. I'll leave two hundred cash with you for the room and be on my way.

INN BOY: The money will do nicely for the room, sir. All my best wishes for a safe voyage ahead. Just pluck up your courage and don't give a thought to that dream. I hope you'll be patronizing us again in your future travels.

KUO-YUNG: (*shouldering his carrying pole and setting out*) I'll be off, then, inn boy.

(*Exit.*)

INN BOY: I thought I noticed some kind of a shadow across his face; that may mean something bad is in store for him. Pah! What business is it of mine?

(*in verse*)

I'll close the gate and ignore the moon before my window;
Let the plum blossoms do what they will.

(*Enter* Chao the Jug *and* P'ieh Chih-hsiu.*)

CHAO: My name's always been the same and always will be: Chao the Jug, that's me. I lost my parents when I was young, and I'm unskilled in anything but robbery and banditry and murder and arson, which I indulge in just enough to scratch out a living of sorts. Otherwise I don't do anything especially improper. Yesterday, after I had had a little too much to drink, I took a nap in the shade of a willow tree and dreamt that a young man came along carrying a couple of heavy bundles. I ran after him and was just about to dispose of him when some white-bearded old man grabbed my arm and yelled for me to stop. Then I woke up with a start and realized it was all a dream. I operate a kiln in Potsherd Village, a little over ten miles from the capital, and an inn on the side, where merchants traveling north and south stay overnight. If they don't have much cash on them, I let them alone, but if they do, then I take off after their[17] money and murder them in the process. Mind the store, wife. I'm going to take a nap. If a traveler comes along looking for a place

---

*"Cast-off blossom," a pun on her former profession and, presumably, her present state of physical beauty.

to stay, say that you have to have the room charge in advance and see how much he has on him when he weighs his silver. If it's a lot, let me know, and I'll take the appropriate measures.

CHIH-HSIU: All you ever do all day long is drink, and now you're drunk again. Go on to bed. If somebody comes looking for a room, I'll take care of it.

CHAO: I'll go have my nap, then.

(*Exit.*)

CHIH-HSIU: I, P'ieh Chih-hsiu, have a background that isn't quite what it should be. I was a prostitute until I married Chao the Jug and teamed up with him in a few underhanded dealings. Nobody lives within a radius of over ten miles from us. The only ones here are we two with our inn, where we put up travelers for the night. And when a rich one comes along, it's the Money God[18] himself stepping through the door. That man of mine Chao the Jug has gone to bed, and for now I'll leave the gate open and wait in the inn to see who comes along.

(*Exit.*) (*Enter* Kuo-yung *carrying his load.*)

KUO-YUNG: I, Yang Kuo-yung, met Chia the Demigod, who predicted that within a hundred days blood would glisten unless I went three hundred miles away. Accordingly I took leave of my father and set off to escape the curse. Since then I have been engaged in commerce, and by the grace of Heaven and Earth, my profits have mounted a hundredfold. Now that I'm just fifteen miles or so from home I'm stepping up the pace a bit. It will be so wonderful to get back and see my father again! (*while walking*) Oh, it's getting dark. I wonder what I should do if I can't reach town. (*counts on his fingers*) Let's see, it's been only ninety-nine days since I left home, and Chia the Demigod told me not to go back until the last day was up. I still have about ten miles ahead of me and couldn't possibly make it. I'd better put up for the night at the pottery village and wait for tomorrow morning, when the hundred days will be over for sure. (*comes to a stop*) Here is Pottery Inn. I'd best call out. Innkeeper!

CHIH-HSIU: Who's there?

KUO-YUNG: A passerby who wants to stay the night.

CHIH-HSIU: Come in, please. We have a clean room with a big bed, just the thing for a good night's rest. (Kuo-yung *steps inside and sets down his load.*) What would you like to eat, sir?

KUO-YUNG: Nothing at all. Just light me a lamp and give me a room for the night. I'm leaving first thing in the morning.

CHIH-HSIU: Very well, let me light it. I'll just tear off some paper here, light it up, pour out some oil, and there now, I've lit the lamp. Here it is, sir.

KUO-YUNG: I won't trouble you any further, then.

CHIH-HSIU: Since my husband isn't home and you're leaving early in the morning, I hate to seem petty, sir, but could you see fit to give me something of a deposit, just to make things nice and tidy and avoid any kind of misunderstanding?

KUO-YUNG: You're perfectly right. I'll count it out. (*opens a basket, takes out some cash, and covers the basket again*) Take these two hundred cash.

CHIH-HSIU: (*with a glance at* Kuo-yung's *bundle*) Now that that's taken care of, sir, please consider yourself right at home. (*aside*) Those two baskets look pretty heavy to me. They must have something in them. I'll just give him a call. Chao the Jug! Oh, Chao the Jug!

(*Enter* Chao.)

CHAO: What are you calling me for?

CHIH-HSIU: A traveler came just now to stay overnight. He's carrying a couple of baskets. I don't know how much money he's got in there, but they're very heavy. He's gone to bed now, and if you're ever going to do anything about it, now's the time.

CHAO: Well then, I'll just go have a look. (*pulls out his knife and kicks the door open*) Where is he?

KUO-YUNG: (*in fright*) Here!

CHAO: (*grabs* Kuo-yung *by the hair*) Straight talk's always better than pussyfooting around. All right, you, what do you have in money and valuables? I want all of it right now and you can go on living!

KUO-YUNG: I'm just a poor street vendor, brother. How do you expect me to have any money or valuables?

CHAO: (*angrily*) You bastard! Let's have it or you're a dead man!

KUO-YUNG: (*in fear*) All right, all right! Here, brother, here's a piece of silver for you.

CHAO: No offense, now. Remember, I never forced it out of you. You gave it to me of your own free will. (*steps out and approaches* Chih-hsiu) I got some silver!

CHIH-HSIU: How much silver?

CHAO: One piece.

CHIH-HSIU: Ai-ya! This business has kept me up the whole night, and all you get out of him is one piece of silver? Ask him for more!

CHAO: Hey, come here. Here's your silver back.

KUO-YUNG: Thank you, brother.

CHAO: It's not enough. I want one of your bundles.

KUO-YUNG: But, brother, they're mine!

CHAO: Pah! I'll kill you if you don't let me have it!

KUO-YUNG: All right, all right, one bundle, then.

CHAO: (*takes one basket out and approaches* Chih-hsiu) I got one of his bundles!

CHIH-HSIU: Still not enough! What's the matter with the other one, does it have the imperial seal on it or something?

CHAO: We've got enough now, don't we?

CHIH-HSIU: That's all very well for you to say, but these are riches sent down from Heaven. Now that you've got him here, are you going to let him go, just like that?

CHAO: You're right, of course. Hey, come here. I was just having some fun with you. I don't want it, take it back.

KUO-YUNG: Thanks a lot, brother.

CHAO: I want the whole load.

KUO-YUNG: (*kneels*) Leave just a little for me, brother!

CHAO: (*shouting*) You bastard! What's more important, your money or your life? Give it to me or I'll kill you!

KUO-YUNG: Take it, brother, take it!

(Chao *picks up the basket.* Kuo-yung *is about to hit* Chao *with the carrying pole, but* Chao *turns around and sees him.*)

CHAO: Hey, what are you up to there?

KUO-YUNG: Take this pole too, brother!

CHAO: (*laughs*) You're a tricky bastard! Wife, I've got the stuff! It's not light out yet; let's go back to sleep.

CHIH-HSIU: (*blocking his way*) Where do you think you're going? Now that we've made off with all his things, do you suppose he's going to let it go at that? Hide in the shadows awhile and find out what he's saying.

CHAO: Fine, fine. "With a virtuous wife in the house, the husband comes to no harm." I'll just give a listen.

KUO-YUNG: Ahh, Yang Kuo-yung, after avoiding calamity for a hundred days, here you are, only ten miles from home, at Chao the Jug's of the pottery village, where they've taken your money and your baskets of goods. What I'm going to do, once I get out of this inn of theirs, is go straight to his Honor Judge Pao and make a complaint. Then I'll get my things back in good time.

CHIH-HSIU: There now, what did I tell you? He's not just saying that, he's really going to go through with it! You let him go now and you'll be falling right into his clutches. If you want things nice and neat, you're going to have to use your knife on him and get rid of him for good.

CHAO: Right you are, wife. Hey, come here. Here are your baskets. You can have them back, I don't want them.

KUO-YUNG: Thank you very much, brother.

CHAO: I'd like something else of yours instead.

KUO-YUNG: What would that be, brother?

CHAO: Your head!

KUO-YUNG: If it isn't one thing, it's another! — Somebody's coming!

CHAO: (*turns around*) Where?

      (Kuo-yung *trips* Chao, *who then gets up and seizes* Kuo-yung.)

KUO-YUNG: Where are you going to have me killed?

CHAO: The kiln will do nicely.

KUO-YUNG:

      (Melody: *Tsuan-sha*)

Murder me in the kiln,
Cast my ghost into the land of the dead?
Who would save me then?
Who could keep this wrong I bear from rising up above?
You have my money, brother; spare me my life at least!
    CHAO: I want both your money *and* your life!
    KUO-YUNG:

Oh, father, your poor eyes, clouded with tears,
Gazing out in hope,
You'll think I'm wandering lost in streams and hills.
Who could guess my corpse will lie ten miles from where
    you are?
He's taken my wealth and will put me to death,
But Yang Kuo-yung will not stop there.

Even though I'm to die, the bandit will taste my fist! (*tries to hit*
Chao) Take that! (Chao *parries* Kuo-yung's *attack with his knife
held high.*) Before I could touch him, his knife slashed my hand!

Oh, where shall my spirit rest this night?

    (Chao *attacks* Kuo-yung, *who falls.*) (*Enter* Chih-hsiu.)
    CHIH-HSIU: Now that you've killed him, it won't do to keep
his body around. You'd better drag him into the kiln and cremate
him.
    CHAO: Good idea. I'll take the head, you take the feet, and
we'll throw him into the kiln. (*They pick* Kuo-yung *up and throw
him offstage.*) Bring me some firewood, wife, and we'll pile it up at
the oven door. Then I'll light the fire. Put a few more good stout
pieces on the leg bones there.
    CHIH-HSIU: Yes, yes, I know. (*arranges the firewood*)
    CHAO: (*blows on the flames*) There, he's all burnt up. Now
ladle out some water to put out the fire. Gather up the bones and
put them in the mortar while I operate the pestle. Have they turned
to powder[19] yet? Then bring me a fine sieve, and we'll sift the
remains. I'll mix in a little clay, fashion it into a pot, and put an
"X" on the bottom. Into the kiln it goes, along with the rest of the
pots. Now for some firewood and a nice big blaze, and then we'll
leave the oven door sealed up for seven days before opening it up

again. My friend, a cremation like this is a dandy send-off indeed!
I just hope Heaven sees fit to reward me with at least half a bowl
of rice for all the charity I'm showing you.

    (*Exeunt.*)

ACT TWO

    (*Enter* Chao the Jug *and* Chih-hsiu.)

CHAO:

    (*in verse*)

    Keeping my place, I ply my trade,

    Content with plain rice and rough tea.

    Do nothing shameful your whole life long,

    And a knock on the door in the dead of the night needn't
        give you a qualm.

I am Chao the Jug. Ever since I murdered Yang Kuo-yung, even
though I got a good deal of money from the deed, a series of dreams
these past couple of days has been turning me topsy-turvy. When
I'm sleeping on my bed, I'm yanked onto the floor, and if I go to
sleep on the floor, then I'm hauled back onto the bed. It's getting a
little hard to take, and if it keeps up like this, I'm going to get hurt.
Wife, shut the inn gate tight, and we'll keep quiet and lie low for a
few days.

    CHIH-HSIU: All right. (*closes the gate*)

    (*Enter the* Spirit of the Kiln.)

    SPIRIT: I am the Spirit of the Kiln. Chao the Jug has committed
an act so monstrous that I am on my way to teach him a good les-
son.

    (*Chung-lü* mode, Melody: *Fen-tieh-erh*)

    As cloud blends with mist, in rank upon rank,

    I send a cold wind to pierce man's soul.

    I press my cap upon my head and adjust my waistband
        of horn.

    Murderer!

    Thief!

Your cruelty and gall know no bounds.
Bad enough to leave a heap of corpses dripping blood,
But, heartless villain, to knead him into a pot?

(Melody: *Tsui ch'un-feng*)
If you grind his bones and burn them to ash,
You must face the heat of your fire.

Inhuman!

Am I to live in this reeking stench?
Am I not to die in the stink?
I'll turn him head over heels,
Grind him down,
Break him apart!

Here I am at his gate. He has it closed up. (*pushes on the gate*)
(Melody: *Ying hsien-k'o*)
I push on the gate,
But he has made it fast.
My heart's fire flares to unquenchable flame,
As I speed forth to question him hard.
A roaring laugh escapes my lips,
And my broad feet smash in the gate.
(Spirit *kicks the gate open.* Chao *in alarm hides under the bed.* Spirit *seizes* Chih-hsiu.)

CHIH-HSIU: (*shouting*) He's hiding under the bed, spirit!
SPIRIT:
(Melody: *Shang hsiao-lou*)
The man of the house wields knife and torch,

Bandit!

And you go along with the wind,
With never a thought that I would come to grab and tear
          at your robe,
Grasp your hair,[20]
Drag you this way and that.
Your crime brought all this about,
This disaster that fills Heaven's breadth.

CHIH-HSIU: Spirit, Chao the Jug committed the murder; I had
nothing to do with it.

SPIRIT: Silence!

You helped at the slaughtering site, that's your crime. Bring out Chao the Jug this instant!

CHIH-HSIU: (*shouting*) Chao the Jug! Come on out! The spirit wants a word with you! (*shouts three times*) Chao the Jug is scared, spirit, and so he won't come out.

SPIRIT: Last night when Yang Kuo-yung came to stay with you, Chao was the first one to bed, yet one call from you brought him out soon enough. He won't come when you call him now. Why is that, I wonder?

CHIH-HSIU: Let me see how much money you've got on you and I'll give him a call.

SPIRIT: That's enough of that! Chao the Jug! Where are all your skills now? Think you can hide under that bed and escape the consequences forever? If you don't come out, I'll chop you into mincemeat, bed and all!

> (Chao *peers out from under the bed.* Spirit *grabs him by the hair and drags him out.*)
> (*Refrain*)
> One hand ahold of your waist,
> How I should like to cast you in flames,
> Gouge out your eyes,
> Clutch at your throat,
> And rip your heart out alive! (*sits on* Chao)
> I'll stay a while
> Upon your back,
> Sitting erect and quite still,
> And ask you why on earth you put an innocent man to
>   death.

CHAO: Tell me what spirit you are, and I'll get the incense and lamps and flowers and fruit together to worship you properly.

SPIRIT: I am the spirit of your kiln.

CHAO: What? You're biting the hand that feeds you.[21] I sacrifice to you twice a year, and instead of looking after me, you cause me trouble. Ingrate!

SPIRIT: Uncouth as ever, I see. Well, I'll just put on a little more pressure and squash you into a persimmon cake.

CHAO: All right, I confess! If you'll only show a little mercy, O holy one!

(Spirit *lets* Chao *up.* Chao *kowtows.*)

SPIRIT:

(Melody: *Man t'ing fang*)

So now you would like a little mercy,
What with "sacrifices twice each year,"
Which you insist on babbling about.
Who told you, potter, to neglect your trade
And study the ways of a thief?
An artful villain you are,
Spurred on by a vicious bitch.
Now a ghost with no place of rest
Will rattle off his appeal,
Like Chuang Tzu beating his pot.*

CHAO: Have pity, your Holiness, and give me pardon!

SPIRIT: If pardon is what you want, you must allow his ghost passage to Heaven. Then pardon you will get.

CHAO: If you will show me mercy, O sacred one, I'll choose a plot on the high ground, chop the wood for his coffin, and invite the most eminent priests of the Buddha and the Tao to perform the Great Service of Land and Sea and transport him to Heaven. What is your august opinion about that? (*with* Chih-hsiu *does a series of kowtows*)

SPIRIT: Chao the Jug, you and your wife listen to what I say.

(Melody: *Shua hai-erh*)

I instruct you both to cease your crimes,
Murder and arson above all.
Man's life is but a dream,
And blessings must wither away.
Just hold to your heart and it will provide;
Riches ill-gained are substance ill-based.

*The philosopher Chuang Tzu, upon recovering from grief at his wife's death and realizing the inevitability of the death of all living things, beat a rhythm on a pot as an expression of acceptance. The allusion here contrasts strongly with the anguish of Kuo-yung's ghost.

Heaven's fate will weigh and choose,
Stay with your simple fare,
What more to seek and win?

(Melody: *Erh-sha*)
If you steal from others on the sly,
Then you must guard against others' hurting you.[22]
Have you no fear? The vengeance of the gods never
    mistakes its mark.
Never think that burglary and brigandage are matters too
    trivial to count.
Consider only why indeed Heaven and Hell exist.
From each is no escape.
You shall hang high from the Sword-branched Tree,
Be pushed into the Vat of Oil.*
Just to think of the misery of Yang Kuo-yung—Chao the Jug, the
both of you are too cruel!
(Melody: *I-sha*)
Pain in the thousands has been his to bear,
And how much cash did that give you?
How could he know that disaster would await him on
    his journey home,
That flames would roast his bones like faggots,
That clay and water would mingle with ash,
That the fire of the kiln would expunge all trace?
Is this the way to avoid trouble?
Better to dive in the river, plunge yourself in a well.
CHAO: (*kowtowing with* Chih-hsiu) Forgive us, and we'll buy
incense, lamps, flowers, and fruit as a sacrifice to you.
SPIRIT: (*shouting*) Silence!
(Melody: *Wei-sha*)
First sweep the blood stains clean,
Then set his soul to rest.

*The Sword-branched Tree and the Vat of Oil are tortures of Hell in popular
Buddhism and Taoism.

That will be your hedge against guilt,
Far better that than flowers and fruit, incense and lamps,
        offerings to me evermore.
    (*Exit.*)

CHIH-HSIU: Now that the god has left, let's open up the kiln
and have a look.

CHAO: (*opens the kiln*) What? Everything's disappeared but
this one pot. Let me see what mark it has on it. (*takes up the pot
and examines it*) Huh! It's his remains, that's what it is! Keeping
it around here might get us into no end of trouble. Better break
the damn thing.

CHIH-HSIU: No, don't break it. Old Chang the Headstrong has
been asking us for a chamber pot. Why not keep it by and give it
to him?

CHAO: Right you are, wife. When old Chang the Headstrong
comes by, I'll give it to him. When he takes it home and puts it to
use, I don't care how much spookery that pot is capable of, the old
boy's prick will put the damper on it for good. Wife, the Spirit of
the Kiln has kept me up all night. After I've checked to see that all
the gates are shut tight, let's be off to bed.
    (*in verse*)
    Here at this kiln I live
    And work to my lot in life.
    I've never swung clubs by the flame of a torch;
    Bare-handed have I sought my wealth.
    What spirits howl, what ghosts cry out?
    What God-sent bailiff have I to fear?
    I'll shut my gate and rest content;
    Let Heaven pronounce my doom.
    (*Exeunt.*)

ACT THREE

(*Enter* Chang the Headstrong.)

CHANG: I am Chang the Headstrong. In my younger days I
was Head Clerk[23] at the K'ai-feng Tribunal, but I'm an old man

now, and his Honor[24] Judge Pao has been kind enough to let me
beg for firewood and rice at the market place. By this means I
keep myself alive in my waning years. That young bastard Chao
the Jug at the pottery village usually sells his stuff through me and
has promised me a chamber pot, but he's been lying all the time
and just won't come up with one. Since I don't have anything in
particular to do right now, I think I'll go to his place and get that
pot.

> (*Yueh-tiao* mode, Melody: *Tou an-ch'un*)
> Empty-handed am I now,
> No firewood or rice to my name.
> I follow my fate in peace of mind,
> Wearing sackcloth, eating gruel.
> I had no children in my prime;
> Then late in life I lost my wife.
> Straight I've walked my path till now,
> Now is time to rest.
> Pitiful only my hair so white,
> My thin frame worn by toil.

> (Melody: *Tzu-hua-erh hsu*)
> I remember in youth my eyes were bright, my hands
>   were swift,
> My movements quick, my body light.
> Now in age I'm bent of back; my head is cast down low.
> In the distance the dogs are barking
> Behind the rickety fence.
> I raise my eyes and have a look:
> A house by a creek in a bamboo grove.
> As I reach the land of Chao the Jug,
> As if my mouth's aflame,
> I pant and puff and pant again.

Here I am at the gate of Chao the Jug at the pottery village. What
is his gate doing closed in broad daylight? I wonder what the
bastard has been up to. Well, I'll just give a call at the gate. (*shouting*) Chao the Jug! Open up! Open up!

> (*Enter* Chao *and* Chih-hsiu.)

CHAO: Who's there? I'll just open the gate and see. (*approaches* Chang) Why, it's Chang the Headstrong! What brings you here, old man?

CHANG: Chao the Jug, you bastard, you promised me a chamber pot. You've been selling your goods through me for some time now, but you won't give me one. What's a single pot worth, to make me come on my own and ask for it?

CHAO: I have the pot; I just forgot about it is all. I see *you* remembered it all right. You know what they say, "To go on living when you're old is to be nothing but a thief." They must have had you in mind when they said it.

CHIH-HSIU: He looks like a thief, sure enough, with that drooping white beard of his.

CHANG:

> (Melody: *Hsiao t'ao hung*)
> So you think me a thief, since I'm old and live on.
> Though I'm not dead yet, what's the good?

CHAO: How old are you, old fellow, and who supplies your rice and firewood?

CHANG:

> With the new year I'll be eighty in full.
> Who provides my kindling and grain?
> Only you juniors. My elders are gone.

CHAO: Tell me, how many cronies of yours are still around?

CHANG: There used to be ten of us.

CHAO: Who?

CHANG: They're either old now or dead. Only three are left: Wang Hung-tao, Li Ts'ung-shan, and myself.

> Alas! Yesterday Wang's fate was cruel,
> And today was Li's turn to go.
> Heavens above, but my white-headed friends are few!

Give me the chamber pot, Chao the Jug, and let[25] me be on my way back home.

CHAO: Bring out the pot, wife, and give it to Old Chang.

CHIH-HSIU: (*bringing out the pot*) Here it is; take it away.

CHANG: (*takes the pot*) Has this thing taken root or what?

CHAO: Pah! You old fool! It's from the kiln out back; how could it put out roots when I've just now set it down on the ground? What are you talking about?

CHANG: You young bastard, after promising me a pot all this time, the least you could do would be to give me a good one. What are you doing, giving me one that sounds cracked? No good, I don't want it. Give me something decent.

CHAO: (*pretending to exchange it for another pot*) I'll substitute another, old man.

CHANG: (*taps the pot*) No good, it doesn't sound right. Another one!

CHAO: (*makes another false exchange*) Now this is a good one.

CHANG: Yes, this one seems all right.

CHAO: (*laughs*) It's all the same to me!

CHANG: (*takes the pot and gestures his thanks*) Well, I'll be getting back then.

CHAO: How did you get here, old fellow, by the main road or on a byway?

CHANG: I came here by the main road, but I think I'll take a pathway back, since it's shorter.

CHAO: It's getting late, old friend. You'd better take the main road after all. The main road doesn't have any ghosts, but the pathway does.

CHANG: Ghosts!? Ghosts indeed! I'll give you a rap on your thieving mouth! I'm Chang the Headstrong, the one who isn't afraid of ghosts. I'm famous in the capital for my incantations: the Heart of Heaven, the Heart of Earth, and the Demon-King.*[26] I write on charms or pray to the rivers, "O Patriarch** on high, I call upon thee for exorcism swift and sure!" And so even if a ghost does happen along, one look at me and he's hightailing it for two or three miles at a stretch!

CHAO: Since you know so many incantations—the Heart of

*Prince Nata from Buddhist mythology.
**Lao Tzu, a patron saint of popular Taoism. Exorcism in popular religion had elements of both Taoism and Buddhism.

Heaven, the Heart of Earth, the Demon-King and all—off with you
then! (*pushes* Chang *out the gate*) Shut the gate again, wife, and
we'll have some wine in the back courtyard.

      (*Exeunt.*) (*Enter* Chang.)

      CHANG: Now that I've gotten a pot out of Chao the Jug, it's
getting late and I'll have to hurry back home. Chao said just now
that there are ghosts on the path, but everybody knows that I'm
Chang the Headstrong, the one who's not afraid of ghosts. I've got
a temper like throwing salt into water.[27] Ah, it's late; I'd better get
moving.

      (Melody: *T'ien ching sha*)

      Anxiously I rush ahead.

(*startled*) What are those footsteps I hear behind me? (*looks back
and shouts*) Hey! Who's there?

      Who is it clomping up behind?

It's enough to scare the life out of me!

      Who is it holds me fast?

Who isn't aware that I'm Chang the Headstrong who is not scared
of ghosts? My temper is like throwing salt into water. I can do all
sorts of incantations: the Heart of Heaven, the Heart of Earth, the
Demon-King. I write on charms or pray to the rivers, "O Patriarch
on high, perform thy exorcism swift and sure!" Whatever ghosts
there are have only to catch sight of me and they're frightened
away for several miles.

      Is it mountain spirit, ogre fierce?

      (Chang *trips.*) (*Enter* Ghost, *who hits* Chang.)

      CHANG: (*gets up, shouting*) Ghost! Ghost! (*gives a close look*)

      Ah, just brambles that clutch at my robe!

Pooh! Some brambles tripped me! (*continues to walk*)

      GHOST: (*following* Chang *and weeping*) Old man!

      CHANG: (*startled*) What's all that crying about?

      GHOST: Old man!

      CHANG: (*stops to listen*) It's not crying at all; it's someone
shouting, "Old man! Old man!" Oh, now I know. It must be the ox
boy, who sent a few oxen out to pasture early in the morning and
can't find them now that it's late. And so now you're asking me,

"Old man! Have you seen my oxen?" Little bastard! So you can't find your oxen. Do you think I give a fart?

> (Melody: *Chai-erh ling*)
>
> To children I'm a thing of sport.
>
> They laugh and say I'm old and dense.
>
> It must be the herdboy, up to his tricks.

(Ghost *weeps.*) Now that's a crying sound, no doubt about it!

> Piteous, mournful,
>
> Weeping, sobbing,

Oh, I've got it!

> Wild geese soaring on gusts of wind.

(Ghost *weeps.* Chang *stops to listen.*) No, it's not wild geese either. Who's crying there?

> (*Refrain*)
>
> At the end of the road, devoid of mankind,
>
> I am seized with fear, my spirit flies.

(Ghost *hits* Chang *on the head.* Chang *shouts.*) Ghost! Ghost!

> I cock my ear for a good long while.
>
> (*looks behind him*)
>
> I gaze about myself.

Ghost! Ghost!

> Senile fool! Just a pile of dirt and bones!

I'm getting stupid in my old age. A pile of dirt and bones and I start shouting "Ghost! Ghost!" I'm Chang the Headstrong, the one ghosts can't scare. I have a temper like scattering salt on water. I know all the incantations: Heart of Heaven, Heart of Earth, Demon-King. I write on charms and pray to the rivers, "O Patriarch on high, I summon thee for exorcism swift and sure!" One look at me and any ghost at all will run several miles in fright.

GHOST: (*calling out*) Old man!

CHANG: Oh, this ghost is getting to be a nuisance! A good thing I'm at my gate. A grass rope is holding it to. I'll just set this pot down here, untie the rope, and open up.

> (Chang *picks up the pot and steps in,* Ghost *following.*
>
> Chang *sighs.* Ghost *also sighs.*)
>
> (Melody: *Huang ch'iang-wei*)

Whence comes that whistling breath?
My head spins 'round with doubt.
I just get home and in my chair,
And something comes to mind.

(Melody: *Ch'ing yuan-chen*)
When I left, the sun deep red was sinking in the west.
Homeward bound, I saw it still; its light had not yet
    gone.
Why then my quaking fear and dread; why be perplexed
    at all?
Hmm, I clean forgot!
It amounts to nothing more
Than foolishness with age.
I never scattered ash outside the gate before I left.
They say if you scatter a handful of ashes in front of your gate,
you'll keep out evil spirits.

    GHOST: But, old man, I've been inside for a long time now!

    CHANG: I'll grab a handful of thatch from the eaves and light
it. (*grabs some thatch*) Here's some thatch. Now, when I left, I had
some cow manure burning in the stove; let's see if it's still there.
(*blows on the flame*) (Ghost *hits* Chang *on the mouth.*) My beard's
on fire! Pooh! It was just a cat jumping out at me, but it almost
burnt up my hair and whiskers! (*curses*) Oh, I know, it's Old Lady
Wang's cat from next door. She never feeds the thing, and it's
always coming over here to steal some food. I'll just give her a
piece of my mind. Old Lady Wang! You won't feed that cat of
yours, and so it comes over here and eats everything in sight—meat,
rice, chickens, ducks, even the ashes out of the stove! Any of your
lip and I'll settle with you tomorrow! (*lights a lamp*) I'll light a
lamp. (*picks up a sheepskin*) I don't know what's on this sheepskin
robe—lice or fleas. Let me have a look here.

    GHOST: Isn't that a flea there, old man?

    CHANG: What the hell business is it of yours? I'll spread this
robe out and get some sleep. (*lays out the sheepskin and goes to
bed*) (Ghost *steals the sheepskin.*) Now that's strange! I lay this

sheepskin out every day for a nice cozy sleep, but now why am I cold as ice all of a sudden? (*feels about him*) Hey, somebody stole my sheepskin! Thief! Police!

> (Melody: *Huang ch'iang-wei*)
> At the top of my voice I call out "Thief!"
> And run out on the street in fright.
> No constable can I find, no patrolman on his round.
> Whom can I get to answer my call?

> (Melody: *Ch'ing yuan-chen*)
> I turn back and dart into the house,
> (*trips*)
> And over the door jamb I fall on my face.
> (Ghost *twists the sheepskin around* Chang's *head.*)

Got him!

> With my hand I grab him by his dirty robe of fur,
> Pound him with my fist,
> Kick him with my foot.
> Pah! Nothing but a worn out skin of wool!

It was just this sheepskin robe covering my head, and I had to start yelling thief! Well, this business has kept me up the whole night, and now I have to get up and relieve myself. There's that pot Chao the Jug gave me; I might as well test it out. (*urinates*) (Ghost *takes the pot away.*) Why is it I don't hear anything hitting the pot? It's landing on the ground instead! (*feels about him*) Damn! I really *am* getting stupid in my old age. The pot's over there, and here I am peeing over here! (*crosses over*) (Ghost *takes the pot away again.* Chang *feels about him once more.*) (*startled*) How did it get over there now? (Ghost *puts the pot on his head.* Chang *gropes about.*) Ai-ya! Now it's dangling in midair!

> (Melody: *T'u ssu-erh*)
> I had thought I'd rise early at night,
> Get all my preparations done,
> But with all that water and all that soup, I had to get
>   myself up at night.
> Who could guess

On this one day
Such weirdness would occur?

(Melody: *Sheng Yao-wang*)
I race over here
And it runs over there.
All I see is something flying to and fro in the air.
Then it runs over here
And I race over there.
My whole body is sweaty, from top to toe.
Ai-ya! And I'm full of a whole night's water as well!
(Ghost *approaches* Chang *with the pot and kneels.* Chang
is startled.)

(Melody: *Kuei san t'ai*)
Right up to me he comes,
As I turn away in fright.
GHOST: Old man, didn't you say you were like salt thrown into
water?
CHANG:
Like salt thrown into water, yes I am.
GHOST: Aren't you Chang the Headstrong?
CHANG:
You know my name, I see.
GHOST: Didn't I hear you say you weren't afraid of ghosts?
CHANG:
Well, I am from this time on!
GHOST: You know the Incantation of the Heart of Heaven.
CHANG:
The Heart of Heaven? Not a shred!
GHOST: The Demon-King?
CHANG:
Nor that as well, O ghost!
GHOST: Then I suppose you can't pray to the rivers or write
charms either.

CHANG:

    Pray to the rivers, write on charms? Not at all!

    Just tricks to cheat the ghosts, to scare them far away.

GHOST: Why don't all those incantations of yours seem to be working, old man?

CHANG:

    (Melody: *T'iao-hsiao ling*)

    Now let *me* ask *you:*

    What is it that you want?

GHOST: Have a guess.

CHANG:

    Are you a forgotten spirit, demanding wine and food?

GHOST: No.

CHANG:

    If then a demon, let me know your name.

GHOST: Nor am I that.

CHANG: No again, eh?

    Then who in hell can you be?

GHOST: I am the pot, and the pot is me.

CHANG:

    Look at all the trouble he's caused with just a chamber
        pot;

That bastard Chao the Jug!

    Now if it were a big water cistern that would really be
        the end!

Just let me ask you something: are you man or ghost, and how did you get in here?

GHOST: You carried me in under your robe.

CHANG: (*curses the door gods**) Let me give those door gods a good talking-to. Door gods! How did you happen to let a ghost get by you? What are you good for anyway?

    (Melody: *Ma lang-erh*)

    On New Year's Day I put you up,

---

*The "door gods" here may be the mythical brothers Shen T'u and Yü Lü.

Offered you sweetmeats and tea,
In hopes that you'd drive out forces malign,
In hopes that you'd guard this my home.
(*Refrain*)
Pah! I had you portrayed
In grim and foul face,
But what do you do but doze off, O gods of the gate!
Both charms of peach wood,* what good do they do?
(*tears off an image of* Chung K'uei, *the demon queller*)
I rip with my hands Chung K'uei of dreams.

GHOST: Help me, old man.

CHANG: Explain yourself and I will.

GHOST: (*weeps*) Have pity on me! My name is Yang Kuo-yung of the capital. After having made a little money selling goods from the south, I was on my way home when, before I knew it, it was nighttime, and so I stayed over at Chao the Jug's in the pottery village. The two of them, husband and wife, stole my money and murdered me. Then they burned me to ashes, pounded up my bones, and made me into a pot. I'd thought I would hold soup or water, but I never dreamed I'd be given to you as a chamber pot! How am I supposed to put up with such filth and pestilence? Pity me, old man, and give me your help!

CHANG: Ah, what a foul fate! The trouble is, pot, you're a ghost and I'm a human; how can I possibly be of any help to you?

GHOST: Take this pot to his Excellency Judge Pao and rap on its edge three times. I'll then rattle off my story.

CHANG: Well then, I'll do what I can for you. It's light out now, and I'll lock up the gate and take this pot off to see Judge Pao. (*goes out the gate*) But hold on a minute. "Practiced in private, polished in public." If he by any chance doesn't say anything once I get to the K'ai-feng Tribunal, what'll I do then? I'll just give it a trial rap. Here's the edge of the pot. (*raps on the pot*) One, two, three!

---

*According to Han legend, Shen T'u and Yü Lü used peach wood to exorcise evil spirits.

GHOST: Just ask me to say my piece, old man, and I'll rattle
away for you.

CHANG:

> (Melody: *Shou-wei*)
> Off to K'ai-feng I carry the pot,
> Straight to the Lung-t'u Judge.
> If Hell's to be avoided, why then, so it shall be.

Pot,

> If you but see justice brought you at last,[28] this time of
> joy you'll die.

> (*Exeunt.*)

ACT FOUR

(*Enter* Judge Pao *with* Chang Ch'ien *and attendants.*)

CHANG CH'IEN: (*shouting*) Yo! Silence, all in court! Bring in
the court desk!

PAO:

> (*in verse*)
> When laws are just, Heaven's heart's in accord,
> With moral purity comes an unblemished world.
> My brush exalts sons loyal and true,
> And my sword beheads the guilty.

My surname is Pao, my given name Cheng, and my courtesy name
Hsi-wen. I come from Lao-erh Hamlet, Ssu-wang Village, Chin-tou
Commandery, Lu-chou. While young I passed my Doctorate of
Letters examination and have since received a good many official
appointments. Because of my honesty of character, competence in
office, devotion to my country, and unselfishness, his Majesty has
been gracious in promoting me to the rank of Academician-in-
waiting of the Lung-t'u Pavilion and the post of prefect of the K'ai-
feng Tribunal. I also have as an imperial gift the Sword of Authority and a Golden Badge, with the right to perform summary executions. I devote my entire attention to investigating corrupt
officials and clerks. At the moment I am about to preside over

early session. Chang Ch'ien, call for the cases to be presented.[29]

    CHANG CH'IEN: Yes, sir. Carry out the sign for appeals!

    (*Enter* Chang the Headstrong *with the pot.*)

    CHANG: Here I am at the gate of the K'ai-feng Tribunal. I'll give a rap on the pot and see what happens. (*raps on the pot*) One, two, three!

    GHOST: I'll rattle off my story.

    CHANG: Then let's go make the accusation.

    (*Cheng-kung*[30] mode, Melody: *Tuan-cheng hao*)

Holding a pot with grievance sore,

I approach the awesome public hall.

All I wish is that the criminal be brought to justice,

And who more famous for that than Old Pao, the
        Lung-t'u?

Let me steal a look by the screening wall.

(Melody: *Kun hsiu-ch'iu*)

I see fierce guards gripping staves,

Glowering clerks stamping papers.

On each side the Sword of Authority and the Bronze
        Blade*

And in the center him with ivory tablet and cap of black
        gauze.

Pot, I wonder if we should have come here at all.

If a matter of false pretenses, you're all but false.

Did I come for a joke? You're certainly no joke!

I'm rousing my courage in the middle of fright;

Am I being made victim for no reason?

Pot, I'd like to impress something on you: when Judge Pao asks you questions, answer him in full detail.

    Pot, if you fail to make your plaint this morn,

I, Chang the Headstrong,

---

*Used to execute criminals by cutting them in half at the waist. It is mentioned occasionally in northern drama as a symbol of special power, along with the Sword of Authority.

Who brags in vain of honest heart,

Must prepare to carry chains and cangue.

I'm going in now, pot, and once I give three raps, you start talking.

GHOST: I'll rattle it off, old man.

CHANG: Injustice!

PAO: Chang Ch'ien, who is that calling out an injustice? Bring him forward.

CHANG CH'IEN: Face the court.

(Chang *steps in and kneels.*)

PAO: The old fellow Chang the Headstrong served many years in the courthouse, and now that he has no one to look after him, I let him beg for firewood and rice in the market place to support himself for the rest of his life. I suspect that one of the people on the street must have treated him badly by refusing to give him some firewood or some rice, and so he's come to make a complaint. What is your grievance, old fellow? Tell me all about it, and I'll do all I can for you.

CHANG: *I* bear no grievance, but this pot does.

PAO: Well, if you bear no grievance, old fellow, tell me about the pot's then.

CHANG: I'll rap on the pot three times, your Honor, and it'll rattle away.

PAO: Indeed! Well then, rap away, old fellow. Listen to it, Chang Ch'ien.

CHANG: (*raps on the pot*) One, two, three—pot!

PAO: Can you hear what it's saying, Chang Ch'ien?

CHANG CH'IEN: (*cocking his ear*) He's lying, sir, I don't hear a sound.

CHANG: He didn't talk!

PAO: I thought the old fellow was getting a little foolish. After all, how can a pot rattle and talk? Throw him out, Chang Ch'ien!

CHANG CH'IEN: Yes, sir. (*pushes* Chang *out*)

CHANG: Why didn't he say anything? I'll try rapping on it. One, two, three!

GHOST: I'll rattle it off.

CHANG: Where were you just now?

GHOST: I had a terrible thirst and went off to find me a cup of tea.

CHANG: Still joking around, are you? When you didn't show up a moment ago, you had me scared so much my face itself was the color of tea.

GHOST: Help me, old man!

CHANG: I'll make your plaint once more, then. (*calls out again*) Injustice!

PAO: Chang Ch'ien, who is making all that fuss at the gate?

CHANG CH'IEN: It's old Chang the Headstrong again, calling out an injustice.

PAO: What, again? Bring him in. (Chang *kneels.*) What is your complaint?

CHANG: Your Honor, this pot really does have a grievance. Outside the courthouse gate just now I beat on it, and it started rattling. (*raps on the pot*) One, two, three—pot!

PAO: What is it saying, Chang Ch'ien?

CHANG CH'IEN: I guess the old boy is the only one who can hear it, because I didn't hear a thing!

CHANG: (*listening himself*) *Now* why didn't he say anything?

PAO: Throw him out, Chang Ch'ien.

CHANG CH'IEN: (*pushing* Chang *out*) This is a court of law, old man, not some place where you can pull shenanigans! Go on home with you!

CHANG: (*steps out and sighs*) Ahh, I, Chang the Headstrong, have had a reputation for honesty my whole life long, and now it's all been ruined by a pot!

(Melody: *Tao-tao ling*[31])

How have I gotten rice and fuel without paying the price?

How do I walk into court and out without being tongue
    lashed?

Because I'm straightforward, fair, with no grain of deceit,

Because I don't speak abuse or play lord of the town.

But you've done me in now,

You've done me in now,[32]

And I'll just have to hold back both anger and tongue
    and wend my way home again.

Let me rap on the pot just one more time. (*raps on the pot*) One, two, three!

  GHOST: What's the matter, old man?

  CHANG: (*angrily*) *Now* where did you go?

  GHOST: I was hungry and went off to eat a roast bun.

  CHANG: Because you didn't show up, Judge Pao came close to beating every last fart out of me!

  GHOST: Help me, old man!

  CHANG:

    (Melody: *Tsui kao ko*)
    In private you rattle away;
    When it counts, you play deaf and dumb.
    I'm going to pick you up,
    And on this very street
    I'll smash you to smithereens!

  GHOST: If you did that, then who would make my case known?

  CHANG: Pot, did you happen to see it?

  GHOST: See what?

  CHANG:

    (Melody: *Hung hsiu-hsieh*)
    That staff just now was as thick as an arm,
    And it fell on me like a hook.
    You ghost, you use an old man for sport!

  GHOST: Go in again for me, old man.

  CHANG:

    It's not that I fear to stride over the sill.
    It's not indolence keeping me out.

  GHOST: If you won't go in, who will help me?

  CHANG:

    Pot, it might mean beating number three.

  GHOST: It's not that I don't want to go in, old man; it's just that the door gods are blocking the way and won't let me in.

  CHANG: Well, why didn't you say so before? I'll call out again. (*shouting*) Injustice!

  PAO: There he goes again! Have him come in. (Chang *steps in and kneels.*) What's your grievance, old fellow?

CHANG: It's actually the pot that has the grievance.

PAO: Doesn't the old man have any idea how to behave at all? He's played a joke on me with that pot two or three times now. Come out with a good reason and all will be forgotten. But speak falsely, and don't expect me to pardon you!

CHANG: Calm your anger, your Honor, and listen to me while I tell you the whole story, item by item.

> (*in verse*)
> Over eighty am I now,
> But I'll go through it all from head to tail.
> When I left, out of the haze and gloom shone the sun;
> When I returned, with darkness and murk the heavens
>   were black.
> On the wall I lit a lamp, flickering but never dying,
> And made ready for a lovely snooze,
> When I heard choking and racking sobs.
> In a state of alarm I got up once again
> And asked, "Are you spirit, are you demon, or are you
>   ghost?"
> He replied, "The pot is my body."
> Hence I make his plaint at court
> And appeal to your Honor to hear the truth.
> By day you've decided in the world of light,
> At night you've heard phantoms in the realms of the
>   dark.
> Thrice for the Wangs you investigated the butterfly
>   dream.
> Singlehanded, you sold rice at Ch'en-chou.
> You used a wise strategem for the boy in the chalk circle.
> With craft you beheaded a lord of *Chai-lang* rank, solved
>   the riddles in the "Flower in the Back Courtyard"
>   songs,
> And recovered both copies of the contract.[33]
> Command those peevish door gods
> Not to block my rattling ghost of the pot.

(Melody: *Hsiao Liang-chou*)
I appeal to your Honor, look into this case.
Would I make schemes and lie?
It's your gods of the gateway, like fierce demon kings,
Broadaxes firmly in grasp.
Your Honor, just look at them!
How can a mere ghost survive terror so stark?

PAO: Yes, of course! Every house, large or small, has its door
gods, and a murdered ghost would be blocked from entering. Chang
Ch'ien, bring me gold and silver paper money.

(*in verse*)
In my mind I've hatched a plan.
Set out the paper cash.
Goblins and demons should not be let past,
But a ghost with a grievance may safely step in.

CHANG CH'IEN: (*burns the paper*) I've burnt the string of
paper money, and just look at that blast of cold wind!

(Ghost *follows the wind in and kneels.*)

CHANG:

(*Refrain*)
The paper cash is burned away.
A whirlwind hovers by.
I'll risk it all and on the pot
Give raps in number three.

(*raps on the pot*) One, two, three—pot!

GHOST: I'll rattle it all off!

CHANG: What a relief!
He says he'll rattle away.
Listen, your Honor,
He's going to tell it right.

PAO: At the foot of the courtroom steps is the ghost of a
murdered man, which no one but I can see. Ghost, what is your
plaint? Tell it in full and I will help you.

GHOST: Your servant is from the capital by birth. I came
upon someone called Chia the Demigod, who foretold that within

a hundred days blood would shine unless I went three hundred miles away. And so I took leave of my father, first, to deal in goods from the south, and second, to escape disaster. Fortunately I did well in business and made some money. By the time I headed back home, it was already the ninety-ninth day, and since the full period was not yet over, I was reluctant to reach home right away. That's why I stayed overnight at Chao the Jug's in the pottery village, about ten miles out. To my surprise the two of them, Chao and his wife, stole my fortune and murdered me. Then they burned me to ashes, ground up my bones, and fashioned me into a pot. Oh, the misery I feel!

> (*in verse*)
> To escape dire fate I set out afar
> And in alien land plied my trade.
> Although my gain was a hundred fold,
> I have suffered in ten thousand ways.
> From my home a scant ten miles
> A stranger's house was my abode.
> That night man and wife, seized with greed,
> Were as cruel as tiger or wolf.
> Murder cast me from the realm of light,
> Then they burned me to ash, pounded my bones,
> Mixed in water and clay, molded a pot,
> And gave it to Old Chang the Headstrong.
> How hope to hold water or broth?
> To avoid the fate of a chamber pot—this request denied.
> Hence I rattle and tell my tale,
> Proclaim my woe for all to hear,
> That you, O lord of justice bright,
> Might aid a ghost of murder dead.

PAO: This is indeed an injustice! Chang Ch'ien! Bring Chao the Jug and his wife here, and give them a stroke of the staff with every step.

CHANG CH'IEN: Yes, sir. (*leaves and calls out*) Is Chao the Jug home?

(*Enter* Chao.)

CHAO: Who's that calling me?

CHANG: Where's your wife?

CHAO: She's an entertainer, I know, but her name's been off the rolls a long time now, and here you are calling her up for service!*

CHANG CH'IEN: Pah! Judge Pao has a summons out for her; get her out here, quick!

(*Enter* Chih-hsiu.)

CHIH-HSIU: Chang Ch'ien, brother! It's been a long time! You're even nastier than you used to be. Come on in and have some tea.

CHANG CH'IEN: Judge Pao is waiting. Get a move on! (*arrives at the courthouse and reports*) Defendants face the court!

(Chao *and* Chih-hsiu *kneel.*)

PAO: Chao the Jug, someone has accused you of killing Yang Kuo-yung.

CHAO: We're both of us vegetarian Buddhists; we never killed any sheep called Yang Kuo-yung or whatever.** Who's the plaintiff? Let me confront him.

PAO: Chang the Headstrong is the plaintiff.

CHAO: That's a fine way to behave, you old dolt! Here I give you a chamber pot as free as you please. What's wrong with that? And then you have to accuse me of homicide! Think you can put the squeeze on me, eh?

CHANG: Blackguard! I thought that pot had a bad ring to it when you gave it to me. I asked you to exchange it, and after three exchanges, you still gave me the same old pot! And after I got it home, its weeping and wailing kept me up all night. That's bad enough, but what's worse, I peed all over the floor! Then it started talking—rattle, rattle—some tall tale or other, something about a Yang Kuo-yung and his money, and how you were out to get it.

CHAO: Do you mean to tell me that pot, after saying nothing at my place, started talking at yours? I don't believe it!

*Chih-hsiu was formerly on the roster of public entertainers (i.e., prostitutes) on call for service at official functions.
**A homophone of the surname Yang is *yang,* "sheep."

CHIH-HSIU: What kind of story is this? The old bird must be after one of our water cisterns!

CHANG:

(Melody: *K'uai-huo san*)
Ah, Chao the Jug!
Did you think me a child?
You gave me a pot for the bedroom
And a horrible shock as well!

(Melody: *Ch'ao T'ien-tzu*)
When I brought you home, pot,
You nearly brought me death from fright!
If you don't believe me, your Honor, just send somebody to take a look.
The piss I spilled like a fool is there still.

PAO: How did he go about committing murder in the kiln?

CHANG: Your Honor,
His pottery village was worse than a bandit lair[34]
That all the troops in the realm could scarcely quell.
He murdered the innocent
And baked them into tile,
Sending their souls into perdition.
If you wish that justice be served aright,
Give him cuts a thousand times ten.
Your Honor,
Even that would barely fit his crimes.

CHAO: It's going to take more than your testimony to put a capital crime on my head. If you can get that pot to rattle off, I'll give in.

CHANG: (*raps on the pot*) One, two, three—pot!

GHOST: Chao the Jug, at last this day has come! (*hits* Chao)

CHAO: Don't you harass me. Let me go home, and I'll give you a service and guarantee your ascent to Heaven. I've got plenty of money to do it, too. I won't let you down.

GHOST: (*hits* Chih-hsiu) You—you heaped those big pieces of firewood on my leg bones and burned me to a fare-thee-well!

CHIH-HSIU: (*in fear*) You were dead as could be; it couldn't have hurt.

PAO: Chang Ch'ien, pick out a large staff and give each one of them a hundred strokes. Then have the secretary get their confessions down on an official form. Once they've signed it, I'll sentence them to death in this very session. On this same day they are to be taken to the execution ground and put to death by a thousand or ten thousand slashes.

CHANG CH'IEN: Yes, sir. (*beats them and has* Chao *sign a piece of paper*)

CHAO: I'll sign, I'll sign! I was the one who killed Yang Kuo-yung, took his money, burnt him to ashes, pounded up his bones, and made him into a pot. I did it then with my eyes open, and I'll take what's coming to me now with my eyes closed. The only thing is, I had to involve you in this, wife.

CHIH-HSIU: In the K'ai-feng Tribunal, if they don't kill you, they beat you. At least they're not going to burn me to ashes, grind up my bones, and make a pot out of me. What have I got to be afraid of? Let them kill me! Let them kill me!

(*Enter* Executioner *with a knife, who ushers* Chao *and* Chih-hsiu *offstage.*)

GHOST: I'm going to the execution ground and watch. I'll serve as the official supervisor of executions! (*kowtows in thanks to* Pao)

(*Exit.*)

PAO: Chang Ch'ien, I want you to confiscate every last scrap of Chao the Jug's property and divide it into two portions. One half goes to Chang the Headstrong as a reward for doing his duty and sounding a plaint for another. The other half is Yang Kuo-yung's father's as his support. Give this pot to him as well to take home and bury. Meanwhile, let this whole matter be announced to the public.

(*in verse*)
It is not that I delight in executions,
But the law of the land knows no favor.
The remaining funds I give to those of old age,

And an empty grave calls to the ghost of the dead.
Never say the righteous exist no more,
The law is here for those in need.
And now let this be known by all
As a tale of marvel in ages hence.

CHANG: (*kowtows in thanks*) If it had not been for your Excellency, this crime would never have found a solution. Truly, your virtue is like Heaven itself, great beyond all conception!

(Melody: *Ssu-pien ching*)
With these white hairs of mine
But for a grieved ghost I would never have come.

Judge Pao,

Your virtue is perfection itself;
The spirits stand in awe.
Let it be known from this time forth
To the end of the sky
As a tale very wondrous and strange.

HOU-T'ING HUA

(The Flower of the Back Courtyard)

by

Cheng T'ing-yü

INTRODUCTION

Like so many other plays of the courtroom type, *Hou-t'ing hua* (The flower of the back courtyard) has no known antecedents in drama or fiction. This play was the principal source for *T'ao-fu chi,* a play in thirty scenes by the prolific Ming dramatist Shen Ching.*

Besides differing from the northern play in some personal names and in a slightly more complex plot, the Ming play also uses a device for bringing the dead back to life: a potion called "soul-restoring cinnabar" (*huan-hun tan*), which Judge Pao administers to revive the dead heroine at the end of the play. *The Flower of the Back Courtyard* is a skillful blending of romantic love with crime, but a preponderant concern for the love story apparently led Shen Ching to sacrifice the power of the northern courtroom play for a happy ending in the tradition of Ming romantic comedy.

Particularly noteworthy in *The Flower of the Back Courtyard* is its central character in the first two acts, Li Shun, who initially is one of courtroom drama's least prepossessing and sympathetic victims but who, through stress, discovers within himself a latent sense of justice. In his Li Shun, Cheng T'ing-yü shows by example that not all characters in northern drama are stereotypes.

This is one of the few Judge Pao plays by a known author, although, as with any other text surviving only in late Ming editions, some elements may date from the Ming. We know very little about Cheng T'ing-yü except that he originated from Chang-te-fu in present-day Honan Province and that he died sometime before 1330. He is known to have written twenty-three plays, six of which are extant; one of these, *Chin feng-ch'ai* (The golden hairpins), also comes under the heading of courtroom drama.**

---

*See chap. 1, n. 35.
**Cheng T'ing-yü was already dead by the time Chung Ssu-ch'eng wrote *Lu kuei pu,* which bears Chung's preface dated 1330. See Chung Ssu-ch'eng, *Lu kuei pu,* p. 107, and Chu Ch'üan, *T'ai-ho cheng-yin p'u,* p. 40.

The Flower of the Back Courtyard is comparatively free of textual problems. Aside from occasional minor differences, the version in *Ku ming-chia tsa-chü* is identical to that in *Yuan-ch'ü hsuan,* the text used for this translation.*

*See Appendix C.

THE FLOWER OF THE BACK COURTYARD

by

Cheng T'ing-yü

ACT ONE

(*Enter* Chao *with* Attendant.)

CHAO:

(*in verse*)

My loyalty and diligence embrace the cares of state,
As I watch my hair grow white with time.
What a shame to be given a girl of flowery grace,
A gift beyond my intentions, a gift I dare not keep.

I, Chao Chung, with the courtesy name of Te-fang, am a man of the capital. There are three of us in my immediate family: my wife, whose maiden name is Chang, has with her a servant's son,[1] Wang Ch'ing. My high repute as an official has earned for me the post of Judicial Inspector,[2] and this morning his Majesty presented me with a girl, Ts'ui-luan, in the company of her mother, to attend to my needs. As yet I have no idea how my wife feels about this, and so I've been somewhat reluctant to take the girl in right away. I'm going to have Wang Ch'ing take her to see my wife and see what she has to say. Attendant, call for Wang Ch'ing.

ATTENDANT: Yes, sir. Wang Ch'ing, the master is calling for you.

(*Enter* Wang.)

WANG: I, Wang Ch'ing, am a steward here in the mansion of his Excellency Inspector Chao, and I handle all the household affairs, inside and out, so that everybody is scared stiff of me. His Excellency is calling for me right now, about what I don't know, and I'll have to get going. No need to announce myself; I'll just go right on in. (*approaches* Chao) You called for me, your Excellency? How may I be of service to you?

129

CHAO: Come here, Wang Ch'ing. Let me ask you something. Where are the mother and daughter that his Majesty gave me?

WANG: They're here in the mansion.

CHAO: Call them here.

WANG: Call for Ts'ui-luan and her mother!

(*Enter* Ts'ui-luan *and* Mother.)

TS'UI-LUAN:

(*in verse*)

Beneath the gate of this great house I have stood for
    days on end,
With never a chance of passage in to let myself be known.
Since favor's gifts rest not with looks,
What need have I to preen?[3]

My name is Wang Ts'ui-luan, and this is my mother. His Majesty has given us to his Honor Inspector Chao, but for the past several days since our arrival here, we haven't been called for once. Why are we being called now, sir?[4]

WANG: You're to go in and see his Excellency.

(*They approach* Chao.)

CHAO: Are these the mother and daughter, Wang Ch'ing? Take them to see my wife, and if she has anything to say about the matter, report back to me.

(*Exit.*)

WANG: Both of you come with me and see Madam Chao.

(*Exeunt. Enter* Wife.)

WIFE:

(*in verse*)

The capital is the post of my lord,
With pay and position to match.
If no woman's help was ever for him,
Who, pray, got him this far?

I am the wife of Inspector Chao. Among the three members of my immediate family is Wang Ch'ing, a servant's son. I'm by nature hard to please, and he always comes to ask me how I want every single household matter taken care of. I wonder why I haven't seen anything of him the last two days?

(*Enter* Wang, *leading* Ts'ui-luan *and* Mother.)

WANG: His Excellency's orders are to take these two to see the Madam. You two stay here by the gate. I'm going in first to see her, and then I'll be out to call you in.

TS'UI-LUAN: Yes, sir.

WANG: (*approaches* Wife) Ts'ui-luan and her mother, whom his Majesty has granted to serve his Excellency, are here. His Excellency has told me to bring them here to see you, Madam.

WIFE: Call them in and let me have a look at them.

WANG: Go in and see Madam Chao.

(Ts'ui-luan *and* Mother *approach* Wife.)

WIFE: The young girl is rather pretty. Now if she attended to his Excellency and any offspring came of it, where would that leave me? This is the only way to handle it—Wang Ch'ing, come here. You take both mother and daughter and strangle them or stab them—I don't care how you do it, I just want them dead, not alive, understand? I'm relying on you to do things right, now. When they're dead, let me know.

(*Exit.*)

WANG: What's so difficult about that? I'll just do them in and that'll be it. You two will stay in the side room for now. (*Exeunt* Ts'ui-luan *and* Mother.) Hold on a minute. I'm eager enough to murder them, all right; the trouble is, I couldn't bear to do the job myself. There's a man, Li Shun, a drunkard, whose wife and I have been having a little affair. Right now I think I'll go to his place and if he isn't home, I'll have a word with his wife. I have an idea.

(*Exit. Enter* Chang.)

CHANG: My name is Chang by birth, and Li Shun is my husband. Our boy, Fu-t'ung, is dumb, can't speak a word. It's my burden to be married to that man of mine; all he does every day is drink and ignore his family. He's a custodian in the official residence[5] here, under the supervision of a certain Wang Ch'ing, with whom I've been having an affair. Now why on earth hasn't Wang Ch'ing shown up in the last couple of days?

(*Enter* Wang.)

WANG: Here I am at the gate. Is Li Shun there?

CHANG: Come on in, Li Shun isn't here. (Wang *approaches* Chang.) Wang Ch'ing, why haven't I seen you in the last few days?

WANG: I've been busy at home.

CHANG: Doing what?

WANG: His Majesty has presented his Excellency the Inspector with a girl named Ts'ui-luan and her mother to serve him. He told me to take them to see his wife, who told me in turn to do away with them, only I can't bear to do it. I'd like to get Li Shun to do it instead.

CHANG: Come here, Wang Ch'ing. I have a plan to make us man and wife for the rest of our lives. When you see Li Shun, tell him Madam Chao wants him to kill the mother and daughter—she wants them gotten rid of for good—and he's to report back to her in three days. He's bound to bring them here to do the job, and when I notice what's going on, I'll say, "Don't you hurt them!" I'll take their valuables off them and make him let them go. On the third day you'll come around and ask Li Shun what's happened to them, and he'll no doubt say he's killed them. Then you'll say, "What I heard is that once you got hold of their jewelry, you let them run away." He's sure to try to squirm his way out of it, and then you'll say, "Your wife must have some knowledge of all this." You then threaten me with your cudgel, and I'll say, "Don't hit me! My husband got their valuables and let them go!" To which you say, "If that's true, I'm hauling you off to see the Madam!" He'll panic, and you'll add, "Would you like to get out of this, Li Shun?" He'll say, "Of course I would!" You say, "Then divorce that wife of yours." He'll say, "Suppose I did, who would want her?" and you'll say, "I would!" If he does divorce me, we two can be husband and wife forever. What do you think?

WANG: What a marvelous plan!

CHANG: I'm going back to my room. Li Shun should be along any moment now.

(*Enter* Li.)

LI: I'm Li Shun. I've just gotten back here at my gate from the official residence.

WANG: Hey there, Li Shun! What's that you're saying? Drunk again, I see!

LI: Oh, it's Mr. Wang Ch'ing! What's on your mind?

WANG: (*hits* Li) Neglecting your duties and spending all your time drinking!

LI: Hey, don't hit me, sir! I haven't been drinking. If I drink another drop, may I drink blood instead!

WANG: Look at him, will you! Drunk as ever, and out he comes with an oath! (*hits* Li again) All you do is drink and neglect your duties!

LI: Mr. Wang,

> (*Hsien-lü* mode, Melody: *Tien chiang-ch'un*)
> Your blather makes my head swim!
> You don't care what you say,
> Just showing off
> To puff yourself up
> And rolling about on the flame![6]

WANG: Where are you off to every day?

LI:

> (Melody: *Hun chiang lung*)
> From the time the bell* rings out,

WANG: When the bell sounds, where are you and what are you up to?

LI:

> I'm standing to attention and don't dare leave the house.
> My spleen is all atremble and my heart is filled with dread.
> 'Round and 'round I go, with flying feet and flailing[7]
>   hands.
> Ai! You stewards with your purple robes
> Lord it over us of tattooed face,** conscripts[8] of lowest
>   rank.

WANG: You never get going with anything, whether it's urgent or not.

LI:

> If the matter be urgent, I speed on my way,
> And if it is not, I slow down,

*The bell to awaken the household.
**Common soldiers were often tattooed on the face to prevent desertion. Li Shun is comparing his status to theirs, one of the lowest in traditional China.

But can any man say my own conscience I've spurned?
Why then are you so angry?
What's the need for wrath?

WANG: Listen, you, I have something for you to take care of.
I want you to get rid of a couple of people for me.

LI: Not me, sir. Get somebody else!

WANG: (*hits* Li) I want *you*! Why won't you do it?

LI:

(Melody: *Yu hu-lu*)

There you go, using privilege and power to play the
          tyrant without cause!

WANG: (*hits* Li) You're looking for a good beating, you
bastard!

LI:

You may land several blows on my back,
But no such foul task for me, no, nor for money as well.

WANG: You're off and running fast enough when it comes to
meat and wine, I notice.

LI:

Vexing enough to go begging for wine and for meat,
Now you come pressing with murder in mind!

WANG: Every day you spend your money on drink.

LI:

Who has the pocket money to mend even a rake?*

WANG: You'd piss on your heels for a drink.[9] No hope for you
at all!

LI:

Who'd piss on his heels for a drink?
When it comes to murder, you're hot enough on mine!
When you want somebody killed, don't go to anybody else, oh no,
just have Li Shun do it!

Tell me, sir, do *my* palms alone bear the dagger's print?

WANG: Just look at the sot, nothing but back talk do I get!

---

*A stock saying, akin to "I don't have a red cent."

LI:

> (Melody: *T'ien-hsia le*)
> What do you know of "He who loves the cup pities the
>   drunk"?

WANG: All right, you, come along with me.

> (Li *follows* Wang.)

LI:

> A plague take you!

WANG: (*looks back at* Li) What are you up to?

LI:

> Think you're so tough?
> With this sharp knife I'll sever your spine.
> One day I'll snap the bones of your legs
> And pulverize your skull!

WANG: Who do you think you're throwing curses at, anyway?

LI:

> You're not worth even the heel of my foot!

WANG: I'm going to let you off for now for talking to me that
way. Right now I have my orders from Madam Chao.

LI: (*startled*) One word about Madam Chao is enough to scare
the wine right out of me! May I ask what this is all about, sir?

WANG: A mother and daughter are staying in this side room,
and Madam Chao wants you to take them away and get rid of them.
You can strangle them or stab them—it's up to you—but she wants
them finished off. You have three days before reporting back. I'm
off now.

> (*Exit.*)

LI: What am I going to do about this? It's getting late.

> (Melody: *Tsui chung-t'ien*)
> By now the sun is fallen behind the sunset clouds,
>   Just at time of dusk.

I'll just open this door here. Where might the mother and daughter
be?

> (Ts'ui-luan *and* Mother *approach* Li.)

TS'UI-LUAN: What are you going to do with us, sir?

LI: Follow me and be quick about it!

We're going to the banks of the River Pien.[10]

TS'UI-LUAN: Have pity on us, please!

LI:

> Your protests sway me not one whit, nor will escape
>> avail.

This is none of my doing.

> I bear the command of the Inspector's wife
> That before the end of the first night watch
> I dispatch your souls* in flight.

For now follow me home. Here's my gate. Now you just stay there. (*calls out*)

(*Enter* Chang *and* Fu-t'ung.)

CHANG: Li Shun, you're drunk again!

LI: I've just had all the wine scared right out of me!

CHANG: How's that?

LI: The Inspector's wife has ordered me to murder that mother and daughter there and report back in three days. I've come to get a piece of rope to strangle them with. At least they'll end up with their corpses in one piece.**

CHANG: Bring them here, Li Shun, and let me have a look at them.

(Ts'ui-luan *and* Mother *approach* Chang.)

TS'UI-LUAN: My greetings to you.

CHANG: What a good-looking girl!

LI: Bring me some rope, son.

(Fu-t'ung *hands* Li *some rope.* Li *is about to strangle* Ts'ui-luan.)

CHANG: A fine girl like that! Li Shun, I tell you, this is no way to build up any merit for yourself. Let's take their valuables and let them go. After all, who's to know? And we'd never spend all the proceeds in a lifetime!

---

*Lit., the "three souls" (*san hun*), which, according to Neo-Taoism, inhabit the human body.

**Dying with one's body intact was held to be necessary for rebirth in paradise; hence the additional horror of decapitation or slicing.

LI: Be quiet!

(Melody: *Chin chan-erh*)

You're mighty quick to mention favors;

Maybe your courage will be your shield.

But my fine skin can't take the rod,

And I implore[11] you to stand by your word.

Don't run against that demon queen.*

Man's gall is money, that we know,

But that mouth of yours is misfortune's own door.

CHANG: Still, who would ever find out?

LI:

Haven't you heard that the walls have ears

And outside every window someone lurks?

CHANG: Just do what I say and everything will be all right.

LI: No matter what happens, then, wife, I'll do what you say.

CHANG: (*to* Ts'ui-luan) Young lady, I've talked my husband into sparing your lives. Take off your jewelry and give it to me, and we'll let you go. How does that strike you?

TS'UI-LUAN: If you could see fit to save us, why should I care about some jewelry? I would be eternally grateful! (*gives* Chang *the jewelry*)

CHANG: Li Shun, take a look at these hairpins and bracelets!

LI: Let me see.

(Melody: *I-pan-erh*)

The bracelet and pin are real silver and gold.

CHANG: It's gold, all right.

LI: I have a question for you, old woman.

Are you two citizens, or are you slaves?

MOTHER: We're full-fledged citizens.

LI:

Then pity shall move our hearts.

Wife,

If but that grasping blackmailer** should hear,

---

*Madam Chao.
**Wang Ch'ing.

> Half of these things might be kept with us, but half
> would go to him.

We're going to save your lives, old woman. Don't you ever forget
this favor; keep it in mind now.

    TS'UI-LUAN: I'll never forget your favor no matter whether I
live or die.

    LI:

> (Melody: *Hou-t'ing hua*)
> My wife's good will
> Has spared your lives.
> Now this may delight my virtuous wife,
> But *me* it throws into a turmoil![12]
> You cannot delay
> At this first watch of night,
> For you'll get no rest tonight.
> My wife and I have talked it through
> And are prepared to save you from grief.
> Tomorrow morning at day's first light
> You'll leave this city's gate
> And search out relations afar
> Or run to your neighbors near home
> Or go to the mountains in shadows to hide.
> Should you meet one fine day the imperial grace
> And leave common status behind,
> High rank will there be for you both to enjoy.[13]
> You'll eat of the finest and sleep on brocade,
> Have piles of jewelry and servants in droves.
> Such will your blessings be.

    TS'UI-LUAN: I could never hope for blessings like those, but if
our lives are spared, I'll never forget you in death or in life.

    LI:

> (Melody: *Ch'ing ko-erh*)
> Oh, you have but to ponder the dangers involved,
> And the thing I fear most is the questions to come.
> The Madam's intent was that I kill you both,
> But from harm I'll deliver you whole,

Release you to sneak well away.

I just want you safe and secure,

So that when I have spent my last coin

And come running along to your side,

Telling the reason—

My life-saving aid—

You won't say that I've forced myself in

But will grant that I once was your friend.

TS'UI-LUAN: My mother and I will always remember your kindness.

LI: You're going to have to make your escape right away.

TS'UI-LUAN: Thank you, sir!

LI:

(Melody: *Tsuan sha*)

The both of you speed from Pien-liang;

I'll send you out fast through East Gate.[14]

If someone should ask, say it's family you seek.

Don't let those tears show one after one;

Just play the rustic, simple and kind.

One day when you marry your man

And arrive at full glory and pride,

Then will your sorrows be brought to an end.

My wife and myself, we mean what we say,

And you and your ma, now, be kind.

When that time has come, you must not forget the man
     who did good for you both.

(*Exit.* Ts'ui-luan *and her mother start walking but become separated by patrolling guards, who have come upon
them by surprise. Exeunt omnes.*) (*Enter* Mother.)

MOTHER: Just as my daughter and I were walking along, we were surprised and separated by guards patrolling the city, and now I don't see Ts'ui-luan anywhere. I'm going to look for her high and low.

(*Exit.*) (*Enter* Ts'ui-luan.)

TS'UI-LUAN: Just as my mother and I were walking together, we were come upon suddenly and separated by city guards, and now I can't find her. (*sadly*) I'll look for my mother no matter where she may be.

> (*in verse*)
> Like rootless weeds we drift away,
> To be parted en route, east and west.
> I shall search and search my whole life through,
> Though we meet on the road of the dead.
> (*Exit.*)

ACT TWO

> (*Enter* Chang.)

CHANG: Li Shun went off this morning to sell a gold hairpin and hasn't come back yet. I'll just wait here. He ought to be by any moment now.

> (*Enter* Li, *drunk.*)

LI: Sorry, brothers, sorry to leave you! My treat next time! I've just had a few cups too many, and it's getting late. I'd better get back home.

> (*Nan-lü* mode, Melody: *I-chih hua*)
> Before you know it, the sun sinks west.
> Before you know it, evening is near.
> Before you know it, you stagger and lurch.
> Before you know it, you're dizzy with drink.
> That I keep my eyes open and my brows raised high
> Owes partly to fate and partly to will.
> All I desire is enough in all things.
> As they say, "With no nighttime fodder a horse can't get
>   fat,
> With mere honest income a man can't get rich."

> (Melody: *Liang-chou ti-ch'i*)
> Those two were as flustered as dogs with no home,
> As anxious as fish that escape from the net.
> In darkness of night they fled, to the corner of the sea,
>   the horizon's distant edge.

They were meant to have fate on their side,
As we were meant to live in style.
Joy will be ours, father and son,
Happiness for us, man and wife!
Our lives I thought to be spent as the poor,
Eternally bound to rude alley and shack.
But the sky has its day and its night, cloudy and bright
    by turns,
As man has luck good and bad.
I too know achievement and loss, and triumph as well as
    defeat.

I think I'll do a little dance here in the back alley. (*dances*)

I sing to myself and I dance for myself,
And what makes me as pleased as all this?
I have a wife for support, as fine as any flower.
Do we hear of Meng Chiang-nü, that paragon of wives?*
Mine outshines them all!

(*arrives home and approaches* Chang) I'm home, wife!

CHANG: Did you sell the hairpin?

LI: (*aside*) I think I'll have some fun with her. (*turns back to* Chang) I lost it.

CHANG: Oh you! Everything we eat and wear depends on that thing! How could you lose that?

LI: I was just having some fun. I sold it.

CHANG: You gave me a start there! If you did sell it, how much did you weigh out to, and what did you get for it? Tell me all about it.

LI:

(Melody: *Mu-yang-kuan*)
Its weight was over half an ounce,
Seventy per cent off made it nine thousand five.**

---

*A legendary heroine, who brought clothing to her husband while he was working as a slave on the Great Wall and, upon learning of his death, washed away with her tears the part of the wall under which he was buried.
**Lit., "nine strings of cash and five." A thousand cash coins made up a string and "five" probably means five hundred additional coins. The "seventy per-

Starting tomorrow you can dress me up fine
In a cap of black gauze
And a waistband of red.*
For our son thin silk trousers his body to guard
And a coat made of cotton to cover his skin.

CHANG: Father and son are well taken care of; now how are you going to dress *me* up?

LI: Wife,
You'll buy two hairpins of copper made from wax
And a comb of date wood lined with gold.

CHANG: You've had too much to drink, Li Shun. Go to bed. (Li *goes to sleep*.) If only Wang Ch'ing were here right now!

(*Enter* Wang.)

WANG: I told Li Shun to strangle Ts'ui-luan and her mother. It's the third day now with no word from him, and I'm going to ask him what happened. So he's shut the gate, has he? Li Shun! Open up!

CHANG: Oh good, good! That's Wang Ch'ing! (*shouts to* Li Shun) Li Shun, somebody's calling at the gate!

LI: (*awakens*) Who's that beating on the gate? Hold off with those donkey hooves, will you? Think it's your own house or something? I'm coming!

WANG: Drunk *again*! Open up, open up, I say!

LI:
(Melody: *Ho hsin-lang*)
A familiar voice that calls at the gate,
Could it be Li Wan or Chang Ch'ien?**

CHANG: I'll go open the gate.

---

cent" deduction may signify that the buyer, intending to make a seventy percent profit, gave Li thirty percent of the value as a wholesale price.

*The "cap of black gauze" and a "waistband of red" were worn by the rich and prominent.

**The "Wan" (lit., "myriad") of Li Wan is parallel to "Ch'ien" ("thousand"). The meaning here is similar to "Tom, Dick, and Harry."

LI: (*grabs hold of* Chang)

> Where you go, wife, so go I.

My good woman, as the proverb says, "With a virtuous wife in the house, —"*

> The gate's been shut for some days now
>
> As a barrier to gossip and talk.[15]

I'll just open it up here. Who's there? You're going to get a licking, whoever you are!

WANG: Hey you! Who are you going to give a licking to?

LI: (*catches sight of* Wang *and becomes frightened*)

> Whatever business you have, sir, don't ever think I'd
>   shirk;
>
> I'll rub in the dirt whomever you want,
>
> Do wrong to whomever you wish.
>
> Whatever the filthy job you want done, I'm ready and
>   willing to do,

(*kneels and falls over*)

WANG: Just look at him, drunk as usual! What will you ever amount to?

LI:

> To snatch a bone from a tiger's jaws,
>
> A pearl from a dragon's maw.

WANG: Drunk again, and how dare you curse me!

LI: Come in the house and have a cup of tea, what's the harm?

WANG: Want me to go in and have some tea, do you? How could somebody in my position ever step into *your* home?

LI: If you did, sir, they'd say Li Shun's superior was having tea at his home, and that would make me look so good!

WANG: You may be drunk, but you do make some sense. All right, I'll have tea at your place and add a little luster to your prestige. Why not? (*enters and sits*)

LI: I have a wife, sir, who's not much to look at, but I'll have her come and pay her respects to you anyway.

---

*"With a virtuous wife in the house, the husband comes to no harm."

WANG: That wouldn't do! If you did that, it wouldn't look right. You'd better not.

LI: It's all right, sir, really!

WANG: Since you mean well, go ahead then.

LI: (*to* Chang) Wife, my boss Wang Ch'ing is here for tea; go pay your respects.

CHANG: I don't think that would be a good thing to do, Li Shun.

LI: It's all right, wife.

CHANG: (*comes out, approaches* Wang, *and bows*) My greetings, sir.

WANG: Li Shun, what about Ts'ui-luan and her mother, the ones I gave over to you?

LI: That mother and daughter, the ones you gave over to me, you mean? I'm not going to make any excuses; I took two pieces of rope and strangled them both. Then I threw them into the River Pien. They must have drifted a thousand miles away by now.

WANG: Listen, you, somebody saw the whole thing and said once you got money out of them, you let them go!

LI: (*in panic*) Oh no I didn't!

(Melody: *Mu-yang-kuan*)

There wasn't a soul who knew.

Who in the world could have told?

Your single question stops me short like a gourd without a mouth.

WANG: How dare you disobey an official order and let them go?

LI:

How dare I indeed disobey

And let mother and child go free?

WANG: I heard you got a bribe from them.

LI:

May punishment be mine if I did.

If you have any proof, I'll confess.

I'm willing enough to taste the sword's edge,

But the stake* won't have proof of my crime.
I would never dare do anything like that! Go ahead and punish me
if you have any proof.

WANG: Won't confess, eh? Well, your wife must have some
knowledge of it. Bring his wife here!

(*Enter* Chang**; *she kneels.*)

CHANG: I had nothing to do with it!

WANG: Your husband released criminals for money, and you
must have known of it. Tell me the truth and everything stops here,
but if you don't, don't expect me to let you off! (*hits* Chang)

CHANG: Stop it, stop it, that's enough! Don't hit me! I'll talk!
My husband took their jewelry and then set the both of them free.

WANG: All right now! Do you still claim you didn't release
them?

LI:

(Melody: *K'u huang-t'ien*)
You have no endurance, peasant wife,
No reticence either, rustic aunt!
They didn't quite beat you with hemp stalks, did they,
      or press on your head with rope,
And yet you're confessing right soon enough, loudly for
      all to hear!
(Wang *furiously clutches* Li's *hair.*)
He's clutching my hair, my hair!¹⁶
I couldn't help it, sir!
We were so miserably poor;
My wife and my son suffered so,
That I fell in love with their money and goods
And let my prisoners go.
You may whip me and cane me
And kill me a thousand times ten;

*The pole fitted with spikes called the "wooden donkey" to which a criminal
was tied. The executioners would then parade him through the streets.
**Previous stage directions fail to indicate that servants enter with Wang
Ch'ing or that Chang ever left the stage.

> You may beat this old drudge till he's gone from this
>   world,
> For what kindness could *you* ever spare?

WANG: Would you like me to get you out of this?

LI: Of course I would!

WANG: If so, then divorce your wife!

LI: An ugly woman like her, who'd want her even if I did?

WANG: I would!

LI:

> Why must you cause me such anger?
> For how dare I act on my own?

I might be[17] willing enough, but I'm not sure how she feels about
it.

WANG: Well, you talk it over with her.

LI:

> (Melody: *Wu-yeh t'i*)
> I'll step up and question my wife.

(*to* Chang) Wife, Mr. Wang Ch'ing said, "If you'd like me to get you
out of this, divorce your wife." Then I said, "If I did, who'd want
her?" And he said, "I would!" Would you be agreeable to that, I
wonder?

CHANG: Don't you worry about me; just worry about your
own life.

LI:

> Oh wonderful! A twenty-year marriage for naught!
> Our child is unable to speak,
> But is he so stupid besides,
> Not to be able to know stranger from kin?
> You'd blithely leave us alone,
> Has Heaven hacked away every feeling you had?
> While his father suffers his grief,
> Our son breaks out in tears.
> Have pity, good sir, on a colleague of yours,
> Hold off on your plots and your schemes!

WANG: Get on with the divorce!

LI: I'd write out the bill of divorce, but I don't have a brush.

CHANG: I have a brush for painting designs here.

LI: There isn't any paper.

CHANG: There's the paper for cutting shoe patterns.

LI: I don't have any inkstone.

CHANG: You can grind some ink in the chamber pot.

LI: She's certainly got everything well prepared! All right, enough!

> (Melody: *Tou ha-ma*)
> Now I'm writing my signature
> And affixing my thumb print as well.
> Even if I kept you, what should I gain?
> I suspect that you have done wrong
> And your lust and desire are what's real,
> That while your husband's back has been turned,
> With another man you've been untrue.
> To speak of how we began
> Is now the source of great shame.
> I can't help but stumble in fright
> And babble and jabber away.
> She rolls her two eyes both at him and at me
> And hesitates, puzzled and vague.
> When I consider, I am so convinced that some kinds of
> murder are just!
> You humiliate me
> And in clearness of mind
> You up and make your demand

Take it away, you ugly whore!

> For the bill of divorcement, dissolving all ties of love
> and tender regard.
> (Chang *feigns tears.*)
> Don't you rain your pearl-like tears!
> Have you no fear of what people will say?[18]
> In K'ai-feng, Judge Lung-t'u holds sway with the law.
> Some day your blood will show forth to your eyes,

And you'll be chastised 'neath the sword.
Don't worry; I'm going straight to the K'ai-feng Tribunal to press
charges against him.

CHANG: Oh-oh! You must have heard that, eh, Wang Ch'ing?

WANG: (*aside*) If he says he'll do something, he'll do it. If I
don't take action first, he'll be the end of me! (*turns back to* Li)
I don't want your wife, Li Shun, but I do want something else of
yours instead.

LI: What's that?

WANG: Just your head!

LI: If it isn't one thing it's another! —Say, isn't that somebody
coming there? (Wang *looks, and* Li *starts to run.* Wang *pulls him to
a stop.*) I give up, I give up!

    (Melody: *Huang-chung wei*)
    Heartless villain, defiant of all,
    With your scheming woman, more vicious still,
    You leave me no chance
    To voice an appeal.
    You're keeping me down
    By use of raw force.
    Wherever you wish,
    There you may go;
    Whatever may suit you
    You feel free to do.
    Using your power
    The way that you do,[19]
    Enjoy your life now,
    For death waits for you.
    You've taken my wife,
    Destroyed father and son.
    I rub my breast raw
    And split open my scalp*
    As I glance at the boy, who can take no revenge.
    I see a hand grasping an instrument vile;

*By knocking his forehead againt the ground in supplication.

Another grabs hold of my head.
Oh, what injustice I bear!
        My throat in constriction can't call out this wrong!
        (Wang *kills* Li. *Exit* Li.)
    WANG: There! I've done the deed. Bring me a sack to put him in, and we'll throw him in the well. My lady, we're going to be husband and wife forever. Heaven's awarded me this half bowl of rice all on account of my fine intentions!
    CHANG: Enough of this idle chitchat. Let's go into the back parlor and enjoy ourselves!
        (*Exeunt.*)

ACT THREE

        (*Enter* Inn boy.)
    INN BOY:
        (*in verse*)
        A seven-foot cloth* drapes the gate of my inn,
        As patrons in flocks come and go.
        Of ten pots of wine made just one day before,
        Nine were vinegary sour.
I'm the inn boy of Lion Inn here in the capital, where traveling merchants going north and south all stay. This evening I'm waiting at the gate to see who will come by.
        (*Enter* Ts'ui-luan.)
    TS'UI-LUAN: Just as I was walking along, I was separated from my mother by some city guards, and I have no idea where she might be. It's getting late; I'll look for a place to stay in this inn. (*approaches* Inn boy) I'd like a room, sir.
    INN BOY: Room Number One is nice and clean, miss.
    TS'UI-LUAN: Give me a lamp, please.
    INN BOY: I'll light this one for you. (*looks her over*) (*aside*) What a beauty! It's late, everybody's resting, and she's all by her-

---

*A sign that the inn is open for business.

self. Why not get her to be my wife? (*turns back*) Nobody's around, miss. How about if we played man and wife?

TS'UI-LUAN: Hunh! What are you talking about?

INN BOY: You're in a trap right now, and you can't even fly your way out of it! You're going to be my woman, no doubt about that!

TS'UI-LUAN: I'd die first!

INN BOY: You really don't want to, then?

TS'UI-LUAN: That's right, I don't!

INN BOY: (*aside*) She won't do it, or so she says, but I'll just take this hatchet out and give her a scare. It's bound to do the trick, her being a girl and all. I've just got to have her! (*takes out the hatchet*) If you really won't go along, I'm going to kill you with one blow of this! (Ts'ui-luan *falls.*) Why hasn't she said anything all this time? (*looks at her closely*) My god, she's died of fright! *Now* what am I going to do? Somebody who's died unnaturally like this is going to start haunting the place. I'll take one of the two peach charms from the gate and stick it in her hair bun here. Then I'll put her in a sack and throw her down this well. (*starts to carry* Ts'ui-luan *off*) I'll put a stone on top of her so that she won't float to the surface.

(*Enter* Mother.)

MOTHER: I don't understand why I can't find my daughter Ts'ui-luan anywhere. It's late now, and I think I'll go look for a room for the night in Lion Inn. (*approaches* Inn boy) Inn boy, I'd like to stay the night.

INN BOY: The room in back is nice and clean. You have a good sleep now.

MOTHER: I'll sleep in the back then.

(*Exit.*)

INN BOY: Oh, what a job this is! I'll just sit down a spell longer; somebody else will probably come by.

(*Enter* Liu.)

LIU:

(*in verse*)

By snow-piled window* I've buried my head;
Belles-lettres and histories, complete in three years.[20]
A scholar today of impoverished means,
Tomorrow an officer in the empire's pay.

My name is Liu T'ien-i; I come from Lo-yang. I have a head full of learning[21] but have yet to try for an official position. The spring notices** are up now, and the examination hall is open. I've gathered up my harp and my sword, my books and my boxes, and have set off for the capital to try my luck. Now that I've arrived here in the capital, it's late and I think I'll try to find a room for the night there in the Lion Inn. (*approaches* Inn boy) I'd like a room, inn boy.

INN BOY: You can stay in the room in front.

LIU: Light me a lamp.

INN BOY: (*gives Liu a lamp*) Here's the lamp.

LIU: Now fix me some wine and something to eat. I'll pour myself a cup and pay you for it tomorrow along with the room charge.

INN BOY: (*brings in wine*) Here's the wine and food. I'm going to bed now.

(*Exit.*)

LIU: I'll close this door and have a few cups of wine.

(*Enter* Ts'ui-luan *as a ghost.*)

TS'UI-LUAN: I am Ts'ui-luan, Mrs. Wang's daughter. I think I'll go to that room there to light my lamp. Would you open your door, sir?[22]

LIU: Here it is, the dead of night, and somebody's calling at the door! Strange business! Who's there?

---

*An allusion to Sun K'ang of the Tsin dynasty, who was too poor to afford a lamp to study by and used instead the moonlight reflected off the snow by his window. This line is echoed by the third, which reads literally, "Today a cold (i.e. poor) scholar."
**The imperial examinations were given in the spring and announced by placards.

TS'UI-LUAN: The daughter of Mrs. Wang. I've come to light my lamp.

LIU: I'll light it for you. The crack in the door is fairly wide. Take my lamp.

TS'UI-LUAN: (*blows out the lamp*) The wind blew it out, sir.

LIU: I'll relight it for you.

TS'UI-LUAN: (*blows it out again*) It's out again.

LIU: I give her my lamp and it's blown out two or three times! All right then, I'll open up and you can light it yourself. (*opens the door and lets Ts'ui-luan in*) Go ahead and light your lamp.—I no sooner get the door open than she's gone! She was just playing a trick on me. I'll put the door to again. (*turns around and sees Ts'ui-luan*)

TS'UI-LUAN: My greetings, sir.

LIU: What a fine looking girl! What family do you belong to? What might your name be?

TS'UI-LUAN: I'm Mrs. Wang's daughter. I heard you were here and have come especially to pay you a visit.

LIU: How do I deserve your kind regard? If you don't mind, I'd like you to share a few cups of wine with me. How would you feel about that?

TS'UI-LUAN: As you wish, with pleasure. (*sits*)

LIU: (*taking up a wine cup*) Take this cup then.

TS'UI-LUAN: (*drinks*) May I ask your name, sir, and where you are from, and why you are here?

LIU: I am Liu T'ien-i, from Lo-yang, here for the examinations. Since it was getting late, I came to this inn for the night, but I never thought I'd meet you here, although I consider it my good fortune that I have.

TS'UI-LUAN: I wonder if I might impose on you for a verse for the occasion?

LIU: I don't really have a great deal of talent, and I hesitate to display my poor efforts in front of you, but I could make do with something to "Flower of the Back Courtyard."[23] I'll recite it to you; listen and see what you think.

(*in verse*)

"Cloudlike hair in raven-green tresses,
   Silken skirt laced with crimson gauze,[24]
   Coyly you knit your willow-like brow,
   As your face takes on a soft, even glow, like the sunset's
      rosy clouds.
   Petite are the tufts of your hair,
   And your stockings of silk seem to skip on the waves.
   Just where in paradise is your home?
   —To the melody 'Flower of the Back Courtyard,' by
      Liu T'ien-i."

TS'UI-LUAN: Oh, but you have great talent indeed! Let me match yours with one of my own in the same rhyme. (*writes*) There, I've written it down. I'll recite it; now you listen and see what you think of it.

(*in verse*)
"As the year has gone by unawares,
   My dream soul has often returned home.
   On the horizon no wild goose* is seen
   Encroaching on frogs in the well's lowest depths.
   The blossom of green peach**[25]
   Worn aslant at my ear
   Is companion to me in my grief.
   —To the melody 'Flower of the Back Courtyard,' by
      Ts'ui-luan."

LIU: That was wonderful, just wonderful! Have another cup of wine.

(*Enter* Mother.)

MOTHER: I'm too depressed to fall back to sleep, and so I've gotten up to take a little stroll. (*listens*)

TS'UI-LUAN: Sir, I beg you not to forsake me!

LIU: I would never forsake you!

MOTHER: Isn't that my Ts'ui-luan talking there? (*shouts*)

*According to a legend, the wild goose brought a message from a lover.
**A common symbol in Sung and Yuan love songs for a secret assignation between lovers. This blossom is the peach wood charm that the inn boy placed in Ts'ui-luan's hair.

Ts'ui-luan! Ts'ui-luan! (Ts'ui-luan *reacts and runs off.*) I'm going to push this door open. (*approaches* Liu) Where is my daughter?

LIU: Nobody's here; I'm all alone.

MOTHER: (*sees the songs*) So you say, but who wrote those two songs there? One of them has my daughter's name on it. You've hidden her away, but don't think you're going to get away with it! There are laws for people like you, and I'm taking you to court!

LIU: Just look at what my fate is doing to me!

(*Exeunt.*) (*Enter* Chao *and* Attendant.)

CHAO: I am Chao Chung. The girl Ts'ui-luan and her mother, who were given to me by his Majesty, I had Wang Ch'ing take to see my wife, and I haven't received any word for some days now. Servant, call for Wang Ch'ing.

ATTENDANT: Where are you, Wang Ch'ing? The master is calling for you.

(*Enter* Wang.)

WANG: I don't know why his Excellency should want me. I'll just have to go and see him. (*approaches* Chao)

CHAO: Several days ago, Wang Ch'ing, I told you to take that girl and her mother to see Madam Chao, but I haven't had a report since then. Where are they right now?

WANG: I handed them over to Madam Chao.

CHAO: Well, since that's the case, ask my wife to come here.

WANG: Madam, his Excellency would like to see you.

(*Enter* Wife. *She approaches Chao.*)

WIFE: Why have you called for me, your Excellency?

CHAO: Madam, I told Wang Ch'ing to take Ts'ui-luan and her mother to see you. Where are they at this moment?

WIFE: After Wang Ch'ing brought them to see me, I entrusted them to him and he took them away.

CHAO: My wife says that she entrusted them to you, Wang Ch'ing. *Now* where might they be?

WANG: That's right, you told me to take them to see Madam Chao, and when she handed them over to me, I handed them over to Li Shun.

CHAO: "Handed them over to Li Shun," he says. There has to

be more to this than meets the eye. Madam, go back to the rear quarters for now.

WIFE:

> (*in verse*)
> A spark from my jealous heart
> Has done that charmer in.
> Let him be confused;
> Let ignorance be my game.
> (*Exit.*)

CHAO: I would inquire into this myself, but there are some difficulties involved. Only Judge Pao, prefect of the K'ai-feng Tribunal, an honest and upright man, can handle this case. Servant, ask Prefect Pao here.

ATTENDANT: Yes, sir. Prefect, his Excellency would like to see you.

(*Enter* Pao *and* Chang Ch'ien.)

PAO: My surname is Pao, my given name Cheng, and my courtesy name Hsi-wen. I come from Lao-erh Hamlet, Ssu-wang Village, Chin-tou Commandery, Lu-chou. I hold the title of Academician-in-waiting of the Lung-t'u Pavilion and have just been given the post of prefect of K'ai-feng Tribunal. Inspector Chao has sent for me for some reason. I'll have to go and see him.

> (*Shuang-tiao* mode, Melody: *Hsin shui ling*)
> With the imperial mandate I sit in my court.[26]
> Having charge of the law, I uncover villainy and crime.
> My clothes are light fur, I ride a fine steed,
> As retainers in file clear the way up ahead.
> Because I am stubborn, because I am brusque,
> Who dares even speak of privilege or guile?
> Commoners, it goes without saying,
> And even officials of worth and of fame
> At the sight of the shadow of Pao Lung-t'u are struck
> > with instant fear.

Servant, report that Pao Cheng is here.

ATTENDANT: (*reports*) I beg to inform you, my lord, that Judge Pao is at the gate.

CHAO: Ask him in.

ATTENDANT: Please go in.

PAO: (*approaches* Chao) What instructions have you for me, your Excellency?

CHAO: Judge, I have one matter with which to trouble you. Several days ago his Majesty presented me with a girl, Ts'ui-luan, and her mother. I had Wang Ch'ing take them to my wife, but I've received no word of them. When I asked my wife, she said that she had entrusted[27] them to Wang Ch'ing, and Wang Ch'ing said that he had placed them in Li Shun's care. There must be more to this than I can see, and I'd like you to make a thorough investigation. It may well be that[28] my wife is guilty in some way of breaking the law.

PAO:

(Melody: *Ch'en-tsui tung-feng*)
Your wife may have broken the law, so you say;
But how dare I place her in chains or the cangue?
Your Excellency,
Your mansion's as vast as the ocean itself,
Your power like Heaven's in scale.
Pao Lung-t'u would be afraid[29]
Ever to cross swords[30] with your wife.
If the defendant so much as popped her eyes at me,
In the very courtroom she'd frighten this old bumpkin
half to death!
Your Excellency, my position is too low to judge this case.

CHAO: Of course, I understand. I'll give you the Sword of Authority and the Bronze Blade and three days to solve the case. If you do come up with a solution, I'll take over from there.

(*in verse*)
I'll have no delay in this affair;
The task must be done in three days.
Discover the whereabouts of mother and child,
And I'll write a memorial in praise to the Throne.
(*Exit.*)

PAO: A fine sword!

(Melody: *Feng ju sung*)

Chill in its menace, it won't leave its scabbard on just
     any excuse at all,
But an unpleasant task[31] has been thrust in my hands.
Should some knave confront[32] me as I step through the
     gate,
This Sword of Authority, this Blade of Bronze I shall be
     bound to flaunt.

As I leave through the gate,

     I spy the panic of Wang Ch'ing
     And his utter viciousness.

Wang Ch'ing, you're responsible for all this!

    WANG: Look at this judge, will you! What do I have to do with
it?

    PAO: Be quiet!

    (Melody: *Hu shih-pa*)

     I don't want your answers,
     I don't want your lies.

Chang Ch'ien, my horse.

    CHANG CH'IEN: Yes, sir. (*brings the horse*) Please mount, your
Honor.

    PAO: (*mounts*)

     Into the jewelled stirrup I step,
     And as I take reins in hand,
     I turn my head and see him, eyeing me with a shifty
       glance.

Chang Ch'ien, arrest Wang Ch'ing!

    CHANG CH'IEN: Yes, sir. (*seizes* Wang)

    WANG: (*hits* Chang Ch'ien) Who do you think you're arrest-
ing?

    PAO:

     You attendants fear him so!

Yet even a third-rank official can be taken to the K'ai-feng Tribunal;
who does he think he is?

    Attendants, all of you, arrest Wang Ch'ing!

Go back to the courthouse, Chang Ch'ien. (*Enter* Ts'ui-luan's *ghost
as a whirlwind.*) What a strong whirlwind!

> (Melody: *Yen-erh lo*)
> A whirlwind pursuing my horse
> Makes me turn 'round in surprise.

Spirit, listen to what I say!

> At dusk present your appeal;
> We cannot talk in light of day.

Spirit, be at the K'ai-feng Tribunal toward evening. Now go, go!

> (*Exit* Whirlwind.) (*Enter* Mother, *pulling* Liu *after her.*)

MOTHER: I have been wronged! Help me, your Excellency!

PAO:

> (Melody: *Kua yü-kou*)
> Clamor and shouts greet my ears; why the fuss?
> I can but examine your case.

Chang Ch'ien,

> Have her come close to make her response.
> Don't shout at[33] her, cause her no fright.
> Though fear's stark chill might pierce your heart,*
> Be frank with me, hold nothing back.

What is your complaint, madam?

MOTHER: This young student has hidden my daughter Ts'ui-luan away. I appeal to your Excellency to help me!

PAO: Who did you say was Ts'ui-luan's mother?

MOTHER: I am.

PAO: What luck! Two cases wrapped up in one! Chang Ch'ien, take everyone to the K'ai-feng Tribunal. (*Court is called to order.*) Bring them all forward, Chang Ch'ien.

CHANG CH'IEN: Yes, sir.

> (*All kneel.*)

PAO: Wang Ch'ing, why aren't you kneeling?

WANG: I haven't done anything wrong!

PAO: If you haven't done anything wrong, then what are you doing here in my K'ai-feng Tribunal?

*This and the following line are directed at Ts'ui-luan's mother.

WANG: All right, I'll kneel and be done with it. (*kneels*)

PAO: Madam, give your testimony.

(Mother *begins to speak.*)

WANG: (*interrupting*) His Excellency told me to take them to see his wife, his wife entrusted them to me, and I entrusted them to Li Shun.

PAO: Who asked you? Madam, your testimony.

WANG: (*interrupting again*) His Excellency told me to take them to see his wife, his wife entrusted them to me, and I entrusted them to Li Shun.

PAO: Chang Ch'ien, take Wang Ch'ing away and give him a beating.

CHANG CH'IEN: Yes, sir. (*beats* Wang)

PAO:

    (Melody: *Ch'uan po chao*)
    I just may shatter[34] every tooth in your mouth.
    This is hardly a family chat
    Where you can go on like a croaking frog,
    Gabbling and prattling,
    Tittling and tattling.
    Right on that lively mouth of his[35]
    Give him a clout if he talks once more.

Chang Ch'ien, make him bite down on your cudgel.

CHANG CH'IEN: Yes, sir.

(Wang *bites the cudgel.*)

PAO: Now, madam, give your testimony.

WANG: (*dropping the cudgel from his mouth and interrupting*) His Excellency told me to take them to see his wife, his wife entrusted them to me, and I entrusted them to Li Shun.

PAO: He just loves to talk, doesn't he?

MOTHER: I was staying last night at Lion Inn, when I heard this student and my daughter Ts'ui-luan talking. I kicked the door open, but my daughter was nowhere to be seen. It's obvious he's hiding her. Help me, your Honor!

PAO: All right now, you, give your testimony.

WANG: His Excellency told me to take them to see his wife,

his wife entrusted them to me, and I entrusted them to Li Shun.

  PAO: Yes, go on.

  WANG: That's it.

  PAO: In that case, what should I do?

    (Melody: *Yeh hsing ch'uan*)

    On all three counts* am I confused, perplexed to an
      inch of my life.

At the very least this case

    Seems to implicate 'most everyone.

    This is a quarrel over human life,

    And it's just like a fight between Guardians of Heaven**

    Which even the Buddha cannot calm.

Chang Ch'ien, put Wang Ch'ing in prison.

  CHANG CH'IEN: Yes, sir. (*takes* Wang *off*)

  PAO: Now, madam, you say he's hidden your daughter away.
Have you any evidence to prove it?

  MOTHER: I have two songs here.

  PAO: Let me see. (Mother *takes out the songs, and* Pao *reads
aloud.*)

    "Cloudlike hair in raven-green tresses,

    Silken skirt laced with crimson gauze,

    Coyly you knit your willow-like brow,

    As your face takes on a soft, even glow, like the sunset's
      rosy clouds.

    Petite are the tufts of your hair,

    And your stockings of silk seem to skip on the waves.

    Just where in paradise is your home?

    —To the melody 'Flower of the Back Courtyard,' by Liu
      T'ien-i."

    (Melody: *Tien-ch'ien huan*)

    You say you've not seen her daughter, the beauty.

*Perhaps Pao means that he is confused by the testimony of all three: Wang
Ch'ing, Ts'iu-luan's mother, and Liu T'ien-i.

**Minor Buddhist deities noted for their ferocity, which is usually directed
against demons and not against each other.

Then who was it who signed this one song?
Haven't you been making a fool out of me?
Do you think that my eyes have grown dim?
Let me have a look at the other song.
"As the year has gone by unawares,
My dream soul has often returned home.
On the horizon no wild goose is seen
Encroaching on frogs in the well's lowest depths.
The blossom of green peach
Worn aslant at my ear
Is companion to me in my grief.
—To the melody 'Flower of the Back Courtyard,' by
Ts'ui-luan."
(*reads aloud again*)
I'll read it again from the start.
"On the horizon no wild goose is seen
Encroaching on frogs in the well's lowest depths."
I'll chant it in closest detail.
"On the horizon no wild goose is seen
Encroaching on frogs in the well's lowest depths."
Alas, there is no hope for the girl! A pity! A pity!
The child may well lie in the world of the shades.
This case seems to have no beginning or end,
And the culprit I can't capture, can't seize.
This is the way in which I'll have to go about it— Chang Ch'ien,
put the woman in prison.

CHANG CH'IEN: Yes, sir. (*takes* Mother *off*)

PAO: Now, Liu T'ien-i, no cause for alarm; I'm letting you go.
Go back to the inn tonight and stay there. If the girl comes, ask her
where she is from and what her name is. If she has any token of
proof, get it from her and I will let you off.

LIU: I understand. I've just got to get a token of proof this
time.

PAO:
(Melody: *Ku mei-chiu*)
Why is the plaintiff in prison, you ask?

Defendant, do not take alarm.
Here is what you must do for me. Just like last night
    draw close to your bed,
And should you be destined to meet up with her,
Do try to get some response.

(Melody: *T'ai-p'ing ling*)
I see him jerk 'round, astonished[36] to hear
That I seem to be awarding him one night of joy.[37]
All I desire is that both be at peace,
And to do this I have but three days.
If the affair comes to light,
Your salvation will owe to me,
To enable you to attain to first rank.[38]
Young man, she is not human, but a ghost.
    (Liu *is frightened.*)
    (Melody: *Yuan-yang sha*)
When I touch upon spirits, he cowers in fright.
I want you, young man, to dally in love.
You need not sit in jail tonight,
You're excused from attendance each day.
They say that a murderer is not far away,
And I already know most of the truth.
Chang Ch'ien,
    Relay to the mother.
    Her outrage is o'er.
    Tomorrow arrests will be made.
    She can watch the sword slice on the donkey of wood[39]
        at the market's execution ground.
    (*Exit.*)
    CHANG CH'IEN: (*walks with* Liu) Here we are at Lion Inn.
Which room was it?
    LIU: This one.
    CHANG CH'IEN: Then you stay here for the night, and I'll be
around tomorrow morning so that I can report back.
    (*Exit.*)

LIU: Heavens above, it's enough to scare the wits out of me! All along I thought she was a human being, and now she turns out to be a ghost! It's the third watch* already. Listen to that, the dirt on the wall going pitter-patter, the tiles on the roof going scritch-scratch! I may die of fright! (*goes to bed*)

(*Enter* Ts'ui-luan *as a ghost.*)

TS'UI-LUAN: I'm going to visit the young student again tonight. (*approaches* Liu) Sir, oh sir!

(Liu *runs away in alarm.* Ts'ui-luan *pulls him to a stop.*)

LIU: Keep away from me and explain yourself! You're a ghost!

TS'UI-LUAN: I'm no ghost.

LIU: His Honor Pao Lung-t'u wants to know where you're from and what your name is.

TS'UI-LUAN: I'm from that household.

LIU: Where might "that household" be?

TS'UI-LUAN: In the well of that household.

LIU: Give me some kind of proof.

TS'UI-LUAN: By my ear is a lovely green peach blossom. Go ahead and take that.

(Liu *takes the flower. Exit* Ts'ui-luan *suddenly.*)

LIU: Well, if that didn't scare the life out of me! She's a ghost, sure enough! Now that I have the token of proof, I can't wait for the morning to come so that I can report back to Judge Pao.

(*in verse*)

I saw last night's beauty with my very own eyes.

From her hair a peach blossom she took.

My try for position for now best forget,

For I'm trembling and numb from the shock!

(*Exit.*)

---

*The third watch was sounded at 11:00 p.m. and lasted until 1:00 a.m.

ACT FOUR

(*Enter* Pao.)

PAO: I, Pao Cheng, have exhausted my mind over this case.

(*Chung-lü* mode, Melody: *Fen tieh-erh*)

For some time now I've had no mind to sleep or eat.

My eyes wide open, I've had no rest the whole night
through

And at morning session am now set to act.

I call Chang Ch'ien

To the bench.

I call for the duty clerks

To bring up no other cases for now;

This one matters the most.

(Melody: *Ying hsien-k'o*)

Despite myself my mind seems blurred, my thoughts
seem in a fog.

In this one case the false seems true.

How to proceed?

I can scarcely cope.

Have the inquisition prepared,

And call for Liu t'ien-i.

(*Enter* Chang Ch'ien *and* Liu T'ien-i. Liu *kneels.*) Young man, did
you see the girl last night? (Liu *says nothing.*) Why won't he say
anything? Make him talk, Chang Ch'ien.

CHANG CH'IEN: He's still in a daze.

PAO:

(Melody: *K'uai-huo san*)

Last night, in gay laughter, you were like fish and water,

Today you tremble, afraid to be man and wife.

Now has advantage turned to loss.

The fair one's intent was yours to test.

(Melody: *Ch'ao T'ien-tzu*)

You must know all there is to know

From the tryst last night of the mandarin ducks.*
Young man,

>Tell me the truth, from beginning to end.

>What's so hard to explain?[40]

>It's in court that I ask you, and you have no reply.

>Did she say naught to you of her past?

>Knowing she's a ghost, your entrapment you fear.**

>As they say, "Fall in love and be caught."

Where is she from, young man, and what is her name?

>LIU: She is from "that household."

>PAO: "That household"? What "household"? This aggrava-tion is going to be the end of me!

>>(Melody: *Hung hsiu-hsieh*)

>>Is "that household" east or west, in village or in field?

>>What is "that household's" name?

>>If this keeps up, when will solution come?

>>Do not hold back,

>>Do not feign doubt;

>>Or interrogation I must perform.

Chang Ch'ien, put him in prison. When he wakes up, I'll question him further. (Chang Ch'ien *takes* Liu *off.*) Chang Ch'ien, bring Wang Ch'ing here.

>CHANG CH'IEN: Yes, sir. (*brings* Wang *forward to face* Pao)

>PAO: You, to whom did you entrust Ts'ui-luan?

>WANG: His Excellency told me to take them to see his wife, his wife entrusted them to me, and I entrusted them to Li Shun.

>PAO: Since you entrusted them to Li Shun— Chang Ch'ien, bring Li Shun here.

>CHANG CH'IEN: Li Shun has run away.[41]

>PAO: Run away!? Now what to do? Take Wang Ch'ing off to one side for now, Chang Ch'ien. (Chang Ch'ien *takes* Wang *off.*) Chang Ch'ien, even though Li Shun has run away, someone must

---

*Symbols of conjugal fidelity.
**The bewitchment of a young man by a seductive female ghost is a common theme in Chinese legend.

still be there at his home. Go there and look around, in ditches or ponds; if there is a well, go down in and drag it. Now why am I having you do this? Li Shun is supposed to have run away, and if he's not in the well, where else are we to look?

CHANG CH'IEN: I'll take care of it, sir. I've left the courthouse, turned the corner, rounded the bend, and here I am at Li Shun's house. No one's here, so I'll just go on in and have a look here in the back of the courtyard. Why is it so quiet? It's scary! Let me just open up this back door. (*stumbles and falls*) Ghost! Ghost! (*picks himself up*) Oh, just the clothesline. That gave me a start! Let me have another look. Here's a well. Good old Judge Pao, he must be a magician. It's a well, sure enough! I'll just take a look here. Why does it smell so bad? I'll have to go down and see, I guess. Now, how can I get down? Well, there's this clothesline. I'll untie it, attach one end to the railing of the well, and drop the other end down in; then I'll hang on to the rope, go down into the well, and have a look. (*enters the well*) Here's a sack. I wonder what's in it. I'll tie the rope around it and once I get back up to the mouth of the well, I'll pull the rope up after me. (*climbs out of the well and pulls the rope*) I've gotten the sack up, but I still don't have any idea what's inside. I'm going to have to take it to his Honor. (*walks away carrying the sack on his back*) (*Enter* Fu-t'ung, *who grabs hold of* Chang Ch'ien.) Who's that grabbing me there? (*turns his head to look*) Oh, just some little bastard or other. (*hits* Fu-t'ung) (*Exit* Fu-t'ung. Chang Ch'ien *walks a while.*) Here we are at the courthouse. (*throws the sack down*) Your Honor, you're a magician, all right! There really was a well. I went down in and pulled out this sack, but what's inside is beyond me. Take a look, your Honor.

PAO: That's fine, just fine; a capable fellow indeed! Open the sack and let me see. (Chang Ch'ien *unties the sack.*) Aha, so it's a corpse. Call the old woman here, Chang Ch'ien, and have her make an identification.

(Chang Ch'ien *calls for* Mother, *who enters and examines the corpse.*)

MOTHER: My lord, this isn't my daughter's body. It has a beard!

PAO: Chang Ch'ien, how did you happen to drag up a bearded corpse?

CHANG CH'IEN: It was in the well, your Honor. How was I supposed to know?

PAO:

    (Melody: *T'i yin-teng*)

    With that I am troubled for a good long while.

    At the sight I'm dumbfounded[42] for a spell.

    If this isn't the body of your daughter, my good woman,
        we'll just resume the search.

    But whose corpse can this be?

    Don't deceive me, madam,

    If you don't know this body, then why not is what I'd
        like to know.

MOTHER: Your Excellency, this is not my daughter's body.

PAO: Chang Ch'ien, whose well did you pull this corpse from?

CHANG CH'IEN: From Li Shun's well.

PAO:

    (Melody: *Man-ching-ts'ai*)

    Then search out the facts at the home of Li Shun.

I have another question for you, Chang Ch'ien.

    When you went to the floor of the well,

    Was there anyone who saw you then?

CHANG CH'IEN: I didn't see anybody. I went to the back courtyard of Li Shun's house and saw a well. I went down in and hauled up this corpse, which I carried away on my back. Oh, now I remember! I saw a little boy.

PAO: Now we have it, Chang Ch'ien!

    Just get the truth from the little boy.

    We'll know almost all the details.

Go and find that boy Chang Ch'ien.

CHANG CH'IEN: Yes, sir. If he's gone by now, I don't know *what* I'll do. I've left the courthouse and walked for a while, and now I'll go into Li Shun's back courtyard again and take a look. Here's the well. (*sees* Fu-t'ung) There he is! Still here, are you? I'll take you on my back to see his Honor. (*carries*

Fu-t'ung) Here we are. Here's the little boy, your Honor.

PAO: Don't frighten him, Chang Ch'ien. See, now that he's here in the K'ai-feng Tribunal, he's so frightened his eyes are rolling. Come up here, my son, and let me ask you a question. Whose boy are you? (Fu-t'ung *gestures.*) He can't speak! Chang Ch'ien, now how did you manage to find someone who can't speak?

CHANG CH'IEN: He's the boy who's living at Li Shun's; how was I to know he'd be dumb?

PAO: You may not be able to talk, my son, but you must understand everything. Do you recognize that body? (Fu-t'ung *approaches the corpse and weeps.*) What a shame!

> (Melody: *Kan ho-yeh*)
> The sight of it brings him heartbroken pain.
> A remarkable business, this!

Let me ask you this, son: how was this person related to you? (Fu-t'ung *gestures.*) What am I going to do?

> I can't comprehend what he means.
> At first I thought his eyes showed doubt,
> But now his hands are giving him aid.
> How true that "The dumb cannot tell of their dreams."
> His agony tears at my heart!

I'm going to ask you some questions, son. If the answer is yes, nod your head; if not, wave your hand. Pay attention now. (Fu-t'ung *listens.*) Could this be your younger paternal uncle? (Fu-t'ung *waves his hand.*) Is it your older paternal uncle? (Fu-t'ung *waves his hand.*) Is it your father? (Fu-t'ung *nods his head and bows.*) So it's your father! My son, who killed your father? (Fu-t'ung *gestures.*) It was a big man, who grabbed his clothing, pulled out a knife, and murdered him, dropping him into the well. Poor child! I have another question, son.

> (Melody: *Shang hsiao-lou*)
> Where is your mother now?
> (Fu-t'ung *points.*)
> Again he seems unsure.
> In a murder such as this of an innocent man,

Am I supposed to leave things as they are?
He might easily go on for the rest of his life with no
  solution[43] at hand.
  (Fu-t'ung *pulls on* Chang Ch'ien, *who panics.*)
Chang Ch'ien must have killed your father then! (Fu-t'ung *waves
his hand.*) Oh, I see! My son,
  You would like
  To go search
  With Chang Ch'ien.[44]

  CHANG CH'IEN: I'll go out and look for your mother with
you. (Fu-t'ung *nods.*) You scared me to death there!
  PAO:
    In your service to your parents you will spare no pains.
Go with him, Chang Ch'ien.
  CHANG CH'IEN: Yes, sir. Let's go look, my boy. Now that
we're out the gate, where are we going to look for her?
  (*Enter* Chang, *drunk.*)
  CHANG: I've had several cups of wine and I'm a little woozy.
  (Fu-t'ung *grabs* Chang.)
  CHANG CH'IEN: This is the woman! (*hits* Chang)
  CHANG: Why did you hit me?
  CHANG CH'IEN: There's a summons out for you from the K'ai-
feng Tribunal.
  CHANG: I haven't done anything wrong, so I'll just go and get
it over with. (*approaches* Pao *with* Chang Ch'ien) I haven't done
anything wrong, your Excellency. What do you want me for?
  PAO: She must be drunk. Woman, do you recognize that
corpse?
  (Chang *recognizes the corpse and pretends to weep.*)
  CHANG: Why, if it isn't my husband, Li Shun! How does he
happen to be dead?
  PAO: You must know how your own husband died.
  CHANG: I don't know how he died!
  PAO:
    (Melody: *Man t'ing fang*)

Don't you evade[45] this way and that!
What do you know of the duties of the hearth?*
What "virtuous wife" in *your* home?
"A piece of tile thrown up high must always hit the
      earth."**
Woman, let me ask you this: in your home
      Did you ever get angry and fight?[46]

    CHANG: Never!

    PAO:
      Didn't you quarrel with tempers aflame?

    CHANG: The two of us were as compatible[47] as you'd ever
want to see!

    PAO:
      Don't try fencing with me!
      It's in court that I'm asking you this,
Just one thing:
      Who might the murderer be?
My son, who killed your father? (Fu-t'ung *gestures as before.*) Can
you recognize the one who did it? (Fu-t'ung *nods.*) Chang Ch'ien,
take these people off to one side and bring the young student here.
(Chang Ch'ien *brings on* Liu T'ien-i *to face* Pao.) You, Liu T'ien-i,
I told you to question the girl in detail last night and get some token
of proof from her, but you haven't brought one back. You're going
to take the responsibility for this whole case!

    LIU: I did get a token of proof from her, your Honor.

    PAO: What is it?

    LIU: A lovely green peach blossom.

    PAO: Let me see it. (Liu *removes it from his tunic.* Pao *takes
it and looks it over.*) So, a peach charm, with "A Rich and Long
Life" written on it. We have the murderer now!

      (Melody: *T'ang hsiu-ts'ai*)
      I thought the murderer would never be found,

---

*Lit., the "Three Obediences," i.e., to father, husband, and son; and the "Four
Virtues," i.e., wifely virtue, speech, demeanor, and household labor.
**I.e., one must bear the consequences of his actions, or, "the truth will out."

But Ts'ui-luan turns out to be here.
'Gainst demons the peach charm was fixed to his door,
To increase his good luck
He painted Chung K'uei.
But how shall his door gods reward him now?

(Melody: *Ai-ku-to*)
"As you do, so you receive,"
And he shall stand to for his crime.
Chang Ch'ien,
    The murderer quickly arrest!
CHANG CH'IEN: Who do you want me to arrest?
PAO:
    Look at each door for "A Happy New Year";
    I have "A Rich and Long Life" in my hand.*
    The language will speak of the fate of mankind,
    The peach charm heralds the tidings of spring.
    Who can deceive the God of Mount T'ai, the Lord of
        Swift Recompense,
    And Judge Pao, the magistrate of the court of K'ai-feng-
        fu?
Chang Ch'ien, take this peach charm and look for the one match-
ing it.
CHANG CH'IEN: Yes, sir. I've gone through the gate, turned
the corner, rounded the bend, and here I am at the restaurant door.
The peach charms are both here. Now I've come to the door of
Lion Inn. Let me have a look. Why does it have "A Happy New
Year" but not "A Rich and Long Life"? I'll compare it with this.
(*compares them*) They're a pair, all right! I'll take them both to
his Honor. (*approaches* Pao) Your Honor, I got the peach charm!
PAO: Where was it?
CHANG CH'IEN: On the door of the Lion Inn.
PAO: Go there and take a look around. If there's a well, go
down in and drag it. I guarantee that you'll get results.

*The two quotations form a pair with one line on each side of the doorway.

CHANG CH'IEN: I've left the courthouse, and here I am at the
inn. In the back is a well, sure enough. I'll go down and drag it.
(*drags up a corpse*) Another corpse! I'll take it to his Honor.
(*approaches* Pao) Another corpse, your Honor!

PAO: Have the old woman come here and identify it. (*Enter*
Mother.) Madam, identify that corpse.

> (Melody: *T'ang hsiu-ts'ai*)
> I feel so entangled in this accursed case!
> If you deny this corpse as well—

MOTHER: This is my daughter's body, your Honor.

PAO: Well then—Chang Ch'ien, bring the inn boy into court,
and give him a stroke of your cudgel with every step.

CHANG CH'IEN: Yes, sir. (*arrests* Inn boy *and beats him onto
the stage to face* Pao)

PAO: Tell me how you murdered the girl. If you're honest
with me, everything will be fine, but if you're not—Chang Ch'ien,
get the cudgel ready.

INN BOY: I killed her!

PAO: Now that we have *that* murderer,

> Will Wang Ch'ing ever confess?

Chang Ch'ien,

> Go summon Wang Ch'ing
> To the courtroom steps
> To listen to my next report.[48]

Chang Ch'ien, bring Wang Ch'ing here.

> (*Enter* Wang.)

WANG: What's this summons all about?

PAO: Good news, Wang Ch'ing! We have the murderer, and
you're not involved. Go on home now.

WANG: Of course it wasn't me. I'll go home then. (*walks
away*)

> (*Enter* Fu-t'ung, *who pulls* Wang *to a stop.*)

PAO: He must be the one who killed your father!

FU-T'UNG: (*with gestures*) That's right. He and my mother
have been "like that." They've been having an affair.

PAO: He isn't dumb after all! Chang Ch'ien, arrest Wang Ch'ing!

(Melody: *Kun hsiu-ch'iu*)

I thought that, being hamstrung,

I'd be setting you free.

But you're now in adultery caught.

"The net of Heaven is opened wide," or so the saying
    goes.

You thought that you would get off

And rejoiced inwardly.

To an honest official you blathered away

That you had no more worries, no guilt.

But "before the fall winds have set out on their course,
    the cicadas sense well in advance,

Yet the sudden reversals[49] of dark, hidden fate may
    never be known until death."

A beating and slicing await you now.

Chang Ch'ien, take charge of these people and follow me to his
Honor the Inspector's.

(*Exeunt.*) (*Enter* Chao *and* Attendant.)

CHAO: "Don't let things concern you, for with concern confusion comes as well." I told Prefect Pao to inquire into that case.
It's been three days now; why hasn't he made a report? (*Enter* Pao
et omnes. Pao *approaches* Chao.) Prefect Pao, how is that certain
matter progressing?

PAO: I have solved it. It turned out that inquiry into one case
solved two.

CHAO: Tell me all about it.

PAO:

(Melody: *Pan tu-shu*)

For your information, my lord,

Wang Ch'ing has confessed to it all.

He had an affair with the wife of Li Shun.

He concocted a plot[50] 'gainst an innocent man,

Had her husband sent off to the land of the dead

After parting them by crude threat of force.

CHAO: What of the other affair?

PAO:

> (Melody: *Hsiao ho-shang*)[51]
> The person who ran the inn
> Tried to force her to act as his wife,
> Ah, such was his wickedness!
> This case have I covered in full;
> No need now to shift any blame.
> Now must I ask Madam Chao to come forth to confess
>   and face up to her crime.*

CHAO: So this is how the case has turned out. I understand everything now. Listen, everyone, to my verdict.

> (*in verse*)
> For his brilliant detection, Judge Pao
> Shall rise by petition three ranks.
> To the poor Madam Wang goes a handsome reward, silver
>   in one thousand taels.
> Liu T'ien-i, now without guilt, is free to try for his post.
> Ts'ui-luan's remains shall be placed in a grave,
> And her soul shall be saved by the Yellow Charm rites.
> In the care of a rich man of K'ai-feng-fu shall Fu-t'ung
>   find a good home.
> The inn boy at execution ground shall be punished
>   according to law.
> Wang Ch'ing had relations with Chang, Li Shun's wife,
> And with guise of false mission he murdered Li Shun.
> May both be beheaded ere autumn arrives.**
> Now do we see how impartial's the law.
> Let a notice be written for all the four gates,
> Telling all that these orders be done.

---

*She is never made to do this, nor does Chao make any mention of her in his verdict. Chao may or may not have some kind of punishment in mind for his wife, but at least the matter is out of Pao's hands.

**Traditionally, executions were carried out in autumn, when Nature's frost "kills" most vegetation.

PAO: (*gives thanks*)
    (Melody: *Wei-sheng*)
    They intended in open to work out their schemes,
    Not expecting that, hidden from them, Heaven and
          Earth were aware.
    Now by the verdict the killers in lust
    Shall repay the two ghosts who bear wrongs.
    (*Exeunt.*)

APPENDICES

NOTES

BIBLIOGRAPHY

GLOSSARY

ABBREVIATIONS

CKKT	*Chung-kuo ku-tien hsi-ch'ü lun-chu chi-ch'eng*
CYSC	*Ch'üan Yuan san-ch'ü*
CYTC	*Ch'üan Yuan tsa-chü*
Jimbun	Kyoto daigaku jimbunkagaku kenkyūjo, *Yuan-ch'ü hsuan shih*
KMC	*Ku ming-chia tsa-chü*
KPHCTK	*Ku-pen hsi-ch'ü ts'ung-k'an*
MWK	*Mo-wang-kuan ch'ao-chiao-pen ku-chin tsa-chü*
SS	T'o-t'o et al., *Sung shih*
YCH	*Yuan-ch'ü hsuan*

Appendix A

COURTROOM PLAYS (*TSA-CHÜ*)

Short Title	*Author*[a]
1. *Chiu hsiao-tzu* (Saving a filial son)[b]	Wang Chung-wen
2. *Hu-tieh meng* (The butterfly dream)	Kuan Han-ch'ing
3. *Tou O yuan* (The injustice of Tou O)	Kuan Han-ch'ing
4. *Wang-chiang-t'ing* (Riverview Pavilion)[c]	Kuan Han-ch'ing
5. *Fei i meng* (The dream of the "conundrum")	Kuan Han-ch'ing
6. *Chien-fu pei* (The inscription of Chien-fu Temple)	Ma Chih-yuan
7. *Ho han-shan* (The matched-up shirt)	Chang Kuo-pin
8. *Hou-t'ing hua* (The flower of the back courtyard)	Cheng T'ing-yü
9. *Chin feng-ch'ai* (The golden hairpins)	Cheng T'ing-yü
10. *Hui-lan chi* (The chalk circle)	Li Ch'ien-fu
11. *Mo-ho-lo* (The Mahoraga doll)	Meng Han-ch'ing
12. *Yuan-chia chai-chu* (The vengeful creditor)[d]	Anonymous
13. *K'an t'ou-chin* (Investigating a head cloth)	Anonymous[e]
14. *Sheng-chin ko* (The tower of fine gold)	Anonymous[f]
15. *Ch'en-chou t'iao mi* (Selling rice at Ch'en-chou)	Anonymous
16. *Sha kou ch'üan fu* (Killing a dog to admonish a husband)	Anonymous
17. *Chu-sha tan* (The load of cinnabar)[g]	Anonymous
18. *Ho-t'ung wen-tzu* (The contract)	Anonymous
19. *Liu hsieh chi* (The sign of the slipper)	Anonymous
20. *P'en-erh kuei* (The ghost of the pot)	Anonymous
21. *T'i sha ch'i* (The uxoricide)[h]	Anonymous
22. *Shen-nu-erh*	Anonymous
23. *Feng Yü-lan*	Anonymous
24. *Ts'un-le-t'ang* (Hall of Country Pleasures)	Anonymous
25. *Yen-an-fu*[i]	Anonymous

26. *K'an chin-huan* (Investigating a golden
    bracelet)   Anonymous
27. *Jen chin-shu* (Acknowledging the golden
    comb)   Anonymous

a Unless otherwise noted, attributions and order of listing (roughly chronolog-
  ical) follow those in Fu Hsi-hua, *Yuan-tai tsa-chü ch'üan-mu* (Complete
  bibliography of Yuan *tsa-chü;* Peking, 1957). Information on editions can
  also be found in this work. All of the editions of these plays are in either
  YCH or *KPHCTK,* Fourth Series (IV), or, with the exception of Play 27,
  CYTC I-III.
b Also called *Pu jen shih* (Failing to recognize a corpse).
c Also called *Ch'ieh-k'uai tan* (The lady who carved a fish).
d Full title: *Ts'ui Fu-chün tuan yuan-chia chai-chu* (Lord Ts'ui judges the case
  of the vengeful creditor).
e The author may be Lu Teng-shan; see Yen Tun-i, *Yuan-chü chen-i* (On problems in Yuan drama; Peking, 1960), I, 322–327.
f There is little reason to suppose the author to be Wu Han-ch'en; see Yen
  Tun-i, I, 281–290.
g Also known as *Fu-ou chi* (A transient existence).
h This is the only play in the table whose extant edition was not printed or
  transcribed in the late Ming. This crudely printed edition, universally
  assumed to be of Yuan date, was once printed separately but is now part of
  a collection of thirty plays commonly named *Ku-chin tsa-chü san-shih-chung*
  (Thirty *tsa-chü* old and new). A modern printing of the thirty texts, additional bibliographical information, and one other text of roughly the same
  background are found in *Chiao-ting Yuan-k'an tsa-chü san-shih-chung* (Thirty
  tsa-chü of Yuan printing, editorially annotated), collated by Cheng Ch'ien
  (Taipei, 1962). The editions in the collection bear no dates, but the print is
  similar in all, four of which mention Ta-tu, the Yuan name for Peking.
i Also known as *Shih t'an-tzu* (The ten scouts).

Appendix B

COURTROOM PLAYS IN YUAN AND
EARLY-MING ACCOUNTS

A. Plays whose titles appear in one or more editions of *Lu kuei pu*
(Roster of ghosts), by Chung Ssu-ch'eng (earliest preface 1330;
subsequently revised by the author).

    Plays 1–11.[a]

B. Plays by anonymous authors, the titles of which appear in Chu
Ch'üan's *T'ai-ho cheng-yin p'u* (The Supreme Harmony authorita-
tive guide to song lyrics; printed 1398).

    Plays 13, 16, 17, 19–22.

C. Plays by anonymous authors, the titles of which appear in the
anonymous *Lu kuei pu hsu-pien* (Supplement to *Lu kuei pu*)
(completed after 1403).[b]

    Plays in B. above and Plays 14, 18, 24.

---

[a] Titles of plays by anonymous authors do not appear in *Lu kuei pu*. Titles of
Plays 2 and 3 are found only in the T'ien-i-ko manuscript edition (also called
the Chia edition). This edition bears a preface dated 1422 by Chia Chung-
ming and is believed to contain his revisions and additions of play titles. See
"*Lu kuei pu* t'i-yao" (Summary of the *Lu kuei pu*) in *Chung-kuo ku-tien hsi-
ch'ü lun-chu chi-ch'eng* (Collection of works on classical Chinese drama)
(Peking, 1959), II, 96–98.

[b] Under Shen Shih-lien is recorded "within the Yung-le" (the Yung-le reign
began in 1403); see *CKKT,* II, 290.

Appendix C

LATE-MING ANTHOLOGIES IN WHICH
COURTROOM PLAYS APPEAR

1. *Ku ming-chia tsa-chü* (*Tsa-chü* by famous authors of old), comp. Ch'en Yü-chiao, ca. 1588.
    Plays 2, 3, 5, 6, 8, 11, 13.

2. *Yuan-jen tsa-chü hsuan* (Anthology of Yuan *tsa-chü*), ed. "Ku-ch'ü-chai" (pseud.), Wan-li period (1573–1619).
    Play 5.

3. *Ku-chin tsa-chü hsuan* (Anthology of *tsa-chü* old and new), comp. "Hsi-chi Tzu" (pseud.), 1598.
    Plays 4, 14, 18, 19.

4. *Yuan–Ming tsa-chü,* ed. "Chi-chih-chai" (pseud.), Wan-li period.
    Play 6.

5. Older printed editions collated by Chao Ch'i-mei in the late Wan-li period and included in his *Mo-wang-kuan ch'ao-chiao-pen ku-chin tsa-chü (MWK)* (*Tsa-chü* old and new as transcribed and collated by "Mo-wang-kuan" [Chao Ch'i-mei]).
    Plays 4, 13, 14, 19.

6. Copies transcribed and collated by Chao Ch'i-mei in the late Wan-li period and included in *MWK* (asterisk indicates copies made in 1615).
    Plays 5, 7*, 9, 12, 16, 17*, 20, 24*, 25*, 26, 27.

7. *Yuan-ch'ü hsuan* (Anthology of Yuan drama), ed. Tsang Mao-hsun, 1616.
    Plays 1–4, 6–8, 10–20, 22, 23.

8. *Hsin-chüan Ku-chin ming-chü, Lei chiang chi* (Newly printed famous plays old and new, *Lei chiang* collection), ed. Meng Ch'eng-shun and Liu Ch'i-yin, 1633.

Play 6.

NOTES

1. Courtroom Plays of the Yuan and Ming Periods

1. Although the precise origins and process of development of this new form are obscure, *tsa-chü* drama of the Sung and its close relation, *yuan-pen* drama of the Kin, may have had a formative influence. Many of their titles survive today in near-contemporary accounts, but their texts (if they ever existed at all) are lost. Hu Chi in *Sung Chin tsa-chü k'ao* (An investigation of Sung and Kin *tsa-chü;* Peking, 1957) gives an exhaustive account of these two genres, but their formal effects on later drama remain unknown. One or several varieties of local northern drama of the Sung and Kin, perhaps slighted by contemporary records and so unknown today, may have been an intermediary stage, but this is mere assumption. One probable, if somewhat far-removed, ancestor is the *chu-kung-tiao* (medley) of the Kin, a long narrative of northern songs and speech to be performed by a single chanteur; a few of their texts are extant either entirely or in part. See Yoshikawa Kōjirō, *Yuan tsa-chü yen-chiu* (original title *Gen zatsugeki no kenkyū*, A study of Yuan *tsa-chü*), tr. from the Japanese into Chinese by Cheng Ch'ing-mao (Taipei, 1960), pp. 17–18.

2. Three plays of the *hsi-wen* genre, with songs of southern origin and rhymes based on southern speech, survive in the *Yung-le ta-tien* (Grand compendium of the Yung-le reign), which was completed in 1408. Their dates of composition have yet to be determined.

   Thirty texts of northern drama are all that can be assigned to the Yuan period with any confidence, and these do not supply the names of authors; see Appendix A, note h, for further details. All of the other texts of so-called "Yuan" drama were printed or transcribed in the late sixteenth or early seventeenth centuries, i.e., the late Ming. The late-Ming anthologies which include courtroom plays are listed in Appendix C. The earlier editions from which the late Ming editors worked may have carried the authors' names; on the other hand, the names may have been lacking. The late-Ming editors may have been forced to turn instead to the late-Yuan list of dramatists' names and corresponding play titles, the *Lu kuei pu* (Roster of ghosts), and attach an author's name to a previously anonymous text. The several demonstrably mistaken attributions in the anthologies are examples. Implicit in the anthologists' approach, in any event, was the assumption that any text bearing, or assigned to, a Yuan author's name was, *ipso facto,* of Yuan date. See also n. 4, this chapter.

3. "Northern drama" reflects the Chinese term *"pei-ch'ü,"* (northern songs), which also includes non-dramatic songs of the *san-chü* type as well as dramatic lyrics and, by extension, whole dramatic texts of the northern *tsa-chü* type. "Northern drama" is convenient in one respect: it avoids the arbitrary and misleading division between Yuan and Ming, which as precise labels apply only to political history. "Northern," however, refers only to the probable origin of the genre and not to the place of composition of any particular play. Toward the end of the Yuan, "northern" plays were being written and performed in southern China, especially in Hangchow. See Yoshikawa, pp. 18–19, 132–139.

4. For this reason, I am by no means convinced that, of the sixteen court-room plays by anonymous authors, fifteen (Plays 12–20, 22–27 of Appendix A) were necessarily written during the Yuan dynasty, al-though many of them have been provisionally assigned to this period by scholars and anthologists since the late Ming. As Appendix B shows, the earliest known mention of seven of the sixteen titles was in 1398. Three more titles did not appear before the decade 1420–1430, and five more were listed much later in the Ming. Indeed, Play 27 is absent from any pre-twentieth century bibliography known to me. The form of the plays themselves is not a convincing factor, since the standard format of four northern song sequences for each play, typical of Yuan *tsa-chü,* con-tinued to be used by some dramatists well into the Ming. When we con-sider that twenty-six of the twenty-seven plays in Appendix A survive only in anthologies printed or transcribed in the late Ming, the dating of the anonymous plays will be uncertain at best. The exception is Play 21, whose only extant edition survives in a Yuan printing; see Appendix A, note h. Skepticism extends even to the plays assigned to known Yuan authors, since their texts may have been changed significantly by actors, producers, or editors before appearing in final form in the late Ming. The gap in time, over two hundred years at least, between the appearance of the texts and the supposed period of composition is simply too large for comfort.

5. The figure 226 is the total number of plays in *Ch'üan-Yuan tsa-chü* (Com-plete *tsa-chü* of the Yuan) I–IV, ed. Yang Chia-lo (Taipei, 1962–1963). *Hsi-hsiang chi* (The western chamber) I count as five plays rather than one. Excluded from the anthology are plays whose authors appeared to Yang to have lived most of their lives in the Ming rather than the Yuan. But no absolute dividing line between the Yuan and the early Ming exists as to dramaturgy.

6. See Cheng Chen-to, "Yuan-tai 'kung-an chü' ch'an-sheng ti yuan-yin chi ch'i t'e-chih" (The reason for the rise of Yuan "crimecase plays" and their characteristics), in Cheng Chen-to, *Chung-kuo wen-hsueh yen-chiu* (Studies in Chinese literature; Peking, 1957; Hong Kong, 1961 ed.), II, 511–534; the article appears in the June, 1934 issue of *Wen-hsueh* (Literature; Shanghai), II, under the name of Ho Ch'ien.

7. This definition is based on a statement in René Wellek and Austin Warren, *Theory of Literature,* 3rd ed. (New York, 1962), p. 231: "Genre should be conceived, we think, as a grouping of literary works based, theoretically, upon both outer form (specifically metre or structure) and also upon inner form (attitude, tone, purpose—more crudely, subject and audience)."

8. I exclude from the category *Lu Chai-lang,* attributed to Kuan Han-ch'ing, and *Yuan-yang pei* (The mandarin duck coverlet), anon. The former is listed as a "crimecase" play by Cheng Chen-to (p. 513), the latter by Ma Yau-woon in his doctoral dissertation "The Pao-kung Tradition in Chinese Popular Literature" (Yale University, 1971), p. 296. In the former play, Judge Pao relates at one point that investigation and punishment have already taken place offstage, and the theme shifts from the crime at this point. The latter play focuses less on a crime than on a romantic entanglement, and the courtroom scene at the very end of Act 4 serves merely to bring the complicated plot to a tidy conclusion. Cheng Chen-to places Play 19 of Appendix A and *K'u-han-t'ing* by Yang Hsien-chih somewhat outside his "crimecase" category but gives no explanation for this arrangement. Patrick Hanan in "The Development of Fiction and Drama," in *The Legacy of China,* ed. Raymond Dawson (London, Oxford, New York, 1971, from the Clarendon Press, 1964 ed.), p. 141, observes Play 3 to be "superficially a crimecase play," which has at its center "a testing or an ordeal" concerning "family obligation." The crux of the problem is where one chooses to locate the center of the play. I find it in the injustice done to the heroine, which results from her self-sacrifice, and in her climactic vindication, both taking place in a context of trial at law.

9. Mystery does appear in short colloquial fiction of the sixteenth century, although not to any great extent. See Patrick Hanan, "The Early Chinese Short Story: A Critical Theory in Outline," *Harvard Journal of Asiatic Studies* 27:193–194 (1967).

10. Cheng K'o's *Che-yü kuei-chien* (Guide to the solution of crime cases)

and Kuei Wan-jung's *T'ang-yin pi-shih* (tr. Robert van Gulik as *Parallel Cases from under the Peartree*).

11. In twenty-two plays, the crime occurs before Act 3. "Act" here is used for convenience only. It is a translation of the term *"che,"* which from 1498 on appears in northern play editions to indicate divisions by song sequence and accompanying dialogue. All of the courtroom play editions but that of Play 21 (i.e., all of the late-Ming editions) are divided into four *che,* plus an optional *hsieh-tzu* (wedge) of one song and, occasionally, a refrain; but the places of division may vary with different editions. As will be seen in the translations, *"che"* and its translation as "act" do not imply the temporal and spatial unities. For a fuller discussion of these terms, see Sun K'ai-ti, "Yüan-ch'ü hsin k'ao" (New research on Yuan drama) in Sun K'ai-ti, *Ts'ang-chou chi* (Peking, 1965), II, 317–328; and Iwaki Hideo, "Gen zatsugeki no kōsei ni kansuru kiso gainen no saikentō" (A reinvestigation into the basic concepts concerning the structure of Yuan *tsa-chü*) in Iwaki Hideo, *Chūgoku gikyoku engeki kenkyū* (Studies on Chinese drama and theater; Tokyo, 1972), pp. 486–515. Iwaki argues on p. 500 that the post-1498 division of the plays into four or five *che* according to song sequence had nothing to do with performance but was conceived for the benefit of readers of the plays as literature.

12. "Character development" in the Western sense is extremely rare in these plays, at least as far as villains are concerned, but the murderer in *P'en-erh kuei* (The ghost of the pot), the second play translated here, does grow in evil under the goading of his wife.

13   Cheng Chen-to was perhaps the first to make the assertion. Others are T'an Cheng-pi, Yen Tun-i, Chu Tung-jun, and Hsu Shuo-fang; see the bibliography for their various works. In every case the theory is presented more as fact than as suggestion.

14. Plays 2, 4, 14, 15, 23, and 25. This number could be expanded by the addition of Plays 1, 10, 11, 13, 22, and 26, in which a judge is incompetent to deal with the testimony and hands the trial over to an evil clerk. Cheng Chen-to (p. 528) jumps to the conclusion that these judges represent Mongols or other foreigners, who were assigned nominal jurisdiction over the courts but were ignorant of Chinese legal procedure and language. This conclusion raises more questions than it answers. For example, where in the plays are the interpreters that officiated in Yuan tribunals? The conniving clerks do not perform this function. Why do the judges always speak Chinese, instead of transliterated Mongolian or

some sort of gibberish standing for a foreign tongue? What of the possibility that the judges portray stupidity in public office per se? Some
courtroom plays may indeed have been topical. Cheng (pp. 514–515)
cites a Yuan anecdote describing how a scandalous court case inspired
the writing of a play (called a *"hsi-wen"* in the original text, not a *tsa-
chü*). Cheng never intended that the example prove his point about the
ethnic origins of incompetent judges, however; actually, the citation
tends to undermine his argument. The judge-hero of the anecdote is a
non-Mongol foreigner, and the villains are, for all we know, Chinese!

15.   Plays 1, 3, 7, 8, 10, 11, 13, 15, 19, 20, 23, 25, and 26.

16.   "Scene" here means any part of a play between the entrance onto a
       bare stage of any character and the first total departure offstage of all
       characters. In contrast to "act," this term does imply unity or con-
       tinuity in time and place. One "act" may include several "scenes," but
       one "scene" may also cover several "acts."

17.   It occurs in Act 2 in Play 2.

18.   Plays 2, 8, 10, and 19. The exception is Play 8. The question of
       whether Pao misjudges the hero of Play 21 can be resolved only by
       knowing if Pao actually goes through with the threatened execution,
       but the play's conclusion is obscure in the edition we now have.

19.   Play 19, Act 4; *Yuan-ch'ü hsuan* (Anthology of Yuan drama), ed. Tsang
       Mao-hsun (Peking, 1953 ed.), III, 1274.

20.   The other two plays are Plays 14 and 22.

21.   These are Plays 11, 13, 17, 24, and 25.

22.   Play 2.

23.   Plays 12 and 17.

24.   Plays 3 and 23. In both plays, the judges are clearly or presumably alone
       when the ghosts appear.

25.   The other two plays are Plays 14 and 22. In Play 8, Pao confronts a
       ghost in the form of a whirlwind and orders it to return to the tribunal
       at dusk. The fact that the clerk Chang Ch'ien, all the while at Pao's side,

makes no comment may indicate either that the spectacle of his master's addressing a whirlwind is a common occurrence or that Chang is oblivious to the whole proceeding.

26. Plays 2, 3, and 5. In Play 27, the murder victim informs his son of the crime by means of a dream; the son later relays these facts to Pao.

27. In Judge Pao's dream of the butterflies in Play 2, the first butterfly caught in the spider web (of the law) represents the two stepsons. A second butterfly (the stepmother) saves this butterfly but forsakes a third (her natural son), also caught in the web. This last Pao in his dream releases.

28. The conundrum is, literally, "Not clothing (but) two handfuls of fire," the graphs of which combine to form the name of the criminal in Play 5, P'ei Yen. An alternate, and more logical, translation is predicated on an alternate form of the first graph: "A court clerk from the nether world with a torch in each hand."

29. *Erh Ch'eng i-shu* (Posthumously collected works of the two Ch'engs), 18.17b, in Ch'eng Hao and Ch'eng I, *Erh Ch'eng ch'üan-shu* (Complete works of the two Ch'engs), *Ssu-pu pei-yao* ed.

30. The Neo-Confucians stressed this view, of course, as does the popular Taoist book on ethical reward and punishment, Li Ch'ang-ling, *T'ai-shang kan-ying p'ien,* of the Sung period.

31. The Sung Neo-Confucians differed sharply on whether man was born with this ability or acquired it later. The school of Ch'eng I and Chu Hsi, which held the former view, dominated the intellectual scene in both north and south China from the end of the Southern Sung on through the Yuan and Ming periods.

32. An example is the mirror as the image for the mind of the detective. One of its origins may lie outside native Chinese tradition. In the Tantric *Surangama sutra* (translated into Chinese in the eighth century as *Ta-fo-ting shou-leng-yen ching*) chüan 8, a "karma mirror" in the Buddhist hell reflects the deeds of previous existences; see *Bukkyō daijiten* (Comprehensive dictionary of Buddhism), ed. Mochizuki Shinkō, 4th ed. (Tokyo, 1967), II, 1034. In Chinese legend of the Sung period, the "karma mirror," used during a trial in a nether world as much Taoist as Buddhist, reproduces on its surface the images of a past injustice; see

Hung Mai, *I Chien chih, Chia* (Shanghai, 1927 ed.), 19.4b. The distin-
guishing feature of the mirror in courtroom drama is that it is not an
instrument exclusive to posthumous judgment in hell, but is rather a
symbol of a human's ethical intelligence in this life; hence its more
Confucian flavor.

33.　Plays 2, 12, 18 (*YCH* ed.), and 19.

34.　Play 24, Act 3, *CYTC* III, vi, 2418–2419.

35.　An example is *T'ao-fu chi* (The peach charm), transcribed copy, *Ku-pen
　　　hsi-ch'ü ts'ung-k'an* (Compendium of drama old and new), First Series
　　　(I), by Shen Ching (1553–1610), which derives, perhaps indirectly, from
　　　The Flower of the Back Courtyard. Judge Pao brings the heroine back to
　　　life by administering a potion called "Soul-restoring Cinnabar." In *Yuan
　　　Wen-cheng huan-hun chi* (The return of the soul of Yuan Wen-cheng,
　　　Wen-lin-ko ed., *KPHCTK,* Second Series (II)), by "Hsin-hsin K'o" (pseud.),
　　　a "Warm and Cool Cap" has the same effect on the male protagonist.
　　　These examples show the lengths to which some Ming dramatists went to
　　　achieve a happy ending. The only material in Yuan or early-Ming northern
　　　drama suggesting the beginning of this trend is the resuscitation of the
　　　hero in Play 19, which remains in the anonymous Ming adaptation *Yen-
　　　chih chi* (The facepowder, Wen-lin-ko ed., *KPHCTK* I). Play 19 in any
　　　case involves only a baseless suspicion of murder; no crime actually occurs.
　　　The practice was also in use in the southern *hsi-wen;* in *Hsiao Sun T'u*
　　　(Young butcher Sun), one of the three *hsi-wen* in *Yung-le ta-tien,* the
　　　protagonist dies in prison, only to be revived later in the play by a super-
　　　natural being. Although he is not strictly a murder victim, the effect is
　　　the same.

2. The Legend of Judge Pao

1.　The earliest known sources for Pao's biography are (1) his memorials to
　　the throne, in 10 *chüan* (171 memorials), compiled in 1065 and usually
　　printed under the title *Pao Hsiao-su-kung tsou-i* (editions surviving today
　　also carry two biographies of Pao); (2) Li T'ao, *Hsu tzu-chih t'ung-chien
　　ch'ang-pien* (Continuation of *Tzu-chih t'ung-chien* [Comprehensive mirror
　　in aid of government] , unabridged) a chronicle compiled in the twelfth
　　century; and (3) various Sung collections of biographies and miscellaneous
　　anecdotes, the earliest being *Lung-p'ing chi* by Tseng Kung (1019–1083).
　　From sources of this type came Pao's biography in the *Sung shih* (History

of the Sung dynasty), written in the Yuan by T'o-t'o (or T'o-k'o-t'o, i.e., Toghto). The highlights of Pao's career, particularly those having to do with the legend, are described in Chapter 1 of this writer's Ph.D. dissertation, "The Judge Pao Plays of the Yuan Dynasty" (Stanford University, 1971).

2.   Pao has appeared even more recently in the world of popular entertainment. An immensely popular series of Judge Pao plays ran on Taiwan television during 1974 and reportedly sparked the construction of temples to Pao in the Taiwan countryside. Reflecting the widespread interest in Pao on Taiwan at the time is an article, "Yuan-jen tsa-chü chung ti Pao Lung-t'u" (Pao Lung-t'u in Yuan *tsa-chü*), by "Hua Lien" (pseud.), in *Lien-ho pao* (United News) (September 9, 10, 11, 1974), p. 12 (all eds.).

3.   For details on Pao's one demotion and two embarrassing incidents in his career, which need not be recounted here, see Li T'ao (Hangchow, 1881 ed.; supplement by Ch'in Hsiang-yeh, 1883), 181.14a and 190.11ab; and Ou-yang Hsiu, "Lun Pao Cheng ch'u San-ssu-shih shang-shu" (Letter submitted on Pao Cheng's promotion to Minister of Finance), in *Ou-yang Wen-chung-kung chi,* 111.13b–17a, in *Ssu-pu ts'ung-k'an, Chi-pu,* ed. Chang Yuan-chi (Shanghai, 1929). The highest rank offered Pao, which he refused prior to retirement, was Vice-minister of Rites (*Li-pu shih-lang*); see the "Kuo-shih pen-chuan" (Original biography in the [Sung] dynastic history), in Pao Cheng, *Pao Hsiao-su-kung tsou-i,* ed. Li Han-chang (1863), "Tsou-i chuan chi" (Biography section of the memorials), pp. 1a–3a.

4.   *Chüan* 316, *Erh-shih-wu shih* (Twenty-five histories) ed. *Erh-shih-wu shih* K'an-hsing Wei-yuan-hui (Twenty-five histories editorial committee; Shanghai, 1935), VII, 5373. For one of the earliest sources of this passage, see Tseng Kung, 11.10b.

5.   The bribery couplet is mentioned in Ssu-ma Kuang (1019–1086), *Su-shui chi-wen,* 10 (Shanghai, 1936 ed.), p. 109. The authorship of this work has been questioned; see Chang Hsin-ch'eng, *Wei-shu t'ung-k'ao* (Investigation into unauthentic works; Shanghai, 1957), pp. 1064–1065. Since the passage mentions Pao's posthumous title, it dates at the earliest from 1062. The joke about Pao's smile is found here and in Shen Kua (1031–1095), *Meng-hsi pi-t'an,* 22 (Shanghai, 1956 ed.), II, 720, which also mentions the Clear-sighted Investigator sobriquet. The latter miscellany is thought to have been written between 1086 and 1093; see the introduction to Hu Tao-ching, I, 22.

6. P'eng Ch'eng (b. ca. 1068–1077), *Mo-k'o hui hsi,* 10.1a, in *Pi-chi hsiao-shuo ta-kuan* (Compendium of anecdotal fiction) (*Ta-kuan*), comp. anon. (Taipei, 1960 fac. of Wen-ming ed.), I, 637.

7. Shen Kua, 22; 720.

8. Li T'ao, 184.14ab. Wang Ch'eng (Southern Sung), *Tung-tu shih-lueh* (A brief account of the Eastern Capital [K'ai-feng]), 73.1b, in *Sung Liao Chin Yuan ssu shih* (Four histories of the Sung, Liao, Kin, and Yuan dynasties), comp. Hsi Shih-ch'en (Sao-yeh-shan-fang ed., preface 1798).

9. Tseng Min-hsing, *Tu-hsing tsa-chih,* 1.1a, in *Ta-kuan,* I, 270.

10. Li T'ao, 184.14b. Shen Kua, 22; 720. Wang Ch'eng, 73.1b.

11. Tseng Kung, 11.9ab. See also the "Kuo-shih pen-chuan."

12. Yuan Hao-wen, *Hsu I Chien chih* (Continuation to the *I Chien chih*), 1.1b, in *Ta-kuan,* I, 1109.

13. For the transcribed text of the inscription and a translation into French, see Edouard Chavannes, *Le T'ai Chan* (Paris, 1910), pp. 361–369. The inscription has as this Pao's place of origin "Lü" (presumably for Lü-chou). Pao Cheng's actual ancestral home was Lu-chou (in present day Anhwei Province), but according to a Yuan rhyming dictionary, the *Chung-yuan yin-yun* (Rhymes of North China), the graphs for both *lü* and *lu* have the same pronunciation: *liu*^{2}. See Hugh M. Stimson, *The Jongyuan in yunn: A Guide to Old Mandarin Pronunciation* (New Haven, 1966), p. 110, Items 1151, 1152. The graph in the inscription, therefore, is probably a mistaken homophone. See the glossary for the graphs in question.

    Chavannes also mentions (p. 113) a pavilion called the "Court of Quick Retribution," of undetermined date, just outside the western gate of the village of T'ai-an-fu on Mt. T'ai. A building with the same name is part of the temple of T'ai-shan in Peking, first built in the Yuan between 1314 and 1320. See Urakawa Gengo, "Pēpin jōgai Tōgakubyō" (Temple of the Eastern Mountain outside Peiping), *Ritsumeikan bungaku,* I, 9, 1307, and Koyanagi Shigeo, *Hakuunkan shi, Tōgakubyō shi* (Account of White Cloud Temple and Temple of the Eastern Mountain; Tokyo, 1934), p. 195.

14. See Ying Shao (Latter Han), *Feng-su t'ung-i* (The comprehensive significance of popular customs), 2, in *Feng-su t'ung-i t'ung-chien* (Index to

ʾeng-su t'ung-i), ed. Chung-Fa Han-hsueh Yen-chiu-so (Sino-French Sinological Institute; Peking, 1943), p. 10. See also Ssu-ma Ch'ien, *Shih chi* (Historical records), 28, in *Erh-shih-wu shih*, I, 114, for the earliest information on the cult of Mt. T'ai as practiced in the Former Han.

15. Liu I-ch'ing (Tsin), *Yu-ming lu,* in Li Fang et al., *T'ai-p'ing kuang-chi* (Extensive records of the T'ai-p'ing reign), 1283.13ab, in *Pi-chi hsiao-shuo ta-kuan hsu-pien* (Continuation to *Pi-chi hsiao-shuo ta-kuan*), comp. anon. (Taipei, 1962 fac. of Wen-ming ed.), II, 872. According to the Ch'ing scholar Chai Hao in *T'ung-su pien* (Collection of popular expressions, Wu-pu-i-chai ed., in 38 *chüan*), 19.3a, the cult of Mt. T'ai did not gain predominance over those of the four other sacred mountains until the middle of the Sung (i.e., ca. 1100). Although documentation connects Pao with Mt. T'ai only from the middle of the thirteenth century, perhaps his appearance in Chinese mythology was in fact earlier than this date and was even allied in some way with the rising popularity of Mt. T'ai.

16. Ch'ang-sun Wu-chi et al., *Sui shu* (Book of the Sui dynasty), 52, biog. of Han Ch'in, in *Erh-shih-wu shih*, III, 2481.

17. As one might expect from the nature of the work, one such source is the voluminous Southern Sung compendium of the supernatural, the *I Chien chih* by Hung Mai.

18. *Chiao-ting Yuan k'an toa-chü san-shih-chung,* p. 435.

19. Title of the song translated below.

20. *Lu Chai-lang* involves the abduction of a man's wife; the crimes in Play 7 are the theft of a contract and assault and battery, although suspected murder is also an issue.

21. *YCH,* III, 1125.

22. *YCH,* II, 572–573.

23. Although its text is not extant, the title *Hu-t'u Pao Tai-chih* (Stupid Judge Pao), found in the *Lu kuei pu* under Chiang (or Wang) Tse-min, seems to indicate the same approach.

24. *CYTC* I, viii, 3909; or *YCH,* IV, 1728 (Pao is struck on the back in this version).

25. The joke, concerning the sword of execution, is translated on pp. 64–65.

26. Plays 2, 3, 6, 8, and 9 of Appendix A.

27. The mandatory punishment for the revenge killing of a father's murderer, an act that Pao holds to be justifiable homicide, is given to someone condemned to die anyway as a donkey thief.

28. Pao vows ties of brotherhood with a criminal in order to give him a false sense of security.

29. Pao adds brush strokes to a fictitious name on a death warrant in order to form the surname and title of the villain, someone whose prominence would have protected him from capital punishment under ordinary circumstances.

30. For a discussion of the Pao legend in the late-Ming and the Ch'ing periods, see Ma Yau-woon. Ma includes the Sung and Yuan periods, but his coverage of the legend from the *Lung-t'u kung-an* onward is more thorough than that of the preceding periods. The recent discovery of chantfable (*shuo-ch'ang tz'u-hua*) texts printed in the 1470s, many of which feature Judge Pao, should, upon their being republished, shed new light on what is now an unclear stage in the growth of the Pao legend, the middle Ming. For bibliographic information on the texts, see Chao Ching-shen, "T'an Ming Ch'eng-hua k'an-pen 'shuo-ch'ang tz'u-hua'" (On "chantfables" printed during the Ch'eng-hua reign [1465–1486] of the Ming), *Wen-wu,* 198:19–22 (November 1972).

3. Selling Rice at Ch'en-chou

1. "Wedge" (*hsieh-tzu*). This term, as used by Chu Ch'üan in *T'ai-ho cheng-yin p'u* (preface 1398) and by Chu Yu-tun in the texts of his plays published by him in the early fifteenth century, indicates the song but, apparently, not the accompanying speech. By the sixteenth century, it had come to include speech as well. By far the most common melodies of the wedge song are, in order of frequency, *Shang hua shih* and *Tuan-cheng hao,* both of the *Hsien-lü* mode. For more detailed discussion, see Cheng Chen-to, "Lun pei-ch'ü ti hsieh-tzu" (On the wedge of northern drama), in Cheng Chen-to, *Chung-kuo wen-hsüeh yen-chiu,* II, 578–595, and the articles by Sun K'ai-ti and Iwaki Hideo cited in Ch. 1, note 11, particularly Iwaki, pp. 509–527, 535–540.

The general pattern of northern drama is that a leading actor or actress sings throughout a play, wedge song inclusive. Thirteen wedge songs that are possibly of Yuan date, among them that of this play, are exceptions in that they are to be sung by supporting players. By and large, these exceptions are peculiar to *YCH;* nine of the songs are in play editions surviving only in *YCH* or are present in *YCH* but are missing from earlier collections.

2. "In service to the realm" (*Feng-huang-ch'ih shang*). Lit., "by the Phoenix Pool." In the Tsin period, this was the name of a pool in the inner palace; in time it came to mean the Secretariat and the Prime Ministry. Here it is a poetic term for high office, derived from the stock phrase: "In ten years I shall reach the Phoenix Pool" (*shih-nien shen tao Feng-huang-ch'ih*).

3. "Plan of Exalted Peace." Apparently the product of the playwright's or the popular imagination, this plan is not mentioned in the biography of Fan Chung-yen in the *Sung shih.*

4. Fen-chou was in present-day Shansi Province.

5. Ch'en-chou was in present-day Honan Province.

6. "Shortage of grain" (*liu-liao pu shou*). Lit., "the six grains are not harvested." "Six grains," a general term, includes rice, millet, barley, and other varieties.

7. The Secretariat was one of the three supreme administrative departments of the Sung government.

8. "An ounce of silver per bushel of hulled rice" (*wu liang pai-yin i shih hsi-mi*). Lit., "five *taels* of fine silver per *shih* of fine rice." The *shih*[a] approximates five bushels.

9. "Me" (*tsa*). This word is defined in modern dictionaries as a first person plural personal pronoun, but number in the personal pronouns of northern drama texts is often vague. Possibly *tsa* was at one time singular only and had as its plural form *tsam* (modern *tsan*) by syncope of *tsa* and the initial of the pluralizing syllable *men.*[a] The pronoun *tsa* is seen from time to time in the songs of northern drama but is comparatively rare in the spoken portions.

10. Hsiang-chou was in present-day Honan Province.

11.   "Approaches" (*chien*). Lit., "sees." This is only an approximate trans-
        lation for what appears to be a movement on stage indicating recogni-
        tion. With few exceptions, instructions to actors in northern dramatic
        texts refer to stage business of various kinds.

12.   "Lord" (*Ya-nei*). Commonly used in northern drama as a hereditary title
        indicating wealth and power, hence its translation here. In the T'ang
        period, *ya-nei* were palace guards, and from the end of the T'ang to the
        beginning of the Sung, the post was passed on to a son or younger
        brother. See Chou Mi, *Ch'i-tung yeh-yü*, 10.18ab, in *Hsueh-chin t'ao-
        yuan*, 14. In northern drama, *ya-nei* are usually villains, but in the verse
        narrative *Liu Chih-yuan chu-kung-tiao*, 11, in the songs *Hsiu-tai-erh* and
        Wei to the *Hsien-lü* mode, *ya-nei* is the title of the hero, Liu Chih-yuan.
        See "Kōchū Ryū Chi-en shokyūchō" (The Liu Chih-yuan chu-kung-tiao,
        collated and annotated), ed. Uchida Michio et al., *Tōhoku Daigaku
        Bungakubu nempō*, no. 14:283 (1964). For a detailed but slightly
        exaggerated discussion of the title's use in northern drama, see Chu
        Tung-jun, "Shuo ya-nei" (An elucidation of *ya-nei*), *Wen-hsueh tsa-chih*
        1.4:23–33 (August 1937).

13.   "Scoundrels" (*hua-hua T'ai-sui*). The latter word is the name of Jupiter
        in ancient Chinese astronomy, a star commonly associated with evil.

14.   The phrase "*yü wo*" (for me) almost always accompanies a command
        from a superior to an inferior. Since no courtesy is intended here, I have
        chosen not to translate it. See Ikeda Takeo, "Genjidai kōgo no kaishi ni
        tsuite" (On co-verbs in Yuan colloquial), *Ritsumeikan bungaku*, no. 180:
        173 (1960).

15.   "I" (*an*). Since Yuan and early-Ming (through the 1430s) texts of north-
        ern drama consistently use this word as a first personal plural or first
        person singular possessive pronoun only, its obviously singular and non-
        possessive meaning here may indicate a later date for at least this part of
        the text.

16.   "Have" (*chao*). This is a causative particle in northern drama and is less
        polite in this context than "ask" (*ch'ing*), which Fan uses above to invite
        his fellow officials.

17.   "Act with compassion" (*shu-chang*). Lit., "bind up (i.e. spare) the rods
        (of punishment)."

18. "Gold" (*tzu-chin*). Lit., "purple (or deep red) gold," gold of the highest
     quality. See Chou Mi, *Kuei-hsin tsa-chih, Hsu* (Supplement), *Hsia* (Sec-
     ond half), 41ab, in *Hsueh-chin t'ao-yuan*, 19. This is the "fine gold"
     (sheng-chin) (lit., "raw gold") of Play 14, Appendix A.

19. "Granary clerks" (*tou-tzu*) A type of clerk or servant employed in
     public granaries. The name possibly derives from the scales used in
     weighing grain, *tou-ch'eng,* as in *T'ieh-kuai Li,* 1, *Chin chan-erh, CYTC*
     I, xiii, 6404. The name dates at least from the Sung. See Chao Yen-wei,
     Yun-lu man-ch'ao (preface 1206) (Shanghai, 1936 ed.), 12:176; and
     Chou hsien t'i-kang (Outline of prefectural and county [administration]),
     anon., 4.6b, in *Hsueh-chin t'ao-yuan*, 8.

20. The original text here does not stipulate which clerk is speaking.

21. "Deduct" (*k'o-lo*). Lit., "deduct and confiscate." This was a common
     legal term for corruption in the disbursement of grain. *Li-hsueh chih-nan*
     (Guide to the study of official administration), i.e., *Chü-chia pi-yung
     shih-lei ch'üan-chi* (Complete collection of household necessities), *Hsin-
     chi,* 15, an anonymous work of the Yuan period, p. 67b (Kyoto, 1951
     ed.), defines it as "taking in more than one gives out and pocketing the
     difference."

22. "Give them a whack" (*ta t'a niang*). The final syllable, *niang* (lit.,
     "mother" or "mother's"), occasionally appears in coarse speech in
     northern drama. It seems to be related to the modern *ma-de.*

23. "Headstrong" (*Pieh-ku*). *Pieh-ku* means "stubborn," "hard to get along
     with." See Chang Hsiang, *Shih tz'u ch'ü yü-tz'u hui-shih* (Definitions of
     vocabulary in poems, lyrics, and songs; Hong Kong, 1962), p. 573. As a
     given name or nickname, it is usually coupled with the surname Chang in
     northern drama and represents a rustic character. See the song sequence
     in the *Cheng-kung* mode "Kao-yin" (Noble reclusion) by Hsueh Ang-fu,
     Kun hsiu-ch'iu, in *Ch'üan Yuan san-ch'ü* (Complete Yuan *san-ch'ü*), ed.
     Sui Shu-sen (Peking, 1964), I, 719.

24. I have translated here the entire proverb, the second half of which is
     absent from the original text but understood from the context.

25. The meaning of this couplet, based on a proverb commonly seen in
     courtroom plays, is that even the most docile citizen will cry out in
     reaction to injustice, which here assumes the image of "uneven ground."

26. "Lung-t'u." Lit., "Dragon Patterns" (i.e., august writings), from the sacred writings in seal script borne by a dragon from the Lo River to the Yellow Emperor in remote antiquity. This was the name of an imperial library in the Northern Sung, in which Pao held the rank of Auxiliary Scholar (*Chih hsueh-shih*) from 1052 to 1055. The Lung-t'u title has been appended to Pao's surname in popular reference since at least the Ming. Ever since Pao's famous administration of the capital, Sung custom used the title *"Tai-chih"* (Academician-in-waiting), which derives from a rank that Pao held earlier in another imperial library, the T'ien-chang Pavilion, from 1050 to 1052. Texts of northern plays attributed to the Yuan period usually conform to the Sung usage, but they frequently confuse the two ranks by appending *"Tai-chih"* to "Lung-t'u." For the sake of convenience, I have translated *"Tai-chih"* as "Judge."

27. Lit., "come to" or "brace up."

28. "Made mincemeat out of him" (*chao t'a pao-pu-ch'eng wang-erh*). Lit., "made him so that a net couldn't wrap him." I am indebted to Professor Patrick Hanan for this interpretation.

29. The "green" of this line puns on its homophone, to mean "pure," "honest."

30. "Chicanery." Lit., "making broth while pointing to a wild goose in the sky," i.e., implying that the wild goose is an ingredient of the broth when in fact it is not. For other occurrences of this expression in northern drama, see Chu Chü-i, *Yuan-chü su-yü fang-yen li-shih* (Examples and definitions of colloquialisms and dialecticisms in Yuan drama; Shanghai, 1956), pp. 171–172.

31. "Face of iron" (*t'ieh-mien*). Although this is used more than once in this play to describe Pao's stern facial expression and impartial attitude, two other figures of the Northern Sung were called "the iron-faced minister": Chao Pien and Wu Chung-fu. See *SS,* 316p. 5333; and Tseng Shu (1073–1135), *Nan-yu chi chiu,* in *Shuo fu* (Shanghai, 1927 ed.), 49.9b.

32. "And still get away with it." Lit., "and it would just be five pairs."

33. "Powderface" (*fen-t'ou*). Lit., "powder head," i.e., "prostitute," "singing girl." Cf. *Shui-hu chuan,* ch. 51 (Shih Nai-an, Lo Kuan-chung, *Shui-*

hu ch'üan-chuan [Variorum edition of *Shui-hu*], ed. Cheng Chen-to [Hong Kong, 1965 ed.], II, 839).

34. "Sword of Authority and Gold Badge" (*shih-chien chin-p'ai*). The first syllable is also written *shih*[b]: "pledge," "vow." See Kyoto daigaku jimbunkagaku kenkyūjō (Kyoto University Research Institute for Humanistic Studies), *Yuan-ch'ü hsuan shih* (The *Yuan-ch'ü hsuan* annotated) I (Kyoto, 1951), ii, 16b. Golden badges, or medallions, were used beginning from 1116 by the Kin dynasty as signs of authority; see T'o-t'o et al., *Chin shih* (History of the Kin dynasty), 58, under "*Fu-yin*" (Emblems), in *Erh-shih-wu shih,* VII, 5973. The Yuan dynasty copied this custom and made heavy gold and silver badges with designs of lion or tiger heads and an inscription entitling the bearer to special privileges while performing imperial duties. See Meng Kung (1195–1246), *Meng-ta pei-lu* (Comprehensive account of the Mongolian Tatars; Changsha, 1939 ed.), pp. 6–7; and *The Travels of Marco Polo,* ed. Manuel Komroff (New York, 1931), bk. 2, ch. 7, p. 121.

35. "Perform summary executions without going through channels before-hand" (*hsien chan hou wen*). Lit., "behead first and report afterward." Northern drama generally has *tsou* (report) for the last syllable. This phrase is widely seen in northern plays as an expression of imperial authority. As such, it derives from actual legal conditions in the Yuan period: see *Ta Yuan sheng-cheng kuo-ch'ao tien-chang* (Dynastic statutes of the sacred administration of the Great Yuan) (*Yuan tien-chang*), anon., ed. Shen Chia-pen (Soochow, 1908), 52.3b (Taipei, 1964 ed.), II, 699.

36. Chang Ch'ien is the name of a servant character commonly seen in northern drama. Other names of characters, always of the menial or rustic type, appearing in more than one play are Chang the Headstrong, as in this play, and Mei-hsiang (lit., "plum fragrance"), who appears so often as a maid that her name is synonymous with the term "maid" itself. Chang Ch'ien's given name, Ch'ien, means "thousand" and may indicate either that he is typical of 999 others like him, or that he is one thousandth in order of birth, i.e., he is a bastard. This play is unusual in giving Chang such a high degree of individuality and dramatic prominence.

37. "Lao-erh Hamlet." In the story "Ho-t'ung wen-tzu chi" (The story of the contract), in the *Ch'ing-p'ing-shan t'ang hua-pen* collection (Peking, 1955 ed., ed. Hung P'ien, p. 28a), Lao-erh hamlet is located thirty li from Pien-liang (K'ai-feng-fu).

"Chin-tou Commandery." During the Sung, Pao's birthplace, Ho-fei, was also known as Chin-niu-ch'eng or Chin-tou-ch'eng. See Yueh Shih, *T'ai-p'ing huan-yü chi* (Geographical record of the T'ai-p'ing Reign), supplement comp. Ch'en Lan-shen (Nan-ch'ang, Kiangsi, preface 1803), 126.4a–5b; and Wang Hsiang-chih, *Yü-ti chi-sheng* (Recorded wonders of the earth), supplement comp. Ts'en Chien-kung (Kan-ch'üan, 1849), 45.8a.

38. "Southern Court" (*Nan-ya*). When an imperial relative during the Sung was prefect of K'ai-feng-fu, he "presided in the Southern Court" (*p'an Nan-ya*). See *Sung pai lei-ch'ao* (A categorized transcription of Sung miscellanies), comp. P'an Yung-yin (n.p., preface 1669), 2.54b, which quotes the anonymous Sung work *Ch'uan-teng lu* (Record of the transmission of the lamp).

39. The location of Wu-nan (lit., "five south") is unknown.

40. "Lu." Lit., "Lu *Chai-lang,*" the villain in the play of the same name. "*Chai-lang*" has the literal meaning of "Master of Sacrifices," but by the Sung period it had become a mere title.
     "Ko." Lit., "Ko *Chien-chün.*" "*Chien-chün*" is roughly equivalent to a military inspector-general. This is a possible reference to Ko Piao in the Pao play *Sheng-chin ko,* but Ko does not have this rank in the extant texts. One courtroom play in which a "Ko *Chien-chün*" is the villain is *Yen-an-fu* (Play 25 in Appendix A), but Pao is not the judge in this play. Perhaps another dramatic version of the same plot did have Pao as the judge.

41. These two lines are a stock couplet expressing renunciation of worldly cares. The first line usually reads "I am well aware of the world's affairs but decline to open my mouth" (*pao-an shih-shih yung k'ai-k'ou*).

42. Stock similes also appearing in *Sheng-chin ko,* Act 4, and *Shen-nu-erh,* Act 4.

43. According to Prof. Tanaka Kenji, *liang* in this line has a self-effacing function.

44. All four men are well-known ministers of history who lost their lives in pursuit of virtue. Ch'ü Yuan drowned himself in a river when his lord, the king of Ch'u, turned against him. Kuan Lung-feng remonstrated against the notorious King Chieh of the Hsia dynasty and was beheaded. Pi-kan had his heart cut out by the evil last monarch of the Shang

dynasty, King Chou. "Marquis Han" is Han Hsin, a general of the Han dynasty and a favorite example in Yuan songs of a worthy man who ignored the signs of danger around him and was destroyed by a powerful enemy.

45. As a prominent official who left the Han court and followed the sage Ch'ih-sung-tzu, Chang Liang was an ideal figure of Yuan eremitism.

46. Fan Li's name appears innumerable times in Yuan plays and songs as a symbol of a man who leaves office just in time to save his own life. Most often his name is coupled with that of Chang Liang. This section of the play is a good example of similar ones in some other plays and in many songs. As a group, the literati of the Yuan (and perhaps the early Ming as well), most of whom could not serve in high office, sang the praises of those in former times who *would* not.

47. Confident that Pao will never go to Ch'en-chou, Liu is speaking with false politeness here.

48. "Hot tempered and stubborn" (*pu-lieh fang-t'ou*). *Pu-lieh* may be a slurred version of *pieh-lieh*, which, like *pieh-ku* in note 23, this chapter, means "irascible." *Fang-t'ou* (lit., "square-headed"), is defined as "crudely straightforward" by Chao Ling-shih (d. 1134) in *Hou ch'ing lu*, 8.1a, in *Ta-kuan*, IV. Chao quotes a poem by the T'ang poet Lu Kuei-meng, also quoted by T'ao Tsung-i in *Ch'o-keng lu*, 17, p. 248, but T'ao gives the definition "out of touch with the times." As used from the T'ang through the Yuan and early Ming, the compound seems to have a connotation of "simple honesty."

49. "Lock horns." *Mao* and *yu*, as symbols for east and west, moon and sun, and dawn and dusk, are mutually opposed. They often comprise the second half of a quadrisyllabic compound with *shen* and *ch'en*.

50. This is the first line of a stock couplet, the second of which occurs in *The Ghost of the Pot*. See p. 85.

51. Pao is making a pun here. "Troubles" indicates not only the troubles *of* granary officials but the trouble *with* them.

52. "Gather up their baskets and stop their weighing" (*shou p'u-lan pa tou*). This stock phrase has the general meaning of "to stop, withdraw," but my translation is literal here because of the intended pun on selling grain.

A version from the Northern Sung has *po-lo* in place of *p'u-lan;* the meaning of *po-lo* is unclear but may be the same as that of *p'u-lan,* "rush basket." See the lyric (*tz'u*) by Ch'in Kuan, "Man yuan hua," in *Ch'üan Sung tz'u* (Complete Sung lyrics), ed. T'ang Kuei-chang, rev. ed. (Peking, 1965), I, 459.

53. "Parasol tree" (*wu-t'ung shu*). This rendering is based on the English translation of the Japanese *aogiri* as "a sultan's (Chinese) parasol" in *Kenkyusha's New Japanese-English Dictionary*, ed. Katsumata Senkichirō (Tokyo, 1954), p. 31. An alternate translation is "plane tree."

For the many variations of this couplet, see Chai Hao, 30.9b–10a, and n. 24 by Ch'ien Nan-yang to Kao Ming, *P'i-pa chi* (Peking, 1965 ed.), p. 176.

54. Rather than reflecting actual practice, this phrase seems to indicate a dramatic convention invented by the playwright in order to provide suspense and a surprise ending.

55. "Disposition" (*hsing-erh*). *Hsing*[a] is corrected in some modern editions to read *hsing*[b].

56. "He." Lit., "you," a rhetorical address to Pao, which I prefer to translate in the third person.

57. "Gruel" (*lo*[a]*-chieh-chou*). The play *Han-kung ch'iu*, 2, *Wei-sheng, CYTC* I, iv, 1843, mentions a gruel called *lo*[b]*-ho-chou*. Both *lo*[a] and *lo*[b] were homophones in the Yuan as now; see Stimson, p. 263, Items 3413a and 3414a. *Chieh* and *ho* may be cognate, but the compound *chieh-chou* appears in a Sung work: Meng Kung, p. 5. I suspect that the compound seen in this play represents a combination of curd (*lo*) and rice gruel (*chieh-chou*). The compound "curd gruel" (*lo-chou*) was used as early as the Northern Wei dynasty; see Yang Hsuan-chih, *Lo-yang ch'ieh-lan chi* (Record of Buddhist temples in Lo-yang), 3.6a, in *Hsueh-chin t'ao-yuan*, 7. During the Ming, northern Chinese commonly ate curd and thin gruel (*hsi-chou*); see Ch'oe Se-jin (1473?–1542), *Pak T'ong-sa on-hae* (Explanations of sayings by Interpreter Bak; Keijō, 1943 ed.), *Chung* (Middle portion), p. 6b.

58. "Tea wine" (*ch'a-hun-chiu*). *Hun-chiu* was a cheap wine, unfiltered and occasionally mixed with tea. See the plays *Huan lao mo*, 4, poem by Juan Hsiao-wu, *CYTC* I, vii, 3493; and *Fan Chang chi shu*, 1, speech by Wang Chung-lueh, *CYTC* II, ii, 1604.

59. "Blabbering away" (*p'i-liu-p'u-la*). Onomatopoetic for incessant and meaningless talk.

60. The syllables *ti* and *che*[b] in this line have no meaning but have been added to fill out the rhythm.

61. "Blink" (*cha*[a]). The modern graph is *cha*[b].

62. "Roll up your sleeves, stick out your fists" (*lo-hsiu hsuan-ch'üan*). Both *lo*[c] (now written *lo*[d]) and *hsuan* mean to tuck back the sleeves and expose the arms, as in preparation for fighting or heavy drinking. The redundancy here is for a rhyming effect. See Jimbun, I, iii, 30b.

63. "All at once." A pun meaning both "while I'm on horseback" and "at once." Chang Ch'ien may have had to dismount each time he was called back. I am indebted to Professor Tanaka for this interpretation.

64. "Throw their money around" (*sa-man*). In the language of prostitutes, this meant to spend lavishly. *Man* originally meant the back of a coin and came eventually to represent money in general. See Jimbun, II, iii, 12b.

65. During the Yuan period, prostitutes were forbidden to ride horses, which were reserved to those with more status.

66. "Animal" (*t'ou-k'ou-erh*). This term seems to have originated in the Yuan period. It occurs commonly in the *Yuan tien-chang*. Chai Hao, *T'ung-su pien,* Wu-pa-i-chai ed. Preface 1751, 28.19a, cites the Han term *sheng-k'ou* as its origin, but this latter refers to humans as well as to livestock. The Yuan compound appears to mean horses and donkeys only.

67. "Leopard tail ranks." By the Sung period, the leopard tail on a red lacquer staff, formerly used to decorate one of the imperial carriages, was replaced by a piece of cloth painted with leopard spots. See *SS,* 149, p. 4837.

68. "Wrestling." *Po*[a] should read *po*[b].

69. "Wine" (*t'ou-nao-chiu*). Lit., "wine that goes to the brain." Some Ming sources have *t'ou*[a] for the first syllable. See *Shui-hu chuan,* ch. 51 (Shih Nai-an, Lo Kuan-chung, II, 840); and Chu Kuo-chen, *Yung-ch'uang hsiao-p'in* (preface 1619), 17.16ab, in *Ta-kuan,* p. 2013. Chu defines the term to mean a mixture of hot wine and meat flavoring to be served in

winter. In *Fan Chang chi shu,* 1, speech by Wang Chung-lueh, *CYTC,* II, ii, 604, *nao-erh-chiu* is contrasted with *hun-chiu* (see n. 58, this chapter) and means wine of good quality. Under *"Nao-erh-chiu"* in Ch'oe Se-jin, *Chung,* p. 3b, this wine is defined as a type made from grain, yeast, and herbs, well-aged, strong, and red. Glutinous rice was also used.

70.   "Brothels" (*ch'ing-lou*). Since the Liang period, this term has meant "house of prostitution," but before then it represented the house of a rich family or the place where the daughter of such a family resided. See Chai Hao, 24.11b.

71.   "Servant" in the original text is expressed by "the tail of a stove," "head man" by its "head." The "head" of a stove is where the fire is located; the "tail" holds the food.

72.   "Charlatan" (Wang Ch'iao). This may refer either to Wang Ch'iao, an official and magician of the Latter Han period, or to the legendary immortal of the Chou period, Prince Ch'iao (*Wang-tzu* Ch'iao). By the fifth century, the two were often confused; see Wang Ch'iao's biography, including a note by Li Hsien, in Fan Yeh, *Hou-Han shu* (History of the Latter Han dynasty), 112 *shang,* in *Erh-shih-wu shih,* I, 888. The play seems to be referring here to a popular legend about which nothing is known.

73.   These very expensive dishes symbolize hedonistic living.

74.   "Liao Hua." The use of these graphs to mean a stupid official may derive from the name of an oily and sticky type of cake, written in the same way, as in Chou Mi, *Hao-jan-chai ya-t'an, Chung,* pp. 5ab, in *Ch'an-hua-an ts'ung-shu.* In Ming fiction, malt sugar (*hsing*[c]), one of its ingredients, is used to mean "stupid."

75.   Pao means that he will scare the life out of Young Liu.

76.   "Time-honored codes." Lit., "Hsiao Ho's codes." Hsiao Ho was the founder of much of the Han legal system.

77.   "Strategist great." Lit., "K'uai T'ung." K'uai T'ung was a wandering theorist of the Ch'u-Han period, i.e., the second century B.C.

78.   "It is only right" (*fei tsa t'e-sha*). Lit., "it is not extreme." *"Tsa"* here may be a particle.

79. "Sly rogue" (*yu-t'ou*). Lit., "greasy head." This expression is coupled with "powder face" (*fen-mien*) as a derogatory term for prostitutes in the play *Ch'ü-chiang-ch'ih*, 2, *Liang-chou, CYTC*, I, ix, 4335. But in the poem "Hsi t'i Hsia-yen" (On the topic of Hsia-yen, in jest) by the Sung poet Huang T'ing-chien, the term refers to extravagantly made-up juveniles of both sexes, whose greased hair gives off a bad odor. See Liang T'ung-shu (1723–1815), *Chih-yü pu-cheng*, p. 10b, in Liang T'ung-shu, *P'in-lo-an i-chi*.

4. The Ghost of the Pot

1. "Capital" (*Pien-liang*). This was not the formal name for K'ai-feng until 1288, but both graphs had been used in previous dynasties as names for the region, as in "Pien-ching" and "Liang-chou." "Pien-liang" was probably a common name during the Sung as well as the Yuan and early Ming.

2. "Yang Kuo-yung." *MWK:* "Yang Wen-yung."

3. An identical prediction, which always comes true, appears in three other courtroom plays: Plays 11, 14, and 17 of Appendix A, as well as in *Shui-hu chuan*, chap. 65 (Shih Nai-an, Lo Kuan-chung, III, 1106).

4. In *MWK* Yang enters with Chao K'o. The prediction of the fortuneteller (unnamed in *MWK*) also applies to Chao, and Yang and Chao borrow money from a third party and leave home together. Later Chao shares Yang's fate.

5. The version in *MWK* of the inn boy's entrance poem can be found in other northern plays. This version in *YCH* seems to be original with this edition.

6. "Wine shop" (*chiu-wu*). In the Sung period, this was the name for member branches of the government alcohol bureau. By the Yuan period, it had become a common name for even the smallest roadside tavern.

7. "Straw broom." A broom as a symbol for wine may have some connection with one of the Eight Immortals (*Pa Hsien*). In the play *Wan-chiang-t'ing*, 1, speech by Chung-li, *CYTC* III, vi, 2450, the Immortal T'ieh-kuai Li is said to be able to brew wine in an instant. In another play,

Yueh-yang-lou, 4, *Shui hsien-tzu, CYTC* I, v, 2050, T'ieh-kuai Li carries a bamboo broom.

8.   "Bumpy" (*chi-ting ke-ta*). The first two syllables probably were pronounced *ki³-teng¹*; see Stimson, p. 81, Item 0664, and p. 351, Item 4874 respectively. This expression is an onomatopoeia for the action of colliding with some object or, more pertinent here, stumbling.

9.   "Stagger my way through life" (*Chieh-chieh pa-pa*). *Chieh-pa* usually means "to stutter, to stammer," but I interpret the phrase figuratively here.

10.   "Peony" (*mu-tan*) (*shao-yao*). Lit., "tree peony" and "herbaceous peony."

11.   "Wine" (*lan-kua*). Lit., "overripe melon," a poetic name for wine.

12.   "Ambrosia" (*liu-hsia*). Lit., "flowing sunset," another poetic name for wine.

13.   "Villain" (*pang-lao*). The technical name for a villain character type in northern drama. *MWK* also designates the real villain, Chao the Jug, as of this type; both he and the villain in the dream may have been played by the same actor. *YCH* prescribes only that Chao is to be performed by a *ching,* a category of actor who often plays villain roles; it makes no mention of character type when introducing Chao.

14.   "Official" (*ku*). A character type for an official. In *MWK* Judge Pao appears here instead. In the *YCH* version Pao is to be played by a *wai,* an actor type; "*ku*" is not used in connection with Pao in this edition. Cf. n. 13 above.

15.   "Bandit" (*t'ai-p'u*). From the official title of the imperial horse and carriage master, but in northern drama the term is usually applied to bandits, sometimes as an honorific. Cf. the play *Li K'uei fu ching,* 1, speech by Wang Lin, *YCH,* IV, 1518.

16.   "Hulk" (*pei-t'ing pan*). Lit., "(as big) as a memorial stone pavilion."

17.   "Their," "them" (*na-ssu*). Third person singular pronoun with a contemptuous tone; sometimes applied to second person.

18. "Money God" (*Ch'ien-lung*). Lit., "Money Dragon."

19. "Powder" (*hui*). Lit., "ash."

20. "Hair" (*t'ou-shao*). Lit., "the top of the head."

21. "You're biting the hand that feeds you" (*wo yang-che chia-sheng shao-li*). Lit., "I've been raising a thug as the son of a slave."

22. "You" (*wo*). The first person pronoun is used here to indicate "oneself."

23. "Head Clerk" (*Wu-ya Tu-shou-ling*). Lit., "Chief of the Five Court (Departments)."

24. "His Honor" (*ta-jen*). In some of its versions of other plays, *YCH* has instead the equivalents *yeh-yeh, hsiang-kung,* and *ta-yeh.* According to Ch'ien Ta-hsin in *Heng-yen lu* (Record of common speech), 4 (Changsha, 1939 ed.), p. 95, calling an official *yeh-yeh* or *lao-yeh* began in the Sung and Kin periods and was northern usage (the former term is referred to in *SS,* 360, biog. of Tsung Tse, p. 5431, specifically as northern). Although *ta-jen* was a general honorific as early as the Han period, it occurs very seldom in *YCH.* Perhaps by the late Ming it had become so commonplace that it had lost any flavor of respect. Hsu Wei (1521–1593) in *Nan-tz'u hsu-lu* (Account of southern drama), in *CKKT,* III, 247, asserts that in the Ming it had replaced the older *hsiang-kung,* but Wang Ying-k'uei (b. 1684) in *Liu-nan hsu-pi,* 2.4ab, in *Chieh-yueh-shan-fang hui-ch'ao,* XV, points out that during the Ming, at least in certain localities, it was insulting in tone.

25. "Let" (*teng*). This extension in meaning of a word usually meaning "to wait" is typical of Yuan–Ming colloquial usage. "*Tai,*" which also means "to wait," can have the same meaning.

26. "Demon-King" (*Na-cha*). Prince Nata from Buddhist mythology, eldest son of Vaisravana, the Celestial King guarding the North.

27. This line is a play on a common expression descriptive of a quick temper: "like throwing salt into fire." Northern drama frequently repeats a joke or an amusing piece of stage business several times; this is no exception.

28. "See justice brought you" (*chien ch'ing-t'ien*). Lit., "see blue sky."

29. "Call for the cases to be presented" (*ho ts'uan-hsiang*[a]). The compound *ts'uan-hsiang* refers to the plaintiff's action of "throwing" (*ts'uan*) the written charge or appeal into a box placed outside the courtroom. In actual Yuan usage, the clerks collected these at noon and read and selected them on the same day. The *hsiang*[a] (box) of *YCH* therefore is preferable to the *hsiang*[b] (chamber) of *MWK*. See Yang Yü (Yuan), *Shan-chü hsin-yü*, 4ab, in *Chih-pu-tsu-chai ts'ung-shu*.

30. In *MWK* the mode is *Chung-lü*, and each song in this sequence bears a different title from its counterpart in *YCH*. The lyrics of the two editions differ the most sharply in this act.

31. These lyrics are absent from *MWK*.

32. The song *Tao-tao ling* repeats the penultimate line.

33. From "Thrice for the Wangs . . ." this poem enumerates six cases solved by Judge Pao, each of which is represented by a northern play. (Plays 2, 15, 10, 8, and 18 respectively in Appendix A; *Lu Chai-lang*, unlisted in Appendix A, is mentioned between Plays 10 and 8.)

34. "Bandit lair." In northern drama the term "bitterweed swamp" often refers to a hideout of the Sung bandit Sung Chiang and his men, heroes of many Yuan and Ming plays, as well as the Ming novel *Shui-hu chuan*. Here it means a bandit hideout in general.

5. The Flower of the Back Courtyard

1. Lit., "a child born in the family," i.e., the son of a family slave.

2. "Judicial Inspector" is a substantive, rather than a literal translation of an administrative title (*lien-fang-shih*) inherited from the Sung, when it was applied briefly to the traveling inspector within a route (*lu*), and given by the Yuan to the official who reviewed legal matters within a circuit (*tao*). The full title is *su-cheng lien-fang-shih*. Neither the full nor the abbreviated form of the title survived the Yuan period.

3. The latter couplet of this quatrain is the second of an eight-couplet poem, "Sorrows of the Spring Palace" (*Ch'un-kung yuan*) by the late-T'ang poet Tu Hsun-ho (846–905). The entire poem is in the well-known Ch'ing anthology *T'ang-shih san-pai-shou* (Three hundred T'ang

poems) under the heading "Five Syllable Regulated Verse" (*wu-yen lü-shih*). The borrowing is apt here; Tu's poem voices the loneliness and nostalgia of a neglected royal consort.

4. "Sir" (*ko* [-*ko*]). Lit., "elder brother," a term of respect inferior to "his (your) Excellency" ([*lao*] *hsiang-kung*) and "his (your) Honor" (*ta-jen*). See *Ghost of the Pot*, n. 24. When not following a personal name, in which case it is rendered as "Mr. . . . ," *ko* is translated as "sir."

5. "Official residence" (*ya-men*). This term is translated elsewhere as "tribunal" or "courtroom," depending on the context. An official and his family lived in the same compound as the office in which he discharged his duties.

6. This line is perhaps the most difficult of several in this play that resist close translation, involving as it does an obscure graph (*pao*[a], probably an alternate form of *pao*[b], "to roast"). The original line is "*Tso i-ko pao chien* ("to fry") *kun* ("to roll about, toss and tumble")."

7. "Flailing" is a surmise from context. "*Tun*" seems to be parallel with "*t'i*" ("to kick"), which is applied to the feet.

8. "Conscripts" (*she-liang chün*). The first graph (Yuan pron. *shiə*[2]) may be a mistaken form for *shih*[c] (Yuan pron. *shiə*[2]), "to eat." The modern "*ch'ih-liang*," lit., "to eat grain," means "to serve as a conscript." See Chu Chü-i, p. 189.

9. If this expression has any logical explanation (and many vulgarities do not), it may be that it describes the effect of bowing low or kowtowing. In any case, it is reminiscent of the saying, "You'd bend over backwards for a drink."

10. The river that gives Pien-liang, or Pien-ching its name (lit., "Capital on the Pien," i.e., present day K'ai-feng, site of the Northern Sung capital).

11. One of the definitions of "*ta-ku-li*" in Chu Chü-i, p. 58, is "*tsung-chih*" ("in short," "all in all"), but it seems to be more emphatic and importunate here.

12. "It throws into a turmoil" (*huo-tuo-sha wu-tsang shen*). Lit., "throws into turmoil the spirit in my five internal organs." *Huo-tuo* is a variant of *hu-t'u*, "to confuse," "confused"; see *Hsiao-shuo tz'u-yü hui-shih*

(Vocabulary in fiction defined), ed. Lu Tan-an (Shanghai, 1964), p. 853. The five internal organs are the heart, lungs, liver, kidneys, and spleen.

13. The translated line is a compression of two in the original text, one referring to Ts'ui-luan as "*hsien-chün,*" the other to her mother as "*t'ai-chün.*" Both are honorific, non-inherited titles conferred upon women.

14. The term translated here as "East Gate" pertained not only to the eastern gate of the capital but also to a region to the east of the city, as well as to a mountain in that region.

15. "*T'a*" here may be a particle, or it may refer to the gate. The translation reflects the latter interpretation.

16. "Hair" (*t'ou-shao*). Lit., "the top of my head."

17. "*P'a-pu*" here, as in modern Chinese, expresses possibility, in contrast to *p'a-pu-tai,* which indicates a rhetorical negative in northern drama.

18. Lit., "Isn't it said that phoenixes fly onto the parasol tree?" This line is the first of a couplet, the second half of which reads, "There will always be another (others) offering his (their) views." For a different connotation of the saying, see p. 62 and n. 53, of *Selling Rice at Ch'en-chou.* This is an example of a type of popular expression, still heard today, which reserves the import of a couplet to the second line, usually left unsaid but assumed to be understood.

    An intriguing question is the possible connection between the flight of the male and female phoenix (*feng-huang*) onto the parasol tree and people's comments or gossip. The saying may be observing that the flight of these mythical birds, although held by most people to be an extremely auspicious event, was still bound to elicit critical comment from some. Or perhaps inevitability is being expressed: just as phoenixes alight on the parasol tree and no other, so the talk of disinterested observers on every subject is unavoidable.

19. For the sake of euphony in translation, the order of this and the preceding line has been reversed.

20. The line "Belles-lettres and histories, complete in three years" (*wen shih san-tung tsu*) derives ultimately from the biography of Tung-fang Shuo in the *Han shu* (History of the Former Han dynasty), 65, by Pan Ku (*Erh-shih-wu shih* ed., I, 521), in which Tung-fang Shuo is said to have

mastered belles-lettres and the histories in three winters ("*san tung wen shih tsu yung*"). A note by Ju-ch'un (surname missing) states that winter was the time in which sons of humble families were able to study. This line reinforces the images of cold, poverty, and diligence in the poem as a whole.

21. A closer translation, "a belly full of learning," has quite a different tone in English from that of the original line.

22. Lit., "young scholar" (*hsiu-ts'ai*).

23. "Flower of the Back Courtyard" (*Hou-t'ing hua*) is the title of a popular melody of the Kin and Yuan periods. Various lyrics of the *san-ch'ü* genre were added to the melody according to set syllabic, tonal, and rhyming standards. The syllabic scheme for this seven-line format is 5, 5, 5, 5, 3, 4, 5, all lines rhyming except the third. The melody, also called *Hou-t'ing hua p'o-tzu* (see *CYSC*, I, 2), was in the *Hsien-lü* mode. The songs of both Liu and Ts'ui-luan follow the format strictly, but the lyrics to *Hou-t'ing hua* in the first song sequence (Act 1) of this play are considerably more free. Dramatic lyrics tended to follow prosodic standards much less closely than did *san-ch'ü* lyrics.

The connection of this song title with Ts'ui-luan and her fate will be apparent when we learn that the well into which the inn boy threw her body is in the back courtyard of the inn.

24. This and the preceding line are almost identical to two lines in the song "On Love" (*T'i ch'ing*) to the melody *I-pan-erh* by Kuan Han-ch'ing (*CYSC*, I, 156).

25. I am indebted to Professor Tanaka Kenji for information concerning the symbolism of this passage.

26. Lit., "Southern Court"; see n. 38 of *Selling Rice at Ch'en-chou.*

27. "Entrusted" (*fen-fu*). This is the same compound translated as "instructions" in Pao's preceding speech, but here it functions as a verb, linked with the succeeding indirect object "Wang Ch'ing" by the complement "*yü*" and with "*yü*" forming a verb phrase which may be placed in completed action, as here, by the syllable "*liao.*" "Placed them in Li Shun's care" below is an alternate translation for the same construction, which to my knowledge is unique to northern drama.

28. "It may well be that" (*to-yin-shih*). The second graph may be a variant or a mistake for *ying; to-ying-shih* in northern drama expresses strong possibility. But the entire phrase may mean "it may very possibly be owing to the fact that," the second graph retaining its usual meaning of "because of."

29. This line is phrased as a disjunctive rhetorical question in the original text: "Would Pao Lung-t'u be afraid or not?" (. . . *p'a yeh pu p'a*) and implies an affirmative answer: "Yes, he would indeed!" "*Tse che*" is emphatic. I am indebted to Professor Tanaka Kenji for these interpretations.

30. "Cross swords" (*tso liang-shih chia*). See Chu Chü-i, p. 140. The translation contains a metaphor not present in the original.

31. "Unpleasant task" (*o-t'ou-erh*). Cf. the plays *Pao chuang-ho*, 2, *Mu-yang-kuan*, 2, *YCH*, IV, 1462; and *Mo-ho-lo*, 4, *Tsui ch'un-feng* 1, *CYTC* I, xiii, 6512.

32. "Confront" (*hu-p'u-ta*). In the play *Jen-tzu chi*, 2, *Wu-yeh t'i*, *YCH*, III, 1070, this phrase means "to make trouble, create a fuss."

33. "Shout at" (*ho-to*). The meaning of the second syllable (Yuan pron. *to*[3]) is unclear. It may mean "to instigate," as in *ts'uan-to,* or it may function in both compounds as a verbal complement of contact or attainment, like the more common *te* (Yuan pron. *tei*[3]), with which it may be cognate. Cognation would have been subsequent to the Sui period, however, when *to* had a *-t* and *te* a *-k* final. See Stimson, Items 1785 (p. 151) and 681 (p. 82) respectively.

34. "Shatter" (*shuo-sui*). The first graph appears often in northern drama with the meaning of "to strike at."

35. A tentative close translation of this line would read "After watching his attitude and his mouth" (*ch'ü liao t'a ching-shen k'ou-mo*) but would leave much to be desired as to meaning and euphony. Particularly puzzling are the last two syllables; they seem to make up a compound which has something to do with Wang Ch'ing's mouth or speech and which was chosen for its rhyme (alternate Yuan pron. *ma* for the last syllable). The final translation, also tentative, assumes that the fourth and fifth syllables, as a compound with the possible meaning of "spirited, energetic, frenetic," modify the last two.

36.   "Astonished" (*hsi-ch'a*). Ch'ien Nan-yang's definition of this compound as "unusual, marvelous, strange" may cover the majority of cases in which it appears, but an extension to a putative connotation seems to be called for here. See Kao Ming, p. 226, n. 3.

37.   "Joy" (*huan-hsia*). This compound, very common in Yuan *san-ch'ü*, seems to be interchangeable with *huan-hsi*. Here it has an erotic connotation; cf. Hung Mai, *I Chien chih, Chih-chia*, 3.1a.

38.   See the proclamation of 1313 by Emperor Jen Tsung instituting the imperial examinations and denying eligibility to anyone ever convicted of a major crime, in Sung Lien et al., *Yuan shih* (History of the Yuan dynasty), 81, under "*K'o-mu*" (Examination Categories; *Erh-shih-wu shih* ed., VIII, 6332).
          This line is the second of a couplet on the subject of the imperial examinations: "You may study for a decade and be ignored by all; in one swift stroke attain your name and all the world will know" (*shih-nien ch'uang-hsia wu jen wen; i-chü ch'eng-ming t'ien-hsia chih*). In this play, the last syllable of the second line has been left off for rhyming purposes.

39.   See Shih Nai-an, *Shui-hu* (Peking, 1963), I, 325, n. 1.

40.   "Explain" (*fen-hsi*). A variant of *fen-shu* or *fen-shuo,* used here to rhyme.

41.   "Run away" (*tsai-t'ao*). A legal term common in the Penal Section (*Hsing-pu*) of the *Yuan tien-chang*.

42.   "Dumbfounded" (*ai-ta-hai*). The last two graphs are used in northern drama as a modifying compound with another word describing a state of mind: *men*[b] ("depressed"). Aoki Masaru in *Genjin zatsugeki* (*Tsa-chü* by Yuan authors; Tokyo, 1957), p. 251, suspects that this compound, with the meaning of "to rest one's cheek on the hand," was once descriptive of the physical appearance of depression or bewilderment. See also Chu Chü-i, p. 123.

43.   "With no solution" (*wu-tui*). The second syllable may instead be a rhyming abbreviation of *tui-t'ou,* to mean (1) "culprit," as in *wu-tui-t'ou kung-an* ("unsolved case") or (2) "enemy." Pao's meaning then would be that the murderer would never be identified.

44.   The order of this and the preceding line has been reversed in translation.

45.   "Evade" (*t'ui-chu*[a]). Variants of the second graph are *chu*[b] and *tsu.*

46.   "Fight" (*mei nan mien pei*). Chu Chü-i, p. 181, mistakenly defines this
      common expression as "enemy." It is always used in relation to hus-
      band and wife or lovers. Since it is parallel to the "quarrel" of the fol-
      lowing line, it seems to describe figuratively the failure of two people,
      ideally as mutually complementary as eyebrows and face, to exist
      peacefully together. But the compound may instead be describing
      graphically an angry facial expression; its literal translation is "eye-
      brows south and face north."

47.   "Compatible" (*shuo-te-chao*). Cf. the modern *shuo-te-lai.*

48.   "Report" (*hsing-hui*). A legal term meaning "to examine into." Here it
      means "report of the results of my examination into this case."

49.   "Sudden reversals" (*wu-ch'ang*). Liu Ts'un-yan in *Buddhist and Taoist
      Influences on Chinese Novels,* I, *The Authorship of the Feng Shen Yen I*
      (Wiesbaden, 1962), p. 210, n. 265, traces "*wu-ch'ang*" to the name of
      the demon sent by King Yama to summon a man's life, but I prefer the
      older and more literal meaning of "impermanence, unpredictability"
      here. See *A Dictionary of Chinese Buddhist Terms,* comp. William Ed-
      ward Soothill and Lewis Hodous (Taipei, 1962 ed.), p. 378.

50.   "Plot" (*t'o-tao chi*). Here this expression is used as a general term for
      any evil plot. Originally, however, it signified a stratagem in combat
      with which, by "dragging the sword" (*t'o-tao*) and withdrawing in
      feigned defeat, one caught the opponent off guard. With this meaning,
      it appears frequently in battle scenes in Lo Kuan-chung's *San-kuo chih
      t'ung-su yen-i* (tr. C. H. Brewitt-Taylor as *The Romance of the Three
      Kingdoms*).

51.   In this song, the first syllable of each line is to be sung three times in
      succession. I have chosen not to attempt to reproduce this effect in
      English.

BIBLIOGRAPHY

A Dictionary of Chinese Buddhist Terms, comp. William Edward
 Soothill, Lewis Hodous, revised by Sheng-kang 聖剛 , Li
 Wu-chung 李武忠 , Tseng Lai-ting 曾萊烶. Taipei,
 1962. Reprint of London, 1937, ed.
Aoki Masaru 青木正兒 . *Genjin zatsugeki* 元人雜劇 .
 Tokyo, 1957.

Bukkyō daijiten 佛教大辭典 , ed. Mochizuki Shinkō
 望月信亨 . 4th ed. Tokyo, 1967.

Chai Hao 翟灝 . *T'ung-su pien* 通俗編 . Wu-pu-i-chai 無不
 宜齋 ed. Preface 1751.
Ch'an-hua-an ts'ung-shu 懺花盦叢書 , comp. Sung Tse-yuan
 宋澤元 . 1887.
Chang Hsiang 張相 . *Shih tz'u ch'ü yü-tz'u hui-shih* 詩詞曲
 語辭匯釋 . Shanghai, 1954. Hong Kong, 1962, ed.
Chang Hsin-ch'eng 張心澂 . *Wei-shu t'ung-k'ao* 偽書通考 .
 Shanghai, 1939. Shanghai, 1957, ed.
Ch'ang-sun Wu-chi 長孫無忌 et al. *Sui shu* 隋書 . *Erh-shih-
 wu shih,* III.
Chao Ching-shen 趙景深 . "T'an Ming Ch'eng-hua k'an-pen
 'shuo-ch'ang tz'u-hua'" 談明成化刊本「說唱詞話」,
 Wen-wu 文物 198:19–22 (November 1972).
Chao Ling-chih 趙令時 . *Hou ch'ing lu* 侯鯖錄 . *Ta-kuan*
 ed., IV.
Chao Yen-wei 趙彥衛 . *Yun-lu man-ch'ao* 雲麓漫鈔 .
 Preface 1206. *Ts'ung-shu chi-ch'eng ch'u-pien* ed. Shanghai,
 1936.
Chavannes, Edouard. *Le T'ai Chan.* Paris, 1910.

218

Cheng Chen-to 鄭振鐸 . *Chung-kuo wen-hsueh yen-chiu* 中
國文學研究 . Peking, 1957. Hong Kong, 1961, ed.

———"Lun pei-ch'ü ti hsieh-tzu" 論北曲的楔子 , in Cheng
Chen-to, *Chung-kuo wen-hsueh yen-chiu*, II, 578–595.

———"Yuan-tai 'kung-an chü' ch'an-sheng ti yuan-yin chi ch'i t'e-
chih" 元代'公案劇'產生的原因及其特質 ,
in Cheng Chen-to, *Chung-kuo wen-hsueh yen-chiu*, II, 511–
534.

Cheng K'o 鄭克 . *Che-yü kuei-chien* 折獄龜鑑. *Mo-hai
chin-hu* ed.

Ch'eng Hao 程顥 and Ch'eng I 程頤 . *Erh Ch'eng ch'üan-shu*
二程全書 . *Ssu-pu pei-yao* ed.

———*Erh Ch'eng i-shu* 二程遺書 , in Ch'eng Hao and Ch'eng
I, *Erh Ch'eng ch'üan-shu*.

Chiao-ting Yuan-k'an tsa-chü san-shih-chung 校訂元刊雜
劇三十種 , collated by Cheng Ch'ien 鄭騫 . Taipei,
1962.

Chieh-yueh-shan-fang hui-ch'ao 借月山房彙鈔 , comp.
Chang Hai-p'eng 張海鵬. Preface 1812.

Ch'ien Ta-hsin 錢大昕 . *Heng-yen lu* 恆言錄 . *Ts'ung-shu
chi-ch'eng ch'u-pien* ed. Changsha, 1939.

Ch'ing-p'ing-shan-t'ang hua-pen 清平山堂話本 , ed. Hung
Pien 洪楩 . Peking, 1955, ed.

Ch'oe Se-jin 崔世珍 . *Pak T'ong-sa on-hae* 朴通事諺解.
Keijō, 1943, ed.

Chou hsien t'i-kang 州縣提綱 . Anon. *Hsueh-chin t'ao-yuan*
ed., *chi* 集 8.

Chou Mi 周密 . *Ch'i-tung yeh-yü* 齊東野語 . *Hsueh-chin
t'ao-yuan* ed., *chi* 14.

———*Hao-jan-chai ya-t'an* 浩然齋雅談 , in *Ch'an-hua-an
ts'ung-shu*.

——— *Kuei-hsin tsa-chih* 癸辛雜識. *Hsueh-chin t'ao-yuan* ed., *chi* 19.

Chu Chü-i 朱居易. *Yuan-chü su-yü fang-yen li-shih* 元劇俗語方言例釋. Shanghai, 1956.

Chu Ch'üan 朱權. *T'ai-ho cheng-yin p'u* 太和正音譜. Printed 1398. *CKKT* ed., III.

Chu Kuo-chen 朱國禎. *Yung-ch'uang hsiao-p'in* 湧幢小品. Preface 1619. *Ta-kuan* ed., VIII.

Chu Tung-jun 朱東潤, "Shuo ya-nei" 說衙內, *Wen-hsueh tsa-chih* 文學雜誌, 1.4:23–33 (August 1937).

Ch'üan Sung tz'u 全宋詞. Ed. T'ang Kuei-chang 唐圭璋. Rev. ed., Peking, 1965.

Ch'üan Yuan san-ch'ü 全元散曲, ed. Sui Shu-shen 隋樹森. Peking, 1964.

Ch'üan Yuan tsa-chü ch'u-pien (I), *erh-pien* (II), *san-pien* (III), *wai-pien* (IV) 全元雜劇初編, 二編, 三編, 外編, ed. Yang Chia-lo 楊家駱. Taipei, 1962, 1963.

Chung-kuo ku-tien hsi-ch'ü lun-chu chi-ch'eng 中國古典戲曲論著集成, ed. Chung-kuo Chü-ch'ü Yen-chiu-yuan 中國劇曲研究院. Peking, 1959, 1960.

Chung Ssu-ch'eng 鍾嗣成. *Hsin-pien lu-kuei pu* 新編錄鬼簿. *CKKT* ed., II.

——— *Lu-kuei pu* 錄鬼簿 ed. Ma Lien 馬廉. Peking, 1957.

——— et al. *Lu-kuei pu (wai ssu chung)* 錄鬼簿 (外四種), ed. Chung-hua Shu-chü Shang-hai Pien-chi-so 中華書局上海編輯所. Peking, 1959.

Erh-shih-wu shih 二十五史, ed. *Erh-shih-wu shih* K'an-hsing Wei-yuan-hui 二十五史刊行委員會. Shanghai, 1935.

Fan Yeh 范曄 . *Hou-Han shu* 後漢書 , annotated by Li Hsien 李賢 in *Erh-shih-wu shih*, I.

Fu Hsi-hua 傅惜華 . *Yuan-tai tsa-chü ch'üan-mu* 元代雜劇全目 . Peking, 1957.

"The Ghost of the Pot," tr. George A. Hayden. *Renditions: A Chinese-English Translation Magazine*, no. 4:31–52 (Autumn 1975).

Hanan, Patrick. "The Development of Fiction and Drama," in *The Legacy of China*, pp. 115–143.

———"The Early Chinese Short Story: A Critical Theory in Outline," *Harvard Journal of Asiatic Studies* 27:168–207 (1967).

Hayden, George A. "The Courtroom Plays of the Yuan and Early Ming Periods," *Harvard Journal of Asiatic Studies* 34:192–220 (1974).

———"The Judge Pao Plays of the Yuan Dynasty," Ph.D. dissertation, Stanford University, 1971.

———"The Legend of Judge Pao: From the Beginnings through the Yuan Drama," *Studia Asiatica*, pp. 339–355.

"Ho-t'ung wen-tzu chi" 合同文字記 , *Ch'ing-p'ing-shan-t'ang hua-pen.*

Hsiao-shuo tz'u-yü hui-shih 小說詞語匯釋 ed. Lu Tan-an 陸澹安 . Shanghai, 1964.

Hsin-chüan Ku-chin ming-chü, Lei Chiang chi 新鐫古今名劇酹江集 , ed. Meng Ch'eng-shun 孟稱舜 and Liu Ch'i-yin 劉啟胤 . *Ku-chin ming-chü ho-hsuan.*

Hsu Shuo-fang 徐朔方 . "Yuan-ch'ü chung ti Pao kung hsi" 元曲中的包公戲 , *Wen shih che* 文史哲 , no. 9:14–17 (1955).

Hsu Wei 徐渭 . *Nan-tz'u hsu-lu* 南詞敍錄 . *CKKT* ed., III.

Hsueh-chin t'ao-yuan 學津討原 , comp. Chang Hai-p'eng
張海鵬 . Chao-k'uang-ko 照曠閣 ed., 1805.

Hu Chi 胡忌 . *Sung Chin tsa-chü k'ao* 宋金雜劇考
Peking, 1959.

"Hua Lien" 華蓮 (pseud.). "Yuan-jen tsa-chü chung ti Pao Lung-
t'u" 元人雜劇中的包龍圖 , *Lien-ho pao* 聯合
報 (September 9, 10, 11, 1974), p. 12 (all eds.).

Hung Mai 洪邁 . *I Chien chih* 夷堅志 . Textual notes by
Chang Yuan-chi 張元濟 . Shanghai, 1927.

Ikeda Takeo 池田武雄 . "Genjidai kōgo no kaishi ni tsuite"
元時代口語の介詞について , *Ritsumeikan
bungaku* 立命館文學 , no. 180:170–189 (1960).

Iwaki Hideo 岩城秀夫 . *Chūgoku gikyoku engeki kenkyū*
中國戲曲演劇研究 . Tokyo, 1972.

———"Gen zatsugeki no kōsei ni kansuru kiso gainen no saikentō
元雜劇の構成に關する基礎概念の再檢討 ,
in Iwaki Hideo, *Chūgoku gikyoku engeki kenkyū*, pp. 486–
515.

Kao Ming 高明 . *P'i-p'a chi* 琵琶記 , collated and annotated
by Ch'ien Nan-yang 錢南揚 . Peking, 1965.

Kenkyusha's New Japanese-English Dictionary, ed. Katsumata
Senkichirō. Original ed., Tokyo, 1954.

"Kōchū Ryū Chi-en shokyūchō" 校注劉知遠諸宮調 ,
ed. Uchida Michio 内田道夫 et al., *Tōhoku Daigaku
Bungakubu nempō* 東北大學文學部年報 , no.
14:240–323 (1964).

Koyanagi Shigeo 小柳司氣太 . *Hakuunkan shi, Tōgakubyō
shi* 白雲觀志 , 東嶽廟志 . Tokyo, 1934.

222

Kracke, E. A. Jr. *Translation of Sung Civil Service Titles.* Paris, 1957.

Ku-chin ming-chü ho-hsuan 古今名劇合選 , comp. Meng Ch'eng-shun 孟稱舜 . Forty-two plays in *KPHCTK* IV. Thirty-two plays in *CYTC* I-III.

Ku-chin tsa-chü hsuan 古今雜劇選, comp. "Hsi-chi Tzu" 息機子 (pseud.). Eleven plays in *KPHCTK* IV. Twenty-three plays in *MWK.* Twenty plays in *CYTC* I-III.

Ku ming-chia tsa-chü 古名家雜劇 , comp. Ch'en Yü-chiao 陳與郊 . Ten plays in *KPHCTK* IV. Fifty-three plays in *MWK.* Thirty-six plays in *CYTC* I-III. Twenty-seven plays in *Yuan Ming tsa-chü.*

Ku-pen hsi-ch'ü ts'ung-k'an (KPHCTK) ch'u-chi (I), *erh-chi* (II), *ssu-chi* (IV) 古本戲曲叢刊初集 , 二集, 四集, comp. *Ku-pen Hsi-ch'ü T'sung-k'an* Pien-k'an Wei-yuan-hui 古本戲曲叢刊編刊委員會 I, Peking, 1953. II, Shanghai, 1955. IV, Shanghai, 1958.

Kuan Han-ch'ing. "T'i ch'ing" 題情 , *CYSC,* I, 156.

Kuei Wan-jung 桂萬榮 . *T'ang-yin pi-shih* 棠陰比事 . Fac. of Yuan hand-copied ed. *SPTK, Tzu-pu.*

Kuei Wan-jung. *T'ang-yin pi-shih, Parallel Cases from under the Peartree; a 13th Century Manual of Jurisprudence and Detection,* ed. and tr. Robert Hans van Gulik. Leiden, 1956.

"Kuo-shih pen-chuan" 國史本傳 . Pao Cheng, *Pao Hsiao-su-kung tsou-i,* pp. 1a–3a.

Kyōto daigaku jimbunkagaku kenkyūjo 京都大學人文科學研究所 . *Yuan-ch'ü hsuan shih* 元曲選釋 . I, Kyoto, 1951. II, Kyoto, 1952.

The Legacy of China, ed. Raymond Dawson. London, Oxford, New York, 1971, from the Clarendon Press, 1964 ed.

Li Ch'ang-ling 李昌齡 (Sung). *T'ai-shang kan-ying p'ien* 太上

感應篇 . *Tao-tsang, T'ai-ch'ing pu* 太清部 . *Tao-tsang* 道藏 . Shanghai, 1923–1926.

Li Fang 李昉 et al. *T'ai-p'ing kuang-chi* 太平廣記 . *Ta-kuan hsu-pien* ed., II–V.

Li-hsueh chih-nan 吏學指南 (*Chü-chia pi-yung shih-lei ch'üan-chi hsin chi* 居家必用事類全集辛集 , 15). Anon. Index by Ikeda Sei 池田誠 and Iwami Hiro 岩見宏 . Reprint of Ming printed ed., preface 1560. Kyoto, 1951.

Li T'ao 李燾 . *Hsu tzu-chih t'ung-chien ch'ang-pien* 續資治通鑑長編 . Submitted 1169. Hangchow, 1881, ed. Supplemented by Ch'in Hsiang-yeh 秦緗業 , 1883.

Liang T'ung-shu 梁同書 . *Chih-yü pu-cheng* 直語補證 , in Liang T'ung-shu, *P'in-lo-an i-chi*.

———*P'in-lo-an i-chi* 頻羅庵遺集 , in Liang T'ung-shu, Liang Yü-sheng, Liang Lü-sheng, *Liang-shih ts'ung-shu*.

———, Liang Yü-sheng 梁玉繩 , and Liang Lü-sheng 梁履繩 . *Liang-shih ts'ung-shu* 梁氏叢書 . N.p., ca. 1796–1821.

Liu Chih-yuan chu-kung-tiao 劉知遠諸宮調 . See "Kōchū Ryū Chi-en shokyūchō."

Liu I-ch'ing 劉義慶 . *Yu-ming lu* 幽明錄 , in Li Fang et al., *T'ai-p'ing kuang-chi*.

Liu Ts'un-yan. *Buddhist and Taoist Influences on Chinese Novels, I, The Authorship of the Feng Shen Yen I*. Wiesbaden, 1962.

Lu-kuei pu hsu-pien 錄鬼簿續編 . Anon. *CKKT* ed., II.

"*Lu kuei pu t'i-yao*" 錄鬼簿提要 . *CKKT*, II, 96–98.

Ma Yau-woon. "The Pao-kung Tradition in Chinese Popular Literature." Ph.D. dissertation, Yale University, 1971.

Meng Kung 孟珙 . *Meng-ta pei-lu* 蒙韃備錄 . *Ts'ung-*

Mo-wang kuan ch'ao-chiao-pen ku-chü 脈望館鈔校本 古今雜劇 , transcribed and collated by Chao Ch'i-mei 趙琦美 ("Mo-wang-kuan" pseud.). Two hundred and forty-two plays in *KPHCTK IV.* One hundred and sixty-five plays in *CYTC I–IV.*

Ou-yang Hsiu 歐陽修 . "Lun Pao Cheng ch'u San-ssu-shih shang-shu" 論包拯除三司使上書 , in Ou-yang Hsiu, *Ou-yang Wen-chung-kung chi*, 111.13b–17a.
——— *Ou-yang Wen-chung-kung chi* 歐陽文忠公集 . Fac. of Yuan printed ed. *Ssu-pu ts'ung-k'an, chi-pu,* 集部.

Pan Ku 班固 . *Han shu* 漢書 . *Erh-shih-wu shih* ed., I.
Pao Cheng 包拯 . *Pao Hsiao-su-kung tsou-i* 包孝肅公奏 議 (*Tsou-i*), comp. Chang T'ien 張田 , 1065, ed. Li Han-chang 李瀚章 . *Hsing-hsin-ko* 省心閣 ed., 1863. Fac. ed., Taipei, 1960.
P'eng Ch'eng 彭乘 . *Mo-k'o hui-hsi* 墨客揮犀 . *Takuan* ed., I.
Pi-chi hsiao-shuo ta-kuan 筆記小說大觀 (*Ta-kuan*), comp. anon. Wen-ming 文明 ed. Fac. ed., Taipei, 1960.
Pi-chi hsiao-shuo ta-kuan hsu-pien 筆記小說大觀續編 (*Ta-kuan hsu-pien*), comp. anon. Wen-ming ed. Fac. ed., Taipei, 1962.

Shen Kua 沈括 . *Meng-hsi pi-t'an chiao-cheng* 夢溪筆談 校證. Annotated by Hu Tao-ching 胡道靜 . Shanghai, 1956, ed.
Shih Nai-an 施耐菴 and Lo Kuan-chung 羅貫中 . *Shui-hu ch'üan-chuan* 水滸全傳 . Peking, 1954. Hong Kong, 1965, ed.
Shuo-fu 說郛 , comp. T'ao Tsung-i 陶宗儀 . 1) Han-fen-lou 涵芬樓 ed., one hundred *chüan*, Shanghai, 1927. 2) Ming printed ed., re-collated by an anon. Ming editor, one hundred and twenty *chüan*.

Ssu-ma Ch'ien 司馬遷 . *Shih-chi* 史記. *Erh-shih-wu shih*, I.

Ssu-ma Kuang 司馬光 . *Su-shui chi-wen* 涑水記聞 . Shanghai, 1936, ed.

Ssu-pu pei-yao 四部備要 , ed. Chung Hwa Book Company, Shanghai, 1936.

Ssu-pu ts'ung-k'an 四部叢刊 , comp. Chang Yuan-chi 張元濟 et al. Shanghai, 1929.

Stimson, Hugh M. *The Jongyuan in yunn: A Guide to Old Mandarin Pronunciation.* New Haven, 1966.

Studia Asiatica: Essays in Felicitation of the Seventy-fifth Anniversary of Professor Ch'en Shou-yi, ed. Laurence G. Thompson. Chinese Materials and Research Aids Service Center Occasional Series No. 29. San Francisco, 1975.

Sun K'ai-ti 孫楷第 . *Ts'ang-chou chi* 滄州集 . Peking, 1965.

———"Yuan-ch'ü hsin k'ao," 元曲新考 in Sun K'ai-ti, *Ts'ang-chou chi,* II, 317–328.

Sung hui-yao chi-kao 宋會要輯稿 . Written 1030–1236, comp. Hsu Sung 徐松 (1781–1848). Peiping, 1936.

Sung Liao Chin Yuan ssu shih 宋遼金元四史 , comp. Hsi Shih-ch'en 席世臣 . Sao-yeh-shan-fang 掃葉山房 ed. Preface 1798.

Sung Lien 宋濂 et al. *Yuan shih* 元史 . *Erh-shih-wu shih* ed., VIII.

Sung pai lei-ch'ao 宋稗類鈔 , comp. P'an Yung-yin 潘永因 . Preface 1669.

Sung Yuan hsi-wen chi-i 宋元戲文輯佚 , comp. Ch'ien Nan-yang 錢南揚 . Shanghai, 1956.

Ta-Yuan sheng-cheng kuo-ch'ao tien-chang 大元聖政國朝典章 (*Yuan tien-chang*). Anon., ed. Shen Chia-pen 沈家本 . Soochow, 1908. Fac. ed., Taipei, 1964.

T'an Cheng-pi 譚正璧 , *Hua-pen yü ku-chü* 話本與古劇 . Shanghai, 1956.

T'ao Tsung-i 陶宗儀 . *Ch'o-keng lu* 輟耕錄. 1) Ming,
  Chin-tai mi-shu 津逮祕書 ed., *Ts'ung-shu chi-ch'eng
  ch'u-pien* ed. Shanghai, 1936. 2) Title: *Nan-ts'un ch'o-keng
  lu* 南村輟耕錄 . Fac. of Yuan ed., reprinted by T'ao
  Hsiang 陶湘 , 1923–1925.

T'o-t'o 脫脫 (T'o-k'o-t'o 托克托) et al. *Chin shih* 金史 .
  Erh-shih-wu shih, VII.

——*Sung shih* 宋史 . *Erh-shih-wu shih,* VI, VII.

The Travels of Marco Polo, ed. Manuel Komroff. New York, 1931.

Tseng Kung 曾鞏 . *Lung-p'ing chi* 隆平集 . Ch'i-yeh-t'ang
  七業堂 ed., 1701.

Tseng Min-hsing 曾敏行 . *Tu-hsing tsa-chih* 獨醒雜志 .
  Ta-kuan ed., I.

Tseng Shu 曾紆 . *Nan-yu chi-chiu* 南遊記舊 , in *Shuo-fu.*
  Shanghai, 1927, ed.

Ts'ung-shu chi-ch'eng ch'u-pien 叢書集成初編 , ed. Wang
  Yun-wu 王雲五 et al. Shanghai, 1935–1937, Changsha,
  1939.

Tu Hsun-ho 杜荀鶴 . "Ch'un-kung yuan" 春宮怨 . *T'ang-
  shih san-pai-shou* 唐詩三百首 .

Urakawa Gengo 浦川源吾 . "Pēpin jōgai Tōgakubyō" 北平城
  外東嶽廟 , *Ritsumeikan bungaku* 立命館文學 ,
  I, ix.

Wang Ch'eng 王稱 (偁). *Tung-tu shih-lueh* 東都事略 .
  Sung Liao Chin Yuan ssu shih ed.

Wang Hsiang-chih 王象之 . *Yü-ti chi-sheng* 輿地紀勝 .
  Supplement comp. Ts'en Chien-kung 岑建功 . Chü-ying-
  chai 懼盈齋 ed., 1849.

Wang Te-hsin 王德信 (T. Shih-fu 實甫). *Hsi-hsiang chi* 西

廂記 . Collated and annotated by Wang Chi-ssu 王季思 .
Shanghai, 1954.

———*Hsi-hsiang chi.* Collated and annotated by Wu Hsiao-ling 吳
曉齡. Peking, 1954.

Wang Ying-k'uei 王應奎 . *Liu-nan hsu-pi* 柳南續筆 .
Chieh-yueh-shan-fang hui-ch'ao ed., *chi* 15.

Wellek, René and Austin Warren. *Theory of Literature.* 3rd ed.
New York, 1962.

Yang Hsuan-chih 楊衒之 . *Lo-yang ch'ieh-lan chi* 洛陽伽
藍記 . *Hsueh-chin t'ao-yuan* ed., *chi* 7.

Yang Yü 楊瑀. *Shan-chü hsin-yü* 山居新語 . *Chih-pu-tsu-
chai ts'ung-shu* 知不足齋叢書

Yen Tun-i 嚴敦易 . *Yuan-chü chen-i* 元劇斟疑 . Peking,
1960.

Ying Shao 應劭 . *Feng-su t'ung-i t'ung-chien* 風俗通儀通
檢 , ed. Chung-Fa Han-hsueh Yen-chiu-so 中法漢學
研究所. Peking, 1943.

Yoshikawa Kōjirō 吉川幸次郎 . *Yuan tsa-chü yen-chiu*
元雜劇研究 . Original ed. in Japanese, Tokyo, 1948,
tr. Cheng Ch'ing-mao 鄭清茂 . Taipei, 1960.

Yuan-ch'ü hsuan 元曲選 , ed. Tsang Chin-shu 臧晉叔 (Mao-
hsun). Prefaces 1615, 1616. Tiao-ch'ung-kuan 雕蟲館 ed.
Peking, 1961, ed.

Yuan Hao-wen 元好問 . *Hsu I Chien chih* 續夷堅志 . *Ta-
kuan* ed., I.

Yuan-jen tsa-chü hsuan 元人雜劇選 , ed. and annotated by
Ku Hsueh-hsieh 顧學頡 . Peking, 1956.

Yuan Ming tsa-chü 元明雜劇 . Reprint of Nanking, 1929, fac.
ed. of twenty-seven plays from an ed. of *KMC* owned by Ting
Ping 丁丙 (1833–1899). Peking, 1958.

Yueh K'o 岳珂 . *K'uei-t'an lu* 愧郯錄 . *Ts'ung-shu chi-*

ch'eng ch'u-pien ed. Changsha, 1939.

Yueh Shih 樂史 . *T'ai-p'ing huan-yü chi* 太平寰宇記 .
  Supplement comp. Ch'en Lan-shen 陳蘭森 . 1803.

Yung-le ta-tien 永樂大典 , ed. Hsieh Chin 解縉 et al.
  Peking, 1959, 1960, ed.

ai-ta-hai 呆打頦
an 俺

cha[a] 詐
cha[b] 貶
ch'a-hun-chiu 茶渾酒
Chang 張
Chang Ch'ien 張千
Chang Liang 張良
Chang Pen 張本
chao 着
Chao Pien 趙卞
chao t'a pao-pu-ch'eng wang-erh 着他包不成網兒
che[a] 折
che[b] 這
ch'en 辰
Ch'en-chou 陳州
chi-ting ke-ta 吉丁疙疸
Ch'i-shih-wu Ssu 七十五寺
Chia-yu 嘉祐
Chieh 桀
chieh-chieh pa-pa 結結巴巴
chien 見
chien ch'ing-t'ien 見青天
Ch'ien 千
Ch'ien-lung 錢龍
Chih hsueh-shih 直學士
ch'ih liang 吃糧

Ch'ih-sung-tzu 赤松子
Chin-luan Hall 金鑾殿
chin-shih 進士
Chin-tou Commandery 金斗郡
ching 淨
ch'ing 請
chiu-wu 酒務
Chou 紂
chu[b] 拄
Chu Hsi 朱熹
chu-kung-tiao 諸宮調
Ch'uan-teng lu 傳燈錄
ch'ü liao t'a ching-shen k'ou-mo 覷了他精神口抹
Ch'ü Yuan 屈原
chüan 卷

Fan Chung-yen 范仲淹
fei tsa t'e-sha 非咱忒煞
Fen-chou 汾州
fen-fu 分付
fen-hsi 分細
fen-mien 粉面
fen-shu 分疏
fen-shuo 分説
fen-t'ou 粉頭
feng-huang 鳳凰
Feng-huang-ch'ih *shang* 丨丨池上

229

Han Ch'i 韓琦
Han Ch'in-hu 韓擒虎
Han Hsin 韓信
Hao-li 蒿里
hsi-ch'a 希詫
hsi-chou 稀粥
Hsi-jen 希仁
hsi-wen 戲文
hsiang[b] 廂
Hsiang-chou 相州
hsiang-kung 相公
Hsiao Ho 蕭和
Hsiao-su-kung 孝肅公
hsieh-tzu 楔子
hsien chan hou wen 先斬後聞
hsien-chün 縣君
hsing[a] 姓
hsing[b] 性
hsing[c] 餳
hsing-hui 省會
hsiu-ts'ai 秀才
Ho Ch'ien 何謙
Ho-fei 合肥
ho-to 喝掇
ho ts'uan-hsiang[a] 喝攛箱
hu-p'u-ta 胡撲搭
hu-t'u 糊塗
Hua-hua T'ai-sui 花花太歲
huan-hsi 歡喜
huan-hsia 歡洽
hui 灰

huo-tuo sha wu-tsang shen 鑊鐸殺五臟神

Jen Tsung 仁宗
Ju-ch'un 如淳

K'ai-feng-fu 開封府
Ko Chien-chün 葛監軍
ko (-ko) 哥丨
k'o-lo 尅落
ku 孤
Ku-chin tsa-chü san-shih-chung 古今雜劇三十種
K'uai T'ung 蒯通
Kuan-chieh pu tao,/Yu Yen-lo Pao-lao 關節不到,/有閻羅包老
Kuan Lung-feng 關龍逢
kung-an 公案

lan-kua 爛瓜
Lao-erh Hamlet 老兒村
(lao) hsiang-kung (老)相公
lao-yeh 老爺
Li-pu Shang-shu 禮部尚書
Li-pu Shih-lang 禮部侍郎
liang 量
liao 了
Liao Hua 蓼花
lien-fang-shih 廉訪使
liu-hsia 流霞
liu-liao pu shou 六料不收

lo^c 攞
lo^d 捋
lo^a-*chieh-chou* 落解粥
lo^b-*ho-chou* 酪和粥
lo-hsiu hsuan-ch'üan
  攞袖揎拳
Lo River 洛河
Lord Liu 劉衙內
lu 路
Lu-chou 廬州
Lü-chou 呂州
Lü I-chien 呂夷簡
"Lung-t'u" 龍圖
Lung-t'u kung-an
  龍圖公案
ma-de 媽的
mao 卯
mei nan mien pei 眉南面北
men^a 們
men^b 悶
ming-ch'a 明察
Mt. T'ai 泰山
mu-tan 牡丹

Na-cha 那吒
na-ssu 那廝
Nan-ya 南衙
nao-erh-chiu 腦兒酒
niang 娘
"Not clothing (but) two handfuls of fire" 非衣兩把火

o-t'ou-erh 惡頭兒
Pa Hsien 八仙
p'a-pu 怕不
p'a-pu-tai 怕不待
p'a yeh pu p'a 怕也不怕
p'an Nan-ya 判南衙
pang-lao 邦老
Pao 包
pao^a 傅
pao^b 炮
pao-an shih-shih yung k'ai-k'ou
  飽諳世事慵開口
Pao Cheng 包拯
pei-ch'ü 北曲
pei-t'ing pan 碑亭般
P'ei Yen 裴炎
Pi Kan 比干
p'i-liu-p'u-la 劈溜撲剌
pieh-ku 憋古
pieh-lieh 憋岁
Pien-ching 汴京
Pien-liang 汴梁
po^a 博
po^b 搏
pu-lieh fang-t'ou 不劣方頭

sa-man 撒鏝
san-ch'ü 散曲
san hun 三魂
San-kuo chih t'ung-su yen-i
  三國志通俗演義

san tung wen shih tsu yung
三冬文史足用

shao-yao 芍藥

she-liang chün 射糧軍

shen 參

Shen T'u 神荼

sheng-chin 生金

shih[a] 石

shih[b] 誓

shih[c] 食

shih-chien chin-p'ai
勢劍金牌

*Shih-nien ch'uang-hsia wu jen
wen,/i-chü ch'eng-ming
t'ien-hsia chih* 十年窗下
無人問,/一舉成名天
下知

*shih-nien shen tao Feng-huang-
ch'ih* 十年身到鳳凰池

shou p'u-lan pa tou
收蒲籃罷斗

shu-chang 束杖

shuo-ch'ang tz'u-hua
說唱詞話

shuo-sui 搠碎

shuo-te-chao 說得着

shuo-te-lai 說得來

Su-cheng lien-fang shih
肅政廉訪使

Sun K'ang 孫康

Sung Chiang 宋江

Ta-fo-ting shou-leng-yen ching
大佛頂首楞嚴經

ta-jen 大人

ta-ku-li 大古裏

ta t'a niang 打他娘

ta-yeh 大爺

t'a 他

tai-chih 待制

T'ai-an-fu 泰安府

t'ai-chün 太郡

t'ai-p'u 太僕

T'ai-shang kan-ying p'ien
太上感應篇

T'ang-shih san-pai-shou
唐詩三百首

tao 道

te 得

teng 等

ti 的

t'i 踢

t'ieh-mien 鐵面

T'ien-chang Pavilion 天章閣

to-yin-shih 多因是

to-ying-shih 多應是

t'o-tao chi 拖刀計

tou-ch'eng 斗秤

tou-tzu 斗子

t'ou[a] 投

t'ou-nao-chiu 頭腦酒

t'ou-shao 頭梢

tsa 咱

tsa-chü 雜劇

tsai-t'ao 在逃
tsan 偺
tse che 則這
tso i-ko pao chien kun
　　做一箇煿煎滾
tso liang-shih chia
　　做兩世家
tsou 奏
tsu 阻
tsung-chih 總之
tui-t'ou 對頭
t'ui-chu[a] 推主
tun 墩
Tung-yueh Su-pao-ssu
　　東嶽速報司
tzu-chin 紫金

wai 外
"Wan" 萬
Wang Ch'iao 王喬
Wang-tzu Ch'iao 王子喬
wen shih san-tung tsu
　　文史三冬足
wo 我
wo yang-che chia-sheng shao-li
　　我養着家生哨裏

wu-ch'ang 無常
Wu Chung-fu 吳仲夫
wu liang pai-yin i shih hsi-mi
　　五兩白銀一石細米
Wu-nan 五南
wu-tui 無對
wu-tui-t'ou kung-an
　　無對頭公案
wu-t'ung shu 梧桐樹
Wu-ya Tu-shou-ling
　　五衙都首領
wu-yen lü-shih
　　五言律詩
ya-men 衙門
ya-nei 衙內
Yang 楊
yang 羊
yeh-yeh 爺爺
yu 酉
yu-t'ou 油頭
yü 與
Yü Lü 欝壘
　yü wo 與我
Yuan Hao-wen 元好問
　yuan-pen 院本
Yung-le 永樂

GLOSSARY OF MODE TITLES

Cheng-kung 正宮　　　　　　Nan-lü 南呂

Chung-lü 中呂　　　　　　　Shuang-tiao 雙調

Hsien-lü 仙呂　　　　　　　Yueh-tiao 越調

GLOSSARY OF MELODY TITLES

Ai ku to 呆骨朵

Chai-erh ling 寨兒令

Ch'ao T'ien-tzu 朝天子

Ch'en-tsui tung-feng
　　沉醉東風

Chi sheng-ts'ao 寄生草

Chin chan-erh 金盞兒

Ch'ing-ko-erh 青哥兒

Ch'ing yuan-chen 慶元貞

Chu-ma t'ing 駐馬聽

Ch'uan po chao 川撥棹

Ch'ueh t'a chih 鵲踏枝

Erh-sha 二煞

Fen tieh-erh 粉蝶兒

Feng ju sung 風入松

Ho hsin-lang 賀新郎

Hou-t'ing hua (p'o-tzu)
　　後庭花(破子)

Hsiao ho-shang 小和尚

Hsiao Liang-chou 小梁州

Hsiao t'ao hung 小桃紅

Hsin shui ling 新水令

Hsiu-tai-erh 繡帶兒

Hu shih-pa 胡十八

Huang ch'iang-wei 黃薔薇

Huang-chung (sha-) wei
　　黃鍾(煞)尾

Hun chiang lung 混江龍

Hung hsiu-hsieh 紅繡鞋

I-chih hua 一枝花

I-pan-erh 一半兒

I-sha 一煞

Kan ho-yeh 乾荷葉

Ko-wei 隔尾

Ku mei-chiu 沽美酒

K'u huang-t'ien 哭皇天

Kua yü-kou 掛玉鈎

K'uai-huo san 快活三

Kuei san t'ai 鬼三台

Kun hsiu-ch'iu 滾繡球

Liang-chou (ti-ch'i) 梁州(第七)

Lu-yao hsu 六么序

Ma lang-erh 麻郎兒

Man-ching-ts'ai 蔓菁菜

234

Man t'ing fang 滿庭芳

Mu-yang-kuan 牧羊關

Na-cha ling 那吒令

Pan tu-shu 伴讀書

Sha-wei 煞尾

Shang hsiao-lou 上小樓

Shang hua shih 賞花時

Shang ma chiao 上馬嬌

Sheng hu-lu 勝葫蘆

Sheng Yao-wang 聖藥王

Shou-wei 收尾

Shua hai-erh 耍孩兒

Shui hsien-tzu 水仙子

Ssu-pien ching 四邊靜

T'ai-p'ing ling 太平令

T'ang hsiu-ts'ai 倘秀才

Tao-tao ling 叨叨令

Te-sheng ling 得勝令

T'i yin-teng 剔銀燈

T'iao-hsiao ling 挑笑令

Tien chiang-ch'un 點絳唇

Tien-ch'ien huan 殿前歡

T'ien ching sha 天淨沙

T'ien-hsia le 天下樂

T'o pu-shan 脫布衫

Tou an-ch'un 鬥鵪鶉

Tou ha-ma 鬥蝦蟆

Tsuan sha(-wei) 賺煞尾

Tsui ch'un-feng 醉春風

Tsui chung-t'ien 醉中天

Tsui kao ko 醉高歌

Ts'un-li ya-ku 村裏迓鼓

T'u ssu-erh 禿廝兒

Tuan-cheng hao 端正好

Tzu hua-erh hsu 紫花兒序

Wei 尾

Wei-sha 尾煞

Wei-sheng 尾聲

Wu-yeh t'i 烏夜啼

Yeh hsing ch'uan 夜行船

Yen-erh lo 雁兒落

Ying hsien-k'o 迎仙客

Yu hu-lu 油葫蘆

Yuan-ho ling 元和令

Yuan-yang sha 鴛鴦煞

GLOSSARY OF PLAY TITLES

Ch'en-chou t'iao mi
陳州糶米

Ch'ieh k'uai tan 切鱠旦

Chien-fu pei 薦福碑

Chin feng-ch'ai 金鳳釵

Chiu hsiao-tzu 救孝子

Chu-sha tan 硃砂擔

Ch'ü-chiang-ch'ih 曲江池

Fan Chang chi shu 范張雞黍

Fei i meng 緋衣夢

Feng Yü-lan 馮玉蘭

Fu-ou chi 浮漚記

Han-kung ch'iu 漢宮秋

Ho han-shan 合汗衫

Ho-t'ung wen-tzu 合同文字

Hou-t'ing hua 後庭花

Hsiao Sun T'u 小孫屠

Hu-tieh meng 蝴蝶夢

Huan lao mo 還牢末

Huan-men tzu-ti ts'o li-shen
宦門子弟錯立身

Hui-lan chi 灰欄記

Jen chin-shu 認金梳

Jen-tzu chi 忍字記

K'an chin-huan 勘金環

K'an t'ou-chin 勘頭巾

K'u-han-t'ing 酷寒亭

Li K'uei fu ching
李逵負荊

Liu hsieh chi 留鞋記

Lu Chai-lang 魯齋郎

Mo-ho-lo 魔合羅

Pao chuang-ho 抱粧盒

P'en-erh kuei 盆兒鬼

P'i-p'a chi 琵琶記

Pu jen shih 不認屍

Sha kou ch'üan fu 殺狗勸夫

Shen-nu-erh 神奴兒

Sheng-chin ko 生金閣

Shih t'an-tzu 十探子

T'ao-fu chi 桃符記

T'i sha ch'i 替殺妻

T'ieh-kuai Li 鐵拐李

Tou O yuan 竇娥冤

Ts'ui Fu-chün tuan yuan-chia
chai-chu 崔府君斷冤
家債主

Ts'un-le-t'ang 村樂堂

Wan-chiang-t'ing 翫江亭

Wang-chiang-t'ing 望江亭

Yen-an-fu 延安府

Yen-chih chi 胭脂記

Yuan-chia chai-chu 冤家債主

Yuan Wen-cheng huan-hun chi
袁文正還魂記

Yuan-yang pei 鴛鴦被

Yueh-yang-lou 岳陽樓

GLOSSARY OF DRAMATISTS

Chang Kuo-pin 張國賓

Cheng T'ing-yü 鄭廷玉

"Hsin-hsin k'o" 欣欣客

Kuan Han-ch'ing 關漢卿

Li Ch'ien-fu 李潛夫

Lu Teng-shan 陸登善

Ma Chih-yuan 馬致遠

Meng Han-ch'ing 孟漢卿

Shen Ching 沈璟

Wang Chung-wen 王仲文

Wu Han-ch'en 武漢臣

INDEX

Act. *See* Sequence, Song

Badge, golden, 6, 25, 202 n.34
Blade, bronze, 6, 25, 114 n
Butterfly Dream (Hu-tieh meng, by
   Kuan Han-ch'ing), 24–26

Category, literary, 3
Chalk Circle (Hui-lan chi, by Li
   Ch'ien-fu), 23–25
Character, dramatic, 2; as singer, 9;
   stylization of, 24, 25
Che-yü kuei-chien (Guide to the
   solution of crime cases, by Cheng
   K'o), 5
Ch'en-chou t'iao mi (Selling rice at
   Ch'en-chou), 24–26, 29–78, 81
Cheng K'o *(Che-yü kuei-chien),* 5
Cheng T'ing-yü *(Hou-t'ing hua),* 127
Clerk, courtroom, 6, 18, 19, 25.
   See also Detective
Contract (Ho-T'ung wen-tzu), 25
Court of Prompt Retribution, 21, 22
Courtroom, 6, 19
Courtroom drama, 2–15, 23; atmos-
   phere of, 2, 3; ingredients of, 3;
   in contrast with "whodunits," 3,
   4; as attack against Mongols, 5;
   philosophical implications of,
   11–15
Courtroom procedure. *See* Jurispru-
   dence
Courtroom scene, 6–8
Crime, 3, 4, 11, 14, 23, 24
Crimecase drama. *See* Courtroom
   drama

Criminal, 4, 11, 13, 24–26; as member of privileged class, 5, 26

Desire, 12, 13
Detection, 3
Detective, 5, 15, 24. *See also* Pao
   Cheng
Dream of judge, 10, 11

*Flower of the Back Courtyard (Hou-
   t'ing hua,* by Cheng T'ing-yü),
   4, 9, 12, 25

Ghost of the Pot (P'en-erh kuei), 4,
   10, 22, 23
Ghost of victim, 10

Han Ch'in-hu, 21
Ho-t'ung wen-tzu (Contract), 25
Hou-t'ing hua (Flower of the back
   courtyard, by Cheng T'ing-yü),
   4, 9, 12, 25
Hsiao Sun T'u (Young Butcher Sun),
   22
Hu-tieh meng (Butterfly dream, by
   Kuan Han-ch'ing), 24–26
Hui-lan chi (Chalk circle, by Li
   Ch'ien-fu), 23–25

Judge. *See* Detective
Judge Pao. *See* Pao Cheng
Judge Pao plays, 23. *See also* Court-
   room drama; Pao Cheng
Jurisprudence, 4, 25, 26, 202 n.35
Justice, 3, 5, 11, 12, 24, 26

K'ai-feng Tribunal, 14, 18–20, 22, 23

Kung-an. *See* Courtroom drama

Law, 3, 6. *See also* Jurisprudence
Liu hsieh chi (Sign of the slipper), 24, 25
Lu Chai-lang, 25, 26
Lung-t'u kung-an (Crime cases of the Lung-t'u judge), 16, 26

Ming drama, 15
Mirror as metaphor for wisdom, 13
Mistrial: with evil judge, 6; with honest judge, 7, 8
Mongols, 5
Murder, 4, 23

Neo-Confucianism, 11–13
Northern drama: structure of, 1; number of plays of, 2; probable origins of, 187 n.1; texts of, 187, n.2, 188 n.4

Pao Cheng (Judge Pao), 16–27; as detective, 8–13, 24–27; as Sung minister, 17; personality of, 17, 18; and humor, 17–19, 25; as magistrate, 18–20; in opposition to courtroom clerks, 18, 19, 24; in opposition to privileged criminals, 19, 23, 24, 26; as judge of dead souls, 20–23; special powers of, 25, 26; cosmological role of, 26; in post-Yuan literature, 26, 27
P'en-erh kuei (Ghost of the pot), 4, 10, 22, 23
Punishment, 3, 23, 25, 26

Selling Rice at Ch'en-chou (Ch'en-chou t'iao mi), 24–26, 81
Sequence, song, 1, 8, 9
Set, song. *See* Sequence, song
Shen Ching (*T'ao-fu chi*), 127
Shen-nu-erh, 24
Sheng-chin ko (Tower of fine gold), 25, 26
Sign of the Slipper (*Liu hsieh chi*), 24, 25
Sub-genre, 3
Sui shu (Book of the Sui dynasty), 21
Sung shih (History of the Sung dynasty), 18, 19
Sword of authority (sword of execution), 6, 25, 202 n.34

T'ai, Mt., 14, 20–22, 26
T'ao-fu chi (Shen Ching), 127
Tower of Fine Gold (*Sheng-chin ko*), 25, 26
Tribunal. *See* Courtroom
Tsa-chü: definition of, 1. *See also* Northern drama

Variety drama. *See* Northern drama
Victim: of crime, 5, 24; of tribunal, 6, 8, 24

Yama, King (King of Hell), 14, 18 21, 26
Yuan-ch'ü hsuan (Anthology of Yuan drama), 32, 82, 128, 182
Yuan dynasty, 5
Yuan Hao-wen, 20, 21

HARVARD EAST ASIAN MONOGRAPHS

1. Liang Fang-chung, *The Single-Whip Method of Taxation in China*

2. Harold C. Hinton, *The Grain Tribute System of China, 1845–1911*

3. Ellsworth C. Carlson, *The Kaiping Mines, 1877–1912*

4. Chao Kuo-chün, *Agrarian Policies of Mainland China: A Documentary Study, 1949–1956*

5. Edgar Snow, *Random Notes on Red China, 1936–1945*

6. Edwin George Beal, Jr., *The Origin of Likin, 1835–1864*

7. Chao Kuo-chün, *Economic Planning and Organization in Mainland China: A Documentary Study, 1949–1957*

8. John K. Fairbank, *Ch'ing Documents: An Introductory Syllabus*

9. Helen Yin and Yi-chang Yin, *Economic Statistics of Mainland China, 1949–1957*

10. Wolfgang Franke, *The Reform and Abolition of the Traditional Chinese Examination System*

11. Albert Feuerwerker ánd S. Cheng, *Chinese Communist Studies of Modern Chinese History*

12. C. John Stanley, *Late Ch'ing Finance: Hu Kuang-yung as an Innovator*

13. S. M. Meng, *The Tsungli Yamen: Its Organization and Functions*

14. Ssu-yü Teng, *Historiography of the Taiping Rebellion*

15. Chun-Jo Liu, *Controversies in Modern Chinese Intellectual History: An Analytic Bibliography of Periodical Articles, Mainly of the May Fourth and Post-May Fourth Era*

16. Edward J. M. Rhoads, *The Chinese Red Army, 1927–1963: An Annotated Bibliography*

17.   Andrew J. Nathan, *A History of the China International Famine Relief Commission*

18.   Frank H. H. King (ed.) and Prescott Clarke, *A Research Guide to China-Coast Newspapers, 1822–1911*

19.   Ellis Joffe, *Party and Army: Professionalism and Political Control in the Chinese Officer Corps, 1949–1964*

20.   Toshio G. Tsukahira, *Feudal Control in Tokugawa Japan: The Sankin Kōtai System*

21.   Kwang-Ching Liu, ed., *American Missionaries in China: Papers from Harvard Seminars*

22.   George Moseley, *A Sino-Soviet Cultural Frontier: The Ili Kazakh Autonomous Chou*

23.   Carl F. Nathan, *Plague Prevention and Politics in Manchuria, 1910–1931*

24.   Adrian Arthur Bennett, *John Fryer: The Introduction of Western Science and Technology into Nineteenth-Century China*

25.   Donald J. Friedman, *The Road from Isolation: The Campaign of the American Committee for Non-Participation in Japanese Aggression, 1938–1941*

26.   Edward Le Fevour, *Western Enterprise in Late Ch'ing China: A Selective Survey of Jardine, Matheson and Company's Operations, 1842–1895*

27.   Charles Neuhauser, *Third World Politics: China and the Afro-Asian People's Solidarity Organization, 1957–1967*

28.   Kungtu C. Sun, assisted by Ralph W. Huenemann, *The Economic Development of Manchuria in the First Half of the Twentieth Century*

29.   Shahid Javed Burki, *A Study of Chinese Communes, 1965*

30.   John Carter Vincent, *The Extraterritorial System in China: Final Phase*

31.   Madeleine Chi, *China Diplomacy, 1914–1918*

32.   Clifton Jackson Phillips, *Protestant America and the Pagan World: The First Half Century of the American Board of Commissioners for Foreign Missions, 1810–1860*

33. James Pusey, *Wu Han: Attacking the Present through the Past*

34. Ying-wan Cheng, *Postal Communication in China and Its Modernization, 1860–1896*

35. Tuvia Blumenthal, *Saving in Postwar Japan*

36. Peter Frost, *The Bakumatsu Currency Crisis*

37. Stephen C. Lockwood, *Augustine Heard and Company, 1858–1862*

38. Robert R. Campbell, *James Duncan Campbell: A Memoir by His Son*

39. Jerome Alan Cohen, ed., *The Dynamics of China's Foreign Relations*

40. V. V. Vishnyakova-Akimova, *Two Years in Revolutionary China, 1925–1927*, tr. Steven I. Levine

41. Meron Medzini, *French Policy in Japan during the Closing Years of the Tokugawa Regime*

42. *The Cultural Revolution in the Provinces*

43. Sidney A. Forsythe, *An American Missionary Community in China, 1895–1905*

44. Benjamin I. Schwartz, ed., *Reflections on the May Fourth Movement: A Symposium*

45. Ching Young Choe, *The Rule of the Taewŏn'gun, 1864–1873: Restoration in Yi Korea*

46. W. P. J. Hall, *A Bibliographical Guide to Japanese Research on the Chinese Economy, 1958–1970*

47. Jack J. Gerson, *Horatio Nelson Lay and Sino-British Relations, 1854–1864*

48. Paul Richard Bohr, *Famine and the Missionary: Timothy Richard as Relief Administrator and Advocate of National Reform*

49. Endymion Wilkinson, *The History of Imperial China: A Research Guide*

50. Britten Dean, *China and Great Britain: The Diplomacy of Commercial Relations, 1860–1864*

51. Ellsworth C. Carlson, *The Foochow Missionaries, 1847–1880*

52. Yeh-chien Wang, *An Estimate of the Land-Tax Collection in China, 1753 and 1908*

53. Richard M. Pfeffer, *Understanding Business Contracts in China, 1949–1963*

54. Han-sheng Chuan and Richard Kraus, *Mid-Ch'ing Rice Markets and Trade, An Essay in Price History*

55. Ranbir Vohra, *Lao She and the Chinese Revolution*

56. Liang-lin Hsiao, *China's Foreign Trade Statistics, 1864–1949*

57. Lee-hsia Hsu Ting, *Government Control of the Press in Modern China, 1900–1949*

58. Edward W. Wagner, *The Literati Purges: Political Conflict in Early Yi Korea*

59. Joungwon A. Kim, *Divided Korea: The Politics of Development, 1945–1972*

60. Noriko Kamachi, John K. Fairbank, and Chūzō Ichiko. *Japanese Studies of Modern China Since 1953: A Bibliographical Guide to Historial and Social-Science Research on the Nineteenth and Twentieth Centuries, Supplementary Volume for 1953–1969*

61. Donald A. Gibbs and Yun-chen Li, *A Bibliography of Studies and Translations of Modern Chinese Literature, 1918–1942*

62. Robert H. Silin, *Leadership and Values: The Organization of Large-Scale Taiwanese Enterprises*

63. David Pong, *A Critical Guide to the Kwangtung Provincial Archives Deposited at the Public Record Office of London*

64. Fred W. Drake, *China Charts the World: Hsu Chi-yü and His Geography of 1848*

65. William A. Brown and Urgunge Onon, translators and annotators, *History of the Mongolian People's Republic*

66. Edward L. Farmer, *Early Ming Government: The Evolution of Dual Capitals*

67. Ralph C. Croizier, *Koxinga and Chinese Nationalism: History, Myth, and the Hero*

68. William J. Tyler, tr., *The Psychological World of Natsumi Sōseki*, by Doi Takeo

69. Eric Widmer, *The Russian Ecclesiastical Mission in Peking during the Eighteenth Century*

70. Charlton M. Lewis, *Prologue to the Chinese Revolution: The Transformation of Ideas and Institutions in Hunan Province, 1891–1907*

71. Preston Torbert, *The Ch'ing Imperial Household Department: A Study of its Organization and Principal Functions. 1662–1796*

72. Paul A. Cohen and John E. Schrecker, eds., *Reform in Nineteenth-Century China*

73. Jon Sigurdson, *Rural Industrialization in China*

74. Kang Chao, *The Development of Cotton Textile Production in China*

75. Valentin Rabe, *The Home Base of American China Missions, 1880–1920*

76. Sarasin Viraphol, *Tribute and Profit: Sino-Siamese Trade, 1652–1853*

77. Ch'i-ch'ing Hsiao, *The Military Establishment of the Yuan Dynasty*

78. Meishi Tsai, *Contemporary Chinese Novels and Short Stories, 1949–1972: An Annotated Bibliography*

79. Wellington K. K. Chan, *Merchants, Mandarins, and Modern Enterprise in Late Ch'ing China*

80. Endymion Wilkinson, *Landlord and Labor in Late Imperial China: Case Studies from Shandong by Jing Su and Luo Lun*

81. Barry Keenan, *The Dewey Experiment in China: Educational Reform and Political Power in the Early Republic*

82. George A. Hayden, *Crime and Punishment in Medieval Chinese Drama: Three Judge Pao Plays*

83.   Sang-Chul Suh, *Growth and Structural Changes in the Korean Economy, 1910–1940*